MARCO

D0300850

NEW YORK

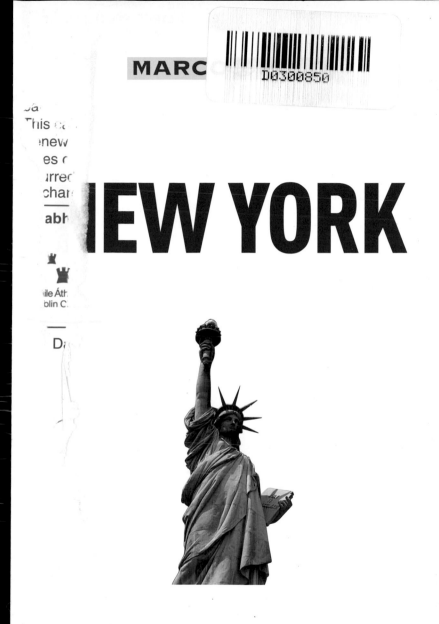

www.marco-polo.com

Sightseeing Highlights

Giant skyscrapers, the Statue of Liberty, the Empire State Building, Grand Central Terminal, Fifth Avenue, Central Park, Brooklyn Bridge and world famous museums – who doesn't know New York's main attractions. There are a few others, too, not quite as well known, but no less worthwhile.

❶ ✶✶ American Museum of Natural History
The largest museum of natural history tells the story of the origins of the universe.
page 180

❷ ✶✶ Brooklyn Bridge
A guaranteed eye-catcher with its 532m/582yd freely suspended deck
page 206

❸ ✶✶ Brooklyn Museum
The second largest museum in New York has a unique Egyptian collection. **page 207**

❹ ✶✶ Central Park
The green oasis in the middle of Manhattan provides an idyllic contrast to the adjacent skyscrapers.
page 213

❺ ✶✶ Chinatown
The largest Chinese city outside China **page 222**

❻ ✶✶ Chrysler Building
One of the most beautiful buildings in the city **page 262**

❼ ✶✶ Empire State Building
The second tallest and most famous building in New York
page 237

❽ ✶✶ Fifth Avenue
The sinfully expensive boulevard is a shopper's paradise. **page 242**

❾ ✶✶ Frick Collection
The collection of old masters is in a grandiose city villa. **page 257**

Do You Feel Like ...

... superb views, interesting churches, historic residences, green parks or excellent street food? Explore New York just as you please.

FAMOUS VIEWS

- **Christopher Street** ▶
  Watch the sun set over New Jersey from piers 45 and 46
- **View on the move**
  On subway line G you get a fantastic view of the skyline before station Smith St./9th St. The same is true on line 7 between 33rd St./Rawson St. and Queensboro Plaza.
- **Brooklyn Promenade**
  From the Esplanade on the East River, the view of the Manhattan skyline is stunning.

HISTORIC HOUSES

- ◀ **Brooklyn Heights**
  One of New York's most romantic neighbourhoods. The narrow-fronted townhouses all date from the 19th century. Truman Capote wrote *Breakfast at Tiffany's* in no. 70 Willow Street.
- **The Row**
  A group of elegant townhouses in the classical Federal style.
- **Orchard Street**
  A historic tenement turned into a museum. See how immigrants lived on the Lower East Side in the late 19th century.

BACKGROUND

**Graffiti is part of
New York**

ENJOY
NEW YORK

Take subway line 7 to explore the city

SIGHTS FROM A TO Z

TOURS

PRICE CATEGORIES
Restaurants
(price of a main dish)
$$$$ = more than 30 $
$$$ = 20 – 30 $
$$ = 10 – 20 $
$ = up to 10 $
Hotels (price of double room)
$$$$ = more than 300 $
$$$ = 250 – 300 $
$$ = 180 – 250 $
$ = up to 180 $

Note
Billable service telephone numbers are marked with an asterisk: *0180…

Times Square, heart of New York City

PRACTICAL INFORMATION

BACKGROUND

New York City is a city of superlatives. Read on for concise information about its inhabitants, economy, politics and history.

Population · Politics · Economy

New York City, in the state of the same name on the north-east coast of the USA, is not America, but the largest city on the continent and the heart of the nation. It is a global symbol of urban life and, although it is 100 per cent American, New York is seen all around the world as the mother of all cities, the ultimate metropolis, a laboratory for urban lifestyle and trends.

POPULATION AND BOUNDARIES

With a little over 8.175 million residents New York is the largest American city, but it developed slowly in the first 200 years after its founding in 1621. At the beginning of the 18th century only 5,000 people lived in Manhattan, by 1790 it had reached 33,000, and by around 1800 the number had almost doubled. But it was only the **mass immigration** of the second half of the 19th century that made New York a city of millions – by 1900 the population had climbed to over three million. Immigration has led to an variety of ethnic groups in New York, many of which live in their own areas, the **neighbourhoods**. Thus Chinese live in Chinatown, Poles and Ukrainians in the East Village, Hungarians and Czechs on the East Side, African Americans in Harlem, Dominicans and Cubans in Washington Heights, while East Harlem and the Bronx are mainly Latin American. In Brooklyn, near Atlantic Avenue, live Arabs, mainly Syrians and Lebanese; orthodox Jews are concentrated in two Brooklyn neighbourhoods, Crown Heights and Williamsburg, Danes and Norwegians in Bay Ridge. Astoria, in the borough of Queens, has a large Greek colony, and many Colombians have found a new home in Jackson Heights. All of these groups have their own shops, restaurants and often their own churches. But the opposite trend is also apparent: apart from the trattoria and ristoranti on Mulberry Street not much is left of Little Italy, and the former German colonies in East Village and on 86th Street have disappeared completely.

Development

? A diverse population

MARCO POLO INSIGHT

Presently 33% of New Yorkers are of European, 25% African American, 28% Latin-American and 12% Asian descent. Only one third were born in the city. There are still American Indians among the residents: in 2008 there were 16,300 Native Americans.

Prospect Park at the heart of Brooklyn is a favourite place for residents of the »suburb« to take some time out

Brighton Beach, Brooklyn, has an eastern European quarter with its own atmosphere

Language variety
The ethnic richness can also be seen in the variety of languages: about 120 – some sources even say 200 – languages are spoken in the city! Some estimates state that about 4.2 million residents of New York speak English poorly or not at all, and approximately 1.5 million speak only Spanish. 30% of all school-aged children in New York speak a language other than English at home. But it works both ways: New York University teaches 25 different foreign languages, one of the most diverse programmes in the country.

ECONOMY

Financial centre and media capital
Even though the economy of New York has lain in ruins several times already, the city has always managed to recover. It is still the **financial capital** of the world, and the **media capital** of the United States. In 1949 New York was still one of the largest industrial centres in the country, but three in five jobs in this sector had been lost by the end of the 1970s. Only the textile industry has remained: located in the Garment District in Chelsea, it employs about a quarter of a million

people. Today, about 85% of jobs in New York are in the **service sector**, above all the retail, finance and real estate sectors as well as in health and education. CHASE (Manhattan) and Citibank, two of the largest banks in the USA, are headquartered in New York, along with six of the world's largest insurance companies and three of the largest American newspapers, the New York Times, the Wall Street Journal and the Daily News. The headquarters of the largest television networks, CBS, ABC, NBC and FOX, are in New York, and the largest number of hotels, theatres, museums, publishers and advertising agencies are located here. **Tourism** is also very important, with about 700,000 people working in this sector. In 2009 New York was host to about 50 million visitors, of which approximately 10 million came from abroad, most of them from Great Britain, Canada, France, Brazil and Germany.

But the »world's capital« has some big problems as well. The reconstruction taking place at Ground Zero with its exploding costs is straining the city. In the past decades the city has only been able to meet its obligations with help from the state and federal governments, and in exchange has had to give up part of its financial autonomy. The unemployment rate is presently about 9% (national average: 8.5%); with more and more businesses leaving the city it is on the increase. The distribution of unemployment also reveals social inequality: almost twice as many Hispanics are unemployed as whites. Of the African Americans between 16 and 19 years old, almost every other one is unemployed, and 50% of adult African Americans and 43% of Hispanics have no income. Overall, every sixth New Yorker is on welfare. Despite the difficult financial situation, significant investment is necessary to counter the neglect which threatens some urban fringe areas, to create jobs in problem areas and for cheap housing. The state schools are in need of repair: people who can afford it avoid sending their children to them. The renovation of the approximately 2000 bridges is very expensive, as is the around 6,000 miles of sewerage, which is 100 years old. Improvements in the infrastructure

Problems of a cosmopolitan city

? MARCO POLO INSIGHT	*The Big Apple*

According to the official explanation the term »The Big Apple« was used for the first time on 18 February 1924 by the horse racing journalist John FitzGerald in a column in *The Morning Telegraph*. He had picked up the term from stable boys in New Orleans and then applied it to New York. A second version states that the term comes from the jazz musicians of the 1920s and 1930s, who apparently used to say: »The tree of success has many apples on it, but when you pick New York you pick the biggest of them all, the Big Apple.« In 1971 the president of the New York City Bureau of Tourism heard the nickname and since then the image has had huge success as the city logo.

Location:
New York City originated in the early 17th century at the place where the Hudson River and the East River flow into New York Bay. The city has a latitude of 40° 43″ north and a longitude of 74° west. By comparison: the latitude of Naples is 40° north.

BRONX
109 sq km/
42 sq mi

MANHATTAN
59 sq km/
23 sq mi

QUEENS
283 sq km/
109 sq mi

Area:
782 sq km/302 sq mi
(by comparison:
Greater London
1579 sq km/610 sq mi)

BROOKLYN
183 sq km/
71 sq mi

STATEN
ISLAND
151 sq km/
58 sq mi

©BAEDEKER

New York City

Population: 8.4 million (2013)
in five boroughs:
Bronx: 1.4 Mio.
Manhattan: 1.6 Mio.
Queens: 2.3 Mio.
Brooklyn: 2.6 Mio.
Staten Island: 0.5 Mio.

Population density
**10,350 per sq km/
26,830 per sq mi**

▶ Economy

New York City is the global financial centre and the media capital of the USA. The service sector is the biggest employer. The rate of unemployment is below 10%.

▶ Government

The city government is headed by the mayor. The City Council consists of 51 members

▶ Climate

The weather in New York is not temperate: cold in winter, very humid in summer. The best times for going there are mid-May to mid-June and mid-September to late October.

▶ Religion

There are over 100 different religious groups with approx. 6,000 churches, temples, mosques and synagogues. The Jewish community, numbering 1.8 million, is the largest outside Israel.

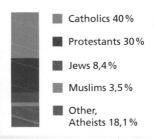

■ Catholics 40 %

■ Protestants 30 %

■ Jews 8,4 %

■ Muslims 3,5 %

■ Other, Atheists 18,1 %

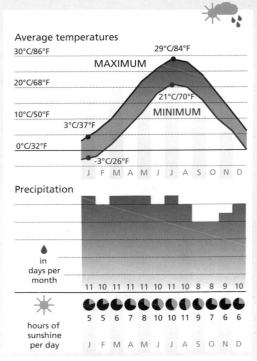

Average temperatures

30°C/86°F

29°C/84°F

MAXIMUM

20°C/68°F

21°C/70°F

10°C/50°F

MINIMUM

3°C/37°F

0°C/32°F

-3°C/26°F

J F M A M J J A S O N D

Precipitation

in days per month

11 10 11 11 11 10 11 10 8 8 9 10

hours of sunshine per day

5 5 6 7 8 10 10 11 9 7 6 6

J F M A M J J A S O N D

▶ Safety

New York is now the safest city in the USA. The murder rate has been falling continuously for years and is below the national average.

Per 100,000 inhabitants

—— New York City
—— USA overall

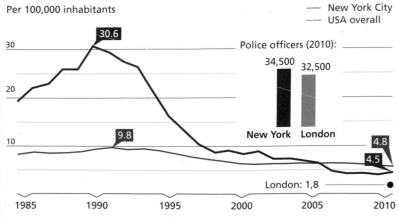

30.6

30

Police officers (2010): _____

34,500 32,500

20

New York London

9.8

10

4.8

4.5

London: 1,8 _____ ●

1985   1990   1995   2000   2005   2010

Welcome to Everyday Life

New Yorkers have a reputation for being bad-tempered. This is not right! People in the »Big Apple« are friendly to visitors, and there are many ways to make contacts with the locals and get to know their everyday life.

Insider Tip

MEETING NEW YORKERS

For a popular service that is also available in other American cities, get in touch with the »Big Apple Greeters«, enthusiastic citizens who tell visitors about their neighbourhood on walks lasting two or three hours. During the walk you have contact with relatives or friends of the greeter and get to look behind the scenes. This service is free of charge. A good way of saying thank you for it is to buy lunch for the greeter.
www.bigapplegreeter.org

PART OF THE FAMILY

Would you like to get to know everyday life and the city culture up close? The website »homestaybooking« puts you in touch with private hosts who are interested in exchanging culture and ideas with their guests. The hosts are sure to show you their favourite restaurant or bar.
www.homestaybooking.com

COOKERY COURSE

Like-minded hobby cooks from the area get together for a cookery course lasting several hours. In fairly small groups you get to know the basics or how to prepare exotic dishes, e.g. recipes from Indian or Thai cuisine. This is an informal way to meet people from New York who are keen on cooking. There are lots of alternatives at: *www.homecookingny.com.*

JACK'S STIR BREW COFFEE

Now we do appreciate Starbucks, especially when we're on the go and need a quick pick-me-up, but let's face it, the omnipresent mega-chain is rather impersonal. New York is teeming with wonderful cafés that have loads of personality and fantastic coffee. Take, for instance, Jack's Stir Brew Coffee in Greenwich Village. Everyone, including celebrity regulars , artists and students, likes to meet here over a cup of Jack Mazzola's famous stir-brewed coffee made of organic fair-trade beans. His special secret is the stir brew coffee machine he designed and had patented; the special brewing process enhances the flavor.

Jack's Stir Brew Coffee
www.jacksstirbrew.com
138 W 10th Street, West Village
222 Front Street, South Street Seaport
425 W 13th Street, Meatpacking District

CLASSES WITH THE LOCALS!

Insider Tip

Look under »Free Classes« in *Time Out* magazine to find a wide range of free courses, (cooking, photography, painting, etc.), which enable you to meet New Yorkers informally. One example: the popular photo courses run by the Swiss photographer Christian Heeb (www.heebphoto.com).
www.timeout.com/newyork/
sport-fitness/free-classes

are overdue: the city is collapsing under street traffic, public transport needs to be expanded and a proportion of the delivery of goods would be better carried out by rail. A large problem here is the deep gap between rich and poor: this city of extremes has the most open trade, the greatest works of art, the world's highest buildings – and the poorest of America's poor.

Transport Thanks to its location, New York was once an important seaport. Manhattan was bordered by piers up to about 100th Street, where up to the middle of the 20th century both shipping and passenger traffic were handled. Once the entrance to the New World, their importance declined with the arrival of the container ships – today these dock mostly on the New Jersey side of New York Bay – and the aeroplane as a means of mass transportation. New York has three airports. The largest and at 26km/16mi away the furthest from the centre of town is John F. Kennedy Airport (JFK), where predominantly international traffic and national flights to the western United States are handled.

Seat of the mayor and the city government: City Hall

La Guardia (LGA), handling exclusively domestic traffic, is only 13km/8mi from the centre. Newark (EWR) is about 25km/16mi away in neighbouring New Jersey: both international and national airlines fly there. Amtrak long-distance trains depart from Pennsylvania (Penn) Station. This is also the terminal for trains of the New Jersey Transit and the Long Island Railroad, the commuter trains with the largest number of passengers in America. Grand Central Terminal is significant for suburban traffic. The most important means of transportation in New York are the subway, busses and ferries (▶Practicalities, Transport).

? MARCO ●POLO INSIGHT

Did you know

In the international ranking of the cost of living in cities, New York took 47th place in 2012. Accommodation is extremely expensive: a one-room apartment of 45 sq m/480 sq ft in Manhattan currently costs about US$2,600 per month, a flat with several rooms at least US$3300.

From an Indian Village to a City of Millions

How did a Native American village named Manahatin become a modern city of millions? Who were the first New Yorkers? Where did the city get its name? Find out here how a small Dutch settlement became one of the most important centres of the Western world.

NEW YORK'S BEGINNINGS

9500 BC	The first American Indians settle the area of what is now New York
1609	Europeans settle on the island
1626	Nieuw Amsterdam founded

About 11,500 years ago the area of today's Manhattan was settled by the Algonquin tribe. They called their territory Manhattan, Manhattes, Manhata or Manhatans, which means »island of hills«. In 1524 Giovanni da Verrazzano from Florence sailed at the command of the French king Francis I along the American east coast and was the first European to reach the Bay of Manhattan, today's New York Bay.
But it was over 80 years later, in the year 1609, that the Englishman Henry Hudson set foot on the southern point of Manhattan. He explored the Hudson River, which was later named after him, on behalf of the Dutch East India Company.

Island of hills

After that more and more Dutch and Walloon emigrants settled on Manhattan, which had a favourable, sheltered location between the Hudson River to the west, the East River and the Harlem River to the north. In 1626 the first governor of the town, Peter Minnewit from Wesel on the Rhine, bought the island of Manhattan from the Native Americans living there for cloth and glass beads worth about 60 guilders and called the settlement Nieuw Amsterdam.

Nieuw Amsterdam

In 1653 Governor Peter Stuyvesant, a man known for his strictness, had a wall built in the north of the city – which had a population of about 1,000 at that time – between the Hudson and East Rivers; Wall Street, which got its name from this wall, runs along here today.

Wall Street

Immigrants on a ferry in Manhattan

ENGLAND CONQUERS THE CITY

1664	England takes Nieuw Amsterdam
1689–1691	Rebellion in the English colonies
1735	The birth of freedom of the press in America

English rule During the second Anglo-Dutch War (1664–65 until 1667) the English took Nieuw Amsterdam without a fight. The English king gave the colony to his brother, the Duke of York, and Nieuw Amsterdam, which in the meantime had a population of 1,500, was renamed New York in his honour. The Glorious Revolution – the overthrow in 1688 of James II of England by Parliament – spread to the colonies in 1689. In New York the German businessman Jacob Leisler led the rebellion, ruling the city for two years. To the very end, he refused to turn the city over to the incoming English governor. He was finally captured and sentenced to death. In 1733 Johann Peter Zenger, who had emigrated from the Palatinate in Germany and founded the *New York Weekly Journal*, was imprisoned after criticizing the governor. He was released in 1735 after a sensational trial. This event is considered to be the birth of freedom of the press in America. By 1709 there was a slave market at the end of Wall Street, and within 34 years around 2,000 black slaves were living in New York.

THE WAR OF INDEPENDENCE

1775–1783	War of Independence against England
1776	Declaration of Independence of New York
1783	England recognizes Independence
1784	New York is made capital of the USA
1789	George Washington takes oath of office

Independence of the colonies New York's population numbered 25,000 at the beginning of the War of Independence of the American colonies, and its harbour handled more cargo than Boston's or Philadelphia's. The headquarters of England's troops was in New York. In order to raise money the English parliament decided in 1764 to impose customs duties on trade goods. In 1765 the **Stamp Act** (every business transaction required a stamp which was liable to a fee) provoked the New Yorkers' protest. The Sons of Liberty, a secret organization which stirred up resistance to the Stamp Act and the English crown, was formed with its motto »no taxation without representation«. The taxation of tea resulted in the Boston Tea Party in December 1773 and in April 1774 the lesser-known New York Tea Party: as in Boston, rebels dressed as American Indians dumped crates of tea that was to be taxed into the harbour. New York signed the Declaration of Independence in 1776, and

George Washington, commander in chief of the Continental Army, moved his headquarters from Boston to New York in April of that year. England sent almost 500 ships with 32,000 troops as reinforcements, which set up camp on Staten Island. On 27 August British and American troops clashed at Brooklyn Heights: in the so-called Battle of Long Island the American troops were at a disadvantage and had to withdraw. New York was left to the British until peace was declared, and the British developed it into their military centre. Over 10,000 American prisoners of war died on ships that had been converted to prisons on the East River.

After the English troops surrendered on 19 October 1781 the British crown recognized the independence of the colonies in the Peace of Paris treaty in 1783. New York had been plundered by the

Immortalized in bronze: statue of George Washington in front of Federal Hall

British after the long occupation and partially destroyed by fire. Nevertheless the city was named the capital of the young nation until Philadelphia took its place in 1790. In 1789 George Washington took his oath of office as the first president of the United States in Federal Hall in New York. The population grew to over 30,000, and the city became capital of the state of the same name until Albany took over that function in 1797. In the same year the most important stock exchange of the financial world was founded. In 1811 the city fathers showed great foresight: even though only the southern tip of Manhattan was inhabited they developed »the grid«, the pattern of 12 avenues that run from south to north and 155 (today 220) numbered cross streets.

THE CIVIL WAR

1827	The city of New York abolishes slavery
from 1850	First mass immigration
1861–1865	Civil War between the North and the South

Prosperity After the opening of the Erie Canal in 1825, connecting New York with the Great Lakes, the city flourished as a seaport. With over 150,000 residents it became the largest city in the country by 1820. When the state of New York abolished slavery in 1827, around 14,000 African Americans were living in New York City. A large fire in 1835 destroyed over 700 houses. From 1850 hundreds of thousands of Germans and Irish fled from poverty and persecution in Europe to New York. In the 1880s Jews from Eastern Europe and Italians streamed into the city (▶MARCO POLO Insight p.336), and New York's population passed the half-million mark.

In February 1860 Abraham Lincoln delivered his famous speech against slavery. When he was elected president in November, 13 states seceded from the union and formed the Confederate States of America. On 12 April 1861 the **Civil War** began, the North fighting against the defected South. Since the city's traders did business with the South, New York at first remained quiet. Then Lincoln enacted a new law on military conscription: it became possible to buy release from military duty for $300. This led to great dissatisfaction among the Irish especially, because they could not raise this much money. The second military draft on 13 July 1863 in New York led to the »draft riots«. An angry mob attacked the police, plundered homes and hunted abolitionists. This hate turned in the end against the African American residents of New York, who as the source of cheap labour were the biggest competition on the job market. When the riots were over 105 people had been killed in what is considered to be the bloodiest uprising in America to this day.

FROM THE CIVIL WAR TO THE STOCK MARKET CRASH

1870	New York's population exceeds one million
1883	The Brooklyn Bridge is completed
1886	Inauguration of the Statue of Liberty
1898	Greater New York City is formed
1904	The first subway runs

Industrializa- After the Civil War, New York became the starting point of industri-
tion alization. The large banking houses were founded, and Wall Street developed into the main business centre of the Western world. The city experienced a building boom. In 1883 the Metropolitan Opera and the Brooklyn Bridge were opened; in 1886 the Statue of Liberty, a gift from France, was erected at the entrance to the harbour. In the 1880s a **second wave of immigration** began, when particularly Jews from Eastern Europe and Italians streamed into the city. Until

1919, Ellis Island was the gateway to the »land of opportunity« for 17 million Europeans (►MARCO POLO Insight p.336).

In 1898 the five until then independent communities of New York – Manhattan, Queens, Brooklyn, Bronx, Staten Island – united to form Greater New York City. With 3.5 million people, this was the world's second-largest city after London. In 1904 the 14.5km/9mi-long first segment of the subway from City Hall in south Manhattan up to 145th Street was opened.

United under a single flag: immigrants from all nations

1930S UNTIL TODAY

1929	Black Friday on the stock exchange causes worldwide depression
1932	Opening of the Empire State Building
1939	World's Fair in Flushing Meadows
1954	Ellis Island is closed
11.9.2001	Attack on the World Trade Center
2008	US financial bank crisis

The boom was only stopped by the crash on Wall Street on »Black Friday« in 1929, heralding an almost ten-year-long depression and sending many residents of New York plummeting into poverty. Around 1930 New York's population had grown to 6.9 million; Harlem with its 220,000 residents was the largest community of African Americans in the USA. It was during the depression – when every fourth New Yorker was unemployed – that the 381m/1,250ft Empire State Building was opened in 1932. For a long time it was the tallest building in the world; today it is still an office building for 25,000 people and a major Manhattan landmark. In the same time period the Chrysler Building, the RCA Building and the George Washington Bridge across the Hudson were built.

Black Friday

New York's recovery began under the Republican mayor Fiorello H. LaGuardia. During his time in office (1932–1945) the city's infrastructure was expanded and social housing was promoted. New York's second World's Fair in Flushing Meadows in 1939–40 attracted 44 million visitors. Between 1933 and 1945 countless Jews, intellectuals, artists, scientists and political refugees fled to the United States;

they influenced the development of architecture and art in New York. In 1941 the USA entered the Second World War. In 1946, when New York became the seat of the United Nations, the city had more than 7 million residents.

In the 1960s and 1970s New York experienced racial riots, the assassination of the African American politician Malcolm X (1965) and the first wave of emigration: more than one million whites left the city and moved to the suburbs. In their place came a new wave of immigrants from Puerto Rico, Central America and the South. During the third New York World's Fair in 1965 there was a 16-hour blackout: nine months later there was an unusually high birth rate. In 1973 the 420m/1377ft-high twin towers of the World Trade Center in the financial district of Manhattan were opened. Many businesses moved out of Manhattan because of the rising cost of real estate. In 1975 New York was not able to pay its bonds; a temporary loan from the federal government prevented **insolvency**, and since then the city has been under a strict austerity programme. In July 1977 New York experienced a second power blackout, which lasted 27 hours. In 1987 »Black Monday« on Wall Street brought about a 30% loss in value of all stocks traded. David Dinkins was the first African American to become mayor of the city and took office on 1 January 1990. In 1994 he was replaced by Rudolph Giuliani, whose »zero tolerance« politics (until 2001) led to an enormous reduction in crime level. Booming stocks brought in increased tax revenue, which were immediately spent on overdue repairs and beautification of the city. But stocks fell shortly afterwards and the city is again close to insolvency.

9/11   On **11 September 2001** the city experienced its greatest catastrophe: two planes flown by terrorists flew into the twin towers of the World Trade Center and caused them to collapse, killing more than 2,800 people. On the fourth of July 2004 the cornerstone of a new building was laid at the site, which is known as **Ground Zero**. The 20t »symbol of American strength and confidence« (George Pataki, governor of the State of New York) made of grey-black granite comes from the Adirondack Mountains, cost $14,000 and was painstakingly carved out by hand, chiselled (it bears the inscription: »to the enduring spirit of freedom«) and polished in order to be buried under 20m/66ft of cement and concrete. The planned height of the so-called **Freedom Tower**, 541m/1,776 feet, symbolizes the year (1776) of the American Declaration of Independence. In February 2005 the artist team Christo and Jeanne-Claude realized the project that they had been planning since 1979, entitled **»The Gates«**: for 16 days saffron-coloured cloth panels coloured 7,500 gates in Central Park. More than four million people streamed into the park to see the art project. On 11 September 2011, ten years after the attack on the World Trade Center, the National 9/11 Memorial was inaugurated. The **worst**

worldwide financial crisis since 1929 began in January 2008 when several large American banks admitted to gambling away billions of dollars on speculations. In September the Lehmann Brothers investment bank went broke, and the crisis overflowed to the rest of the world. The complete collapse of the system was only prevented through bail-out packages worth several billion dollars. Nevertheless, the future is seen optimistically in New York. Today, New York is considered the safest city in the USA — and one of the most popular ones, too. Around 50 million visitors flock to New York every year. And add to that the 9.1 million residents expected by 2030 in the already overcrowded city. But not even this can deter New Yorkers. The city already has a plan in place, »PlaNYC 2030, a growth, resiliency and sustainability blueprint that addresses the city's long-term challenges. It is an effort to improve the city's overall infrastructure and enhance the quality of life for all New Yorkers

11 September 2001: the World Trade Center is burning

On 1 January 2014, Democrat **Bill de Blasio**, a veteran to city government , assumed office as the Mayor of New York City. De Blasio has taken up the cause to close the gap between the rich and poor in NYC, to create affordable housing, to push for a law extending paid sick leave and to expand community health services and other social benefits and services for all to diminish inequality and make New York a more liveable city.

Arts and Culture

City Development and Architecture

New York's spectacular skyline with about 200 skyscrapers is a gigantic panopticon of historical building styles – from New York's first skyscraper, the Flatiron Building, through the neo-gothic Woolworth Building, the Art Deco ornaments of the Chrysler Building and the rationality of the Seagram Building by Mies van der Rohe, to the figurative neo-renaissance of Philip Johnson's AT & T Building.

How did the »vertical city« (the description comes from the French Swiss architect Le Corbusier) come about? New York's rise to become an international city began at the end of the 18th century after declaring its independence from England. At that time the city covered an area from the southern tip of Manhattan to around today's Canal Street, largely still on the street map that had been designed by the Dutch. Because of the rapid rise in population (New York was in 1800 already the largest city of the still young USA) the growth of the city threatened to get out of control. In order to make up for the lack of building land, landfills were created early on around the southern tip of Manhattan. Thus, for instance, the round **Castle Clinton** in today's Battery Park was built at that time only 100m/110yd from the shoreline in the harbour.

Vertical city

In the same way, today's Water Street near South Street Seaport got its name because it was originally right next to the water. Even though New York only took up the southern tip of Manhattan, the city council developed a plan in 1811 that was supposed to control the future development of Manhattan. The **street grid** covers the whole island like a net with its twelve avenues running north to south and the cross streets numbered 1 to 220. Only the older parts of the city south of 14th Street and the path of today's Broadway, which was already established by the Algonquin Indians as a hunting trail, were integrated into the plan. The decision for this quite regular grid was the consequence on the one hand of economic pragmatism (in the sale of plots of land there were to be no »good« or »bad« locations), but also of democratic convictions: the city was supposed to offer all of its residents the same living conditions.

Architecture from the drawing board

No job for the faint-hearted: constructing the
Empire State Building in 1931

The city
centre shifts
away

Manhattan grew quickly and by 1864 more than half of the population of the island lived north of **14th Street**. As a consequence of the
expansion northwards the centre of the city shifted away from the
southern tip. This was possible due to the improvement of the inner
city means of transportation (at first horse-drawn trams, later street-
cars and subways). After the completion of **Central Park** around
1870 its southern edge (the northern part of the park was in an area
that was for the most part undeveloped) quickly became a centre for
building projects and encouraged the city to expand northwards.
During the second half of the 19th century 14th Street became the
meeting point for elegant New York society: Tiffany's jeweller's shop
was located on Union Square, and the city opera house, the Academy
of Music, was a few blocks away. By the turn of the century the centre
of activity had already shifted. The construction of the Flatiron Building (1902) and the Metropolitan Life Tower (1909) on Madison
Square hinted at this development. In the 1930s and 1940s
42nd Street developed into a centre for theatre and nightlife, and at
the same time **Fifth Avenue** changed from a sleepy side street to a
city boulevard. In the meantime the construction of luxury hotels like
the Plaza or the Savoy had changed the southern edge of Central Park
to a centre for the elegant world of New York. As of the 1960s the
most expensive shops in the city can be found on **58th Street** as well
as on **Fifth** and **Madison Avenue**. The two areas with the greatest
density of skyscrapers today are the southern edge of Central Park
(**Midtown**) as well as the southern tip of Manhattan (**Downtown**).
This concentration in two places can above all be attributed, next to
the already described city development, to the character of the
ground: in both of these areas the massive bedrock is directly at the
surface of the ground and thus guarantees the secure foundation of
very tall buildings.

FOUR GENERATIONS OF SKYSCRAPERS

Origins

MARCO
POLO Insight
p.238, 350

With the invention of the skyscraper towards the end of the 19th century, American architecture began to free itself from the until then
dominant European influence. The skyscraper has been the symbol
of American entrepreneurial spirit and optimism ever since. This development was made possible by two decisive technical innovations:
steel skeleton construction and the improved security of the **eleva-
tor** which had been developed earlier (the New York engineer Elisha
Otis proved the reliability of his new security system in 1853 at the
New York World's Fair in a spectacular experiment on himself).
While the first skyscrapers needed especially thick supporting walls,
with steel skeleton construction the façade was simply hung in front
of the supporting steel frame like a curtain. This light and stable

building method allowed buildings to be erected with heights that had never been reached before. Shortly after the turn of the century the use of steel concrete also gave new stimulus to construction. The centres of this development were the cities New York and Chicago. After the Great Fire of 1871 a building boom began in Chicago which led to a series of new buildings, among them the first skyscraper with a steel frame, built in the year 1884. Inspired by these buildings the first towers began to grow into the heavens in New York as well. Yet the first New York skyscraper was imported from Chicago: in 1897 the Chicago architect Louis Sullivan built the **Bayard Building**, 65 Bleecker Street, a 12-storey steel frame with a terracotta façade. From then on the two cities entered into a competition for height that still continues today (though in the meantime the tallest buildings in the world are found in Southeast Asia).

The architectural style of the early skyscrapers in New York is clearly different from that of the buildings in Chicago. While a modern and functional style predominated in the latter quite early on, New York buildings imitated traditional European models for a long time. A typical example of this tendency for decoration is the neo-gothic **Woolworth Building** of 1913 (Cass Gilbert) or the **Metropolitan Life Tower** (on Madison Square) of 1909, which is styled after the campanile on Saint Mark's Square in Venice. The sight of these towers may be romantic, but it should not be forgotten that there is a modern steel skeleton and building technology inside. Perhaps the most famous of the very early skyscrapers is the 200m/657ft-tall **Singer Tower** built in 1908 in the Beaux-Arts style on lower Broadway, the tallest building in the world at that time. In spite of great protest it was torn down in 1970 in order to build 1 Liberty Plaza (incidentally, it is to this day the tallest building ever torn down, a task presenting considerable technical problems).

Tendency for decoration

The Woolworth Building reaches for the sky

Luxurious lobby of the Woolworth Building

1916 Zoning Law

As early as 1916 the growing number of skyscrapers was beginning to disturb the residents of New York. The reason was the completion of the **Equitable Building** (120 Broadway, near Wall Street), which rises 39 storeys in a massive block on a small lot and completely overshadows lower Broadway. In order to preserve air and light in the streets the city fathers passed the Zoning Law, the first building regulation. From then on, newly constructed buildings had to taper off after a certain height. This model for skyscrapers made architectural history.

1920s Art Deco

In the middle of the 1920s, in the jazz period, New York discovered its love for Art Deco. During this time the elegant **Chrysler Building** (William van Alen, 1930) was built, which appears to be the embodiment of speed and energy with its shining steel tip and the gigantic waterspouts in the form of eagle heads. After its completion the 319m/1047ft Chrysler Building was for a few weeks the tallest building in the world until the title was taken by the **Empire State Building**, which was under construction at the same time. The Empire State captivates less through stylistic detail than its measurements. It stands more or less unobstructed and thus its tower dominates the Midtown skyline and is visible throughout the entire city in ever changing profiles. With its slowly receding stories from a broad base (like a wedding cake) and the slender point set onto the tower, the building is the definitive New York skyscraper. The steel point was incidentally conceived as the anchor point for airships, and a small lobby for airship passengers was even provided. For reasons of safety (the Hindenburg catastrophe in Lakehurst) the installation was never used.

Further highlights of New York Art Deco are the **Waldorf Astoria Hotel** on Park Avenue or the Radio City Music Hall complex in the **Rockefeller Center**, whose foyer and hall are furnished with extravagant ornaments and the most exquisite materials. The Rockefeller Center, which was conceived in 1927, is especially significant in the development of the skyscraper, since for the first time towers are joined together instead of being built separately, forming a »city in the city«. The buildings of the central area (the last buildings of the Rockefeller were only completed toward the end of the 1960s) already point to the abandoning of the romantic skyscraper of earlier years. With its cubic forms and the relatively undecorated facades, the central **RCA** (today GE) Building, designed by Raymond Hood, already foreshadows the period of architectural rationalism.

City in the city

From the middle of the 1930s European modernism also began to gain influence in New York architecture. The exhibition initiated by Philip Johnson in 1931, **The International Style** in the Museum of Modern Art, was the first to introduce the American public to the architectural tendencies of the European avant-garde. The exhibition catalogue introduced the principles of modern architecture: »Not symmetry but order are to give clarity to the design, instead of arbitrarily applied decoration the natural elegance of the material, the technical perfection and the proportions appear«. No longer decorative inclination but **functionality** and **progress** were the new leitmotifs. In the following years many architects of the Bauhaus (among others Walter Gropius, Mies van der Rohe) and other European schools of architecture emigrated to the United States and began to work there. For many it was the first opportunity to realize their designs.

International Style

The decisive technical innovation of this time was the so-called curtain wall or curtain façade, in which the stone covering of the steel skeleton structures used up to this point was replaced by a light outer skin of glass and steel. The first skyscraper in New York with a curtain wall was the **United Nations Headquarters** on the East River with its covering of green glass designed in 1950 by an international group of architects under the leadership of W. K. Harrison (based on the concept of Le Corbusier). The **Lever House** on Park

Curtain wall 1950s

Avenue, built two years later by Gordon Bunshaft (from the office of Skidmore, Owings & Merrill, S.O.M.), is clearly inspired by the UN Building. Next to the light and elegant façade the slab-shaped high-rise Lever House is an innovation primarily because of its setting. Instead of occupying the entire (very expensive) plot area the building leaves an open area on Park Avenue which is surrounded by arcades. Only a few blocks away, an indisputable masterpiece of the late 1950s is the **Seagram Building** by Mies van der Rohe and Philip Johnson, from the year 1958. With its elegant façade of vertical bronze profiles and the glass-covered two-storey entrance hall, the beverage company Seagram's simple 38-storey tower is a classic example of Mies van der Rohe's architectural minimalism. Its location, set back from Park Avenue, allows the viewer »room to breathe«. This type of building was copied countless times in New York in the following years, but only rarely were the delicacy and elegance of the original attained.

1960s and 1970s – trade-off of height for public space

Inspired by the Seagram, the New York city planners decided to revise the Zoning Law of 1916. This allowed additional storeys if the constructors created **public spaces** in return. Whoever wanted to build higher had to construct a so-called plaza on his property, and it was in this way that most of the large open areas in the city came about. At the end of the 1950s the era of the skyscrapers seemed to be finished: only a few large projects were completed. In addition to economic reasons, attitudes toward the »dinosaurs« of architecture had changed. The harsh public criticism of the **Pan Am Building** completed in 1963 (today the **MetLife Building**), in which Walter Gropius also took part, seems to exemplify the altered zeitgeist. The Pan Am tower, which rises over Grand Central Terminal, was accused primarily of overshadowing the entire area as well as distorting the view along Park Avenue (the building is the only Manhattan high-rise on a street corner). New York had bid farewell to the boundless 1930s enthusiasm for its towers and now viewed them much more critically. Nevertheless in 1973 the largest building complex of the city to date, the **World Trade Center** with its smooth, 420m/1377ft-high twin towers, was opened. In the course of the 1970s, when the city was close to bankruptcy, construction all but stopped in Manhattan.

New record 1980s

It was only in the **boom of the 1980s** that the climate for the building of new high rises seemed to improve. New paths of form were followed as well: Philip Johnson's **AT&T** Building (1984; today **Sony**) with its meanwhile famous Chippendale gable clearly marks the end of the simple, pragmatic »box with glass curtain façade« that had predominated in New York for decades. Other buildings from that time are the **Lipstick Building** (1985; also by Johnson) or the silver

Citicorp Tower with its concise triangle as a concluding element (1977; both on Lexington Avenue), the **Trump Tower** (1983) and the **World Financial Center** in Battery Park City. The curious side of the boom is the fact that many owners of lower buildings sold the air rights over their buildings to the owners of skyscrapers, in doing so accepting a shadowy existence in exchange for financial reward. In this way the Museum of Modern Art among others financed the building of the Museum Tower (architect: Cesar Pelli) in 1984, which is attached to the main building.

After some years of economic stagnation a boom caused in large part by the new medium of the internet began in the middle of the 1990s, giving the architectural development of New York new momentum. The markedly reduced crime rate and the increased involvement of the city fathers in the renovation of the subway as well as countless parks and squares (Bryant Park went from a notorious drug dealing site to a green oasis in a few years) provided the city with a breathtaking boom in real estate. Even the ensuing collapse in profits in the

New momentum 1990s until today

The most famous skyline in the world, seen from Queens. The Pepsi logo in the foreground is protected heritage.

internet industry, as well as the tragic events of 11 September 2001, only temporarily weakened this development. The **Time Warner Center** on Columbus Circle (architects: S.O.M.), completed in 2004, was the first spectacular construction of the internet age. With its two angled glass towers, the building both continues the course of Broadway and at the same time continues the tradition of the double towers on the western edge of Central Park. Another project from this time is the 48-storey tower of the publishing house **Condé Nast** (4 Times Square; architects: Fox & Fowle) completed in 1999. The building is noteworthy above all for its energy-saving building engineering, which set new standards worldwide.

Pushing westward

The transformation of **Times Square** and **42nd Street** between Seventh and Eighth Avenues, furthered for the most part by Disney, points to Manhattan's newest large civic project: the development of the long neglected West Side between 42nd and 34th Street. So for example the New York Times gave up its headquarters on Times Square (which gave it its name) and moved into the highly modern **New York Times Tower** at the corner of Eighth Avenue and 42nd Street (2007, Renzo Piano in cooperation with Fox & Fowle).

The new push westward is manifest in the plans for **Penn Station**. The former main post office on Eighth Avenue is to be transformed into the new entrance to Moynihan Station. The main element of the entrance (architects: S.O.M.) is a fan-shaped, 40m/132ft-high glass hall. The almost completed **greenways** between Battery Park to the

The right angle has become obsolete: view from High Line Park to Frank O. Gehry's IAC Building

south and Riverside Park to the north add a great deal of value to community life in the West Side of Manhattan. The old commercial district of wharves on Hudson River was turned into a public space, **Christopher Street Pier**, which is now part of the Hudson River Park. The waterfront area has green lawns and playgrounds, mostly around Pier 45. Especially notable architecture in the Chelsea neighbourhood of Manhattan are two modern buildings designed by one of the most acclaimed architects of our time Frank O. Gehry: the somewhat futuristic-looking **IAC Building** with its curving sail-like façade that resembles sails on the Hudson River completed in 2007 (555 West 18th Street/11th Avenue) and the twisting and rippling **New York by Gehry** (also known as 8 Spruce Street and Beekman Tower), a 76-storey skyscraper completed in 2010 and, at 265m (870ft), one of the tallest residential towers in the USA (8 Spruce Street, between William and Nassau Streets, in Lower Manhattan. Also spectacular is the **Hearst Tower** (182m/597ft) designed by world-famous English architect Norman Foster (Lord Foster of Thames Bank) in 2006. The unique triangular framing pattern of the glass and steel structure erected on a 6-storey base built in the 1920s creates a distinctive faceted silhouette in the midst of New York's skyline (57th Street/8th Avenue). There are many other interesting buildings near **High Line Park** (▶p. 277), such as the **Whitney Museum of American Art** (▶p. 347).

> **!** *Sunset* **Insider Tip**
>
> MARCO ⊕ POLO TIP
>
> Christopher Street Pier in the West Village (Greenwich Village) on Manhattan's West Side is an especially good place to watch the sun set. Simply follow Christopher Street to the Hudson. Two former piers, numbers 45 and 46, have been converted to parks, and their lawns, promenades and playgrounds are attractive places to spend some time.

After years of trying to get the reconstruction of the World Trade Center off the ground, the rebuilding of the main tower, **One World Trade Center** (▶p. 348), started in 2006 at Ground Zero, and the final piece of the spire was ceremoniously placed on the top of the building in May 2013. It stands tall at 1776 ft (541.3 m), which is a symbolic reference to the 1776 adoption of the United States Declaration of Independence. The architects were Daniel Libeskind of Studio Daniel Libeskind and David Childs of Skidmore, Owings & Merrill. The **National September 11 Memorial & Museum** commemorating the 9/11 attacks of 2001 is the centrepiece of the WTC complex and consists of a museum and a plaza with a field of trees around two large square pools, where once the Twin Towers of the World Trade Center stood (Architect: Michael Arad). **One57** , Manhattan's luxury high-rise is getting its first residents. This 90-storey skyscraper is the tallest residential building in the city (157 West 57th Street; Architect: Christian de Portzamparc).

Latest
develop-
ments

One57 will not, however, be the tallest residential skyscraper for long, because the **building boom in New York must go on**. Soon the number of residents in New York will exceed the 9 million mark, and there will be a dire need for more housing and living spaces. Entire neighbourhoods are undergoing redevelopment, including infill development. The Hudson Yards Redevelopment Project is currently the largest rezoning effort. The aim is the turn the far West Side into a chic new neighbourhood called Hudson Yards. If all goes according to plan, approximately seventeen skyscrapers will shoot up in this area, especially around West Side Yard, a rail yard, and some structures are planned to cantilever over railway tracks. The redevelopment project is estimated to be completed in 2018. One residential tower is currently under construction (architects: Kohn, Pedersen and Fox). Building over an existing railway system is nothing new to New Yorkers. To a large extent, railway tracks run in a tunnel underneath Park Avenue. Current residential redevelopment projects in Manhattan also include St. Vincent's Hospital (33rd Street/9th Avenue) and the East River area south of the United Nations complex. The construction of seven super skyscrapers on the southern edge of Central Park is planned. These luxury residential towers, up to 450m/1476ft in height, are, along with One57, part of the so-called billionaires' belt. This building megalomania is however provoking more and more criticism. One of the major concerns is that these new giants will cast huge shadows over the **southern part of the Central Park**. Experts warn that superstorms are a real danger, as evidenced in 2012 when the construction crane on the One57 tower partially collapsed during Hurricane Sandy. However, gentrification is generally the most controversial issue. The irony is that more and more luxurious first and second homes (mostly flats in NYC) are available to wealthy Americans and foreigners and less and less affordable housing for middle and low-income earners. During his tenure, former Mayor Bloomberg, a billionaire himself living on the Upper East Side of Manhattan, one of the most affluent neighbourhoods in New York City, fully supported this. It remains to be seen if the newly elected Mayor de Balsio keeps his promise to create affordable housing and whether he really meant it when he said, »Our city does not belong to any individual or set of individuals. It belongs to all the people«.

PRESERVATION OF HISTORICAL MONUMENTS

Precious
heritage

In 1963 the Pennsylvania Railroad Company had its train station, a masterpiece by McKim, Mead White, torn down. The broad public outrage led to the Landmark Preservation Act of 1965, in which 900 buildings and 55 so-called historical districts with 18,000 houses were placed under preservation orders. The Landmarks Preservation

Commission, which has been founded in the meantime, keeps strict watch over New York's architectural heritage. Thus the historic **Grand Central Terminal** can be admired in its original state since the detailed renovation was completed in 1998. With its many shops and restaurants the train station now functions both as a hub of transportation and a shopping mall in historical garb. But not only is the architecture of the turn of the century being preserved; buildings of the modern age, the 1950s and 1960s, which for a long time had gone unnoticed, are also being placed under protection, now considered to be of historical value at the beginning of the 21st century.

New York, City of Culture

What is running on Broadway or the studio theatres in the Village? What treasures await you in New York's famous museums?

With one world famous opera hous, around 250 theatres, several orchestras, ballet and dance companies, more than 150 museums and 400 art galleries, cinemas, universities and colleges, New York is the

Cultural hub of the USA

A big choice of musicals

MARCO ⊕ POLO INSIGHT

?

Did you know …?

In New York there are about 40 Broadway, 20 Off-Broadway and over 200 Off-Off-Broadway theatres. While on Broadway between 41st and 53rd Street the long-running successes (especially musicals) are on the bill, the more unusual productions are at home Off-Broadway, and the completely experimental pieces in the Off-Off-Broadway theatres. But boundaries are flexible: some successful Off-Broadway plays have already made the jump from one of the theatres in Midtown or the Village to Broadway.

cultural centre of the USA. Most of the US publishing houses are here and the publishers of almost all large US periodicals. Alongside the public library, incidentally the second largest library in the USA, there are many smaller libraries for every field of interest. More than 50 cable programmes provide television for New Yorkers. There are about 130 **universities**, schools of higher learning and **colleges** with around 300,000 students. The oldest and perhaps best known is Columbia University, founded in 1754 as King's College, and the largest is New York University with more than 40,000 students, which was founded more than 150 years ago.

MUSIC AND THEATRE

New York's music and theatrical life with its opera houses, theatres, concert halls and jazz bars takes the indisputable lead in the USA and is an important economic factor: behind the scenes is the machinery of organizations, unions, agents, producers and an industry that meets the stage's every need. The aforementioned 250 **theatres** are divided into the 40 established Broadway theatres north of Times Square (between 40th and 50th Streets) and the remaining playhouses, the so-called Off-Broadway and Off-Off-Broadway theatres, of which most have settled in Greenwich Village or Chelsea. There are around 600 premieres every season.

Drama   The theatre tradition goes back to the time when New York was slowly growing to be one of the largest cities in North America. In the first half of the 18th century only amateur groups played in temporary buildings. In 1750 the first professional performance took place, of Shakespeare's Richard III in the New Theatre in Nassau Street. At the beginning of the 19th century a popularization began, which finds its culmination in to-day's perfectly marketed mainstream musicals. 200 years ago **melodramas**, **variety shows**, **Vaudeville shows** and **acts from fairs** dominated the stages. When the wave of immigrants increased at the end of the 19th century, the **theatre** offered the immigrants an ideal home: thus Jewish theatre and Irish **musicals** were established. In the years after the First World War the dramas were about the unique ethnic variety in New York. After the years of war, which were marked by patriotic restorative tendencies, new avant-garde streams could only prevail again in the 1950s and 1960s. Acting societies, among them the »Living Theatre«, took to the streets with their pieces, making political theatre and creating the world of **Off-Broadway**. Soon, in the 1960s, more experimental stages formed, the so-called **Off-Off-Broadway**, which presented completely new, frequently provocative and highly original forms of theatre: performances, happenings and improvisations.

Nowadays, the musical predominates on Broadway: after all, the form was born here. Elements of variety shows and melodrama, minstrel shows, ballad opera and borrowings from America's own music, ragtime and jazz, have all contributed to this glamorous form of musical theatre. The **first real musical** was The Black Crook (1866). Shining with spec-

The Lion King – first a cartoon film, now a successful musical

tacular effects, the mixture of song, dance and entertainment was performed 475 times in a row. The boom on Broadway made the city on the Hudson River the music and theatre centre of the United States. The real success only came in the 1930s, when underscoring was introduced and more modern music such as jazz entered into the productions. The scores were made simpler, the texts more meaningful and dance became a regular part of the narrated story. After the Second World War the musical scene boomed: many musicals whose melodies we still hear today were box office successes in the 1940s and 1950s, among them Annie Get Your Gun (1946), Kiss me Kate (1948), Guys and Dolls (1950) and My Fair Lady (1956), which broke all records. Finally the critical and meaningful musical found its place on Broadway: West Side Story opened at the Winter Garden Theatre in 1957, in which Leonard Bernstein carried the story of Romeo and Juliet over to the world of the Puerto Ricans in New York. Presently significantly more musicals than dramas are being performed in Broadway theatres. 33 of the theatres belong to three men, the so-called landlords, who make all decisions and collect all profits

New York, City of Cinema

Could it be that you fully expect to come across a rampaging gorilla or a screaming lady in white on the Empire State Building? If you have to describe the view from a skyscraper on Manhattan, do you imagine that you're on top of the Chrysler Building with its stainless steel water-spouts? Do you imagine your taxi being driven by Robert de Niro, and is the quintessence of Manhattan for you the black and white Queens-boro Bridge in the fog? Do you think of the Marilyn Monroe's blowing white chiffon dress when you walk over the grating of subway shafts, and does the name Tiffany's remind you not of lamps but of Audrey Hepburn's almond eyes?

If the answer to these questions is yes, then you are like all cinema lovers: even if you have never been there, New York lives in your mind predominantly through cinema images burned into the brain. Not only the most famous movies like *King Kong*, *The Bonfire of the Vanities*, *Taxi Driver*, *Manhattan*, *The Seven-Year Itch* and *Breakfast at Tiffany's*, but also countless other movies that take place in New York have left a lasting impression on their audiences. At any moment a feeling of déjà vu might come over you on the streets of New York. At www.newyorkinthemovies.com you can find out why.

A Setting in Demand

With more than **40,000 approved locations** New York is the most sought-after cinema setting in the world. More than 1,500 films play in the Big Apple, most of them in the streets of Manhattan. In the meantime it has become common to film the location shots in New York and the rest of the scenes in the studio in Hollywood. It was all rather different when the nickel-odeon was still young. In April 1896, a few months after cinema

history had begun with the Lumière brothers' presentation in the Grand Café in Paris, **the first film was shown** on the American continent in Koster and Bial's Music Hall in New York. New York remained the centre of the American film industry until the First World War. Soon the producers – with Thomas A. Edison leading the way – tried to control the quickly growing market: they founded a trust in 1908, the Motion Picture Patents Company, that did everything to secure a monopoly. Although even mafia tactics could not get the better of independents in the cinema industry – among them Charlie Chaplin, Douglas Fairbanks, William Fox, Samuel Goldwyn, Carl Laemmle and Mary Pickford – the future studio bosses chose to move their places of work to the quieter and sunny California, where they found ideal production conditions. New York's commercial film scene dwindled.

Independent Movies

Away from the mainstream along the Hudson River however, one of the most important centres of **underground films** developed. What today is known as ethnic film be-

A scene from *King Kong*, 1930

came established as early as the 1920s: Jewish films came from the Lower East Side and Harlem became the centre of black cinema. After 1945 New York moved on to be the international **capital of avant-garde cinema**. The New York school of filmmakers features names like Maya Deren, Jonas Mekas, Michael Snow, Robert Crumb with *Fritz the Cat* and of course **Andy Warhol**, who dedicated one of his static 24-hour films to the Empire State Building. Since 1955, the New York periodical Film Culture has accompanied the various movements of independent film. Representative of the intellectual role that New York plays in the film industry is the fact that the **Museum of Modern Art** began to build a collection of films in the early 1940s, a collection which contains more than 22,000 films today.

Hollywood Musicals

If films were produced in New York after 1920 then it had something to do with the inexhaustible dramatic potential of **Broadway**. Moreover, Hollywood's producers were fascinated by the success and the aesthetics of the extravagantly staged musicals. A new film genre was born: the Hollywood musical. And – how could it be any different – some of the best took place in New York. In **42nd Street** (1933) Busby Berkeley made Manhattan's skyline dance. **On the Town** in 1949 – three sailors on shore-leave in town – conveyed the euphoric post-war mood and was also the first Hollywood musical which was not filmed only in a studio but also on location in New York. **West Side Story** turned attention to the backyards of Manhattan in 1960, when the Jets and the Sharks danced in

West Side Story with music by Bernstein

neighbourhoods that have now been demolished. , and was filmed in 1977 **Hair** showed that flower power didn't just exist in San Francisco. Indeed, the declarations of love to New York just don't stop flickering across the screen: they existed as early as 1928 when Josef von Sternberg, in the exquisitely shot silent film **The Docks of New York**, immersed the dark harbour scenery into soft, transfiguring light. They lie in the small everyday gestures, when every morning Harvey Keitel in **Smoke** (1994) steps in front of his tobacco shop in Brooklyn and photographs the opposite street corner. Spike Lee's **Do the Right Thing** (1988) is another declaration of love, in which he makes the atmosphere of a humid summer day in black Brooklyn so thick that you can smell the pizza, tap your foot to the rap and feel the brooding heat, and – like the kids in the film enjoy – the cool water when the fire hydrant is opened.

They are full of poetry like the brilliant opening scene in Woody Allen's **Manhattan**: set against breathtaking black-and-white pictures of New York, with Gershwin's **Rhapsody in Blue** in the background, a New Yorker offscreen tries to formulate his relationship to his city. He hovers between kitsch, pathos and irony: »Chapter One: He was as tough and romantic as the city he loved. Behind his black rimmed glasses was the coiled sexual power of a jungle cat... New York was his town, and it always would be«. Recently the producer Martin Scorsese, with his powerful and violent historical epic film **Gangs of New York** (2002), illustrated how in the middle of the 18th century the development of the city was also shaped by violence and crime. The American Museum of the Moving Image in ►Brooklyn, the first ever American museum of film, has information on the history of American cinema.

Inside Tip

in their theatres. The producer of the show is actually just a tenant. Broadway musicals like Cats, Phantom of the Opera, Miss Saigon, The Lion King and 42nd Street suffer from their immense technical and financial complexity and radiate an almost sterile perfection. Moreover they can also be seen on musical stages in London, Toronto or Sydney. Insiders say that only two in ten shows make a profit. The actual profit is made on tours through the USA and in royalties – including the soundtracks and film rights.

Tip Open Rehearsals   *Insider Tip*

MARCO ⊕ POLO TIP

Most of the New York Philharmonic Orchestra's rehearsals are open to the public. They generally start at 9.45am and last until about 12.30pm; times and programme are available on tel. 212-875-5656 or at www.nyphil.org. Tickets cost $18.

Concerts

Those who would rather indulge in the pleasures of a **concert** are spoilt for choice in this city. Concert halls like Carnegie Hall, where the crème de la crème of classical music meets, or Radio City Music Hall – here lighter tastes are satisfied – and of course the Lincoln Center with Avery Fisher Hall, the home of the New York Philharmonic Orchestra, are all near Broadway, north of 50th Street. New York had the first permanent symphony orchestra in the USA, the Philharmonic Society founded in 1842. But not only the large orchestra is promoted here – anything goes: choir concerts, gospel music, chamber music, every kind of avant-garde music and a rich selection for children and young people, a tradition in which Leonard Bernstein, long time conductor of the New York Philharmonic Orchestra, with his »Young People's Concerts«, played a pivotal role.

Opera

The glittering highlight of classical music is the opera. Performed at many locations in New York, above all it has the most significant stage in the New World at its disposal: the Met. When the opera house befitting their social class, the Academy of Music, became too small for the wealthy families of John Pierpont Morgan and William H. Vanderbilt, they remedied the situation as only the rich can: by having the Metropolitan Opera House built – with enough boxes – on 40th Street in 1883. In 1966 the Met moved to the new Lincoln Center. The Met has no real competition in the city but there are numerous ensembles that offer unusual programmes, of which the New York City Opera (also in Lincoln Center) has managed to establish itself.

Ballet

In the 20th century New York also became a metropolis of ballet. Isadora Duncan, Ruth Saint Denis and Martha Graham developed expressive dance into its American form, modern dance. Later innovators in ballet were George Balanchine, who in 1934 founded the

School of American Ballet – which later developed into the New York City Ballet (Lincoln Center) – and Merce Cunningham. He and his ensemble worked closely with contemporary composers and painters from 1952. There is also a broad scene of ethnic dance, in which dancing styles from all over the world are represented.

Jazz The USA's real autonomous contribution to musical history is jazz, an art form which developed out of the tension between oppression, pressure to assimilate and self-awareness: the music of African Americans. Even though jazz had its first strongholds in New Orleans and Chicago, New York quickly became the focal point at the beginning of the 20th century, and the first jazz phonograph record was produced here in 1917. However it took another 20 years for the music to become successful in its pure form. Until then jazz was either reviled as »negro music«, abused as dance music or treated as a curiosity in minstrel shows, in which white people with blackened faces played supposedly black music for exclusively white audiences. Jazz finally became an avant-garde art form in the 1940s: in New York, jazz saxophonist Charlie Parker and trumpeter Dizzy Gillespie created the nervous and technically brilliant bebop, making the city

Dee Dee Bridgewater in the legendary Blue Note in Greenwich Village

the world's jazz capital. The various styles existed alongside each other; even New Orleans jazz was dusted off again. In one single street, 52nd Street, also called Swing Street or simply »the Street«, one could find a bar for every variety of jazz. At the end of the decade the trumpeter Miles Davis transformed bebop to what he called cool jazz. Even though it was first developed in New York and studio recordings made here, this new direction was less important for the city. The cool jazz scene moved to the West Coast; in 1959 the jazz saxophonist Ornette Coleman came from there and brought free jazz to New York. In the legendary **Village Vanguard**, a lively venue in Greenwich Village that still exists today, he and John Coltrane became the stars of the scene. Jazz became accepted by the establishment when in 1991 the Lincoln Center opened a separate department within the performing arts. Since 2004, jazz events have been taking place at Jazz at Lincoln Center, a venue designed especially for the purpose. Meanwhile hip hop, born in the ghettos of the Bronx, has become one of the important means of musical expression for African Americans. The DJs Grandmaster Flash, Kool Herc and Africa Bambaataa mixed records in the middle of the 1970s and moved them back and forth by hand on the turntable, a method known as »scratching«. Their raps or rhymes were as rhythmic as possible: spoonerisms, lyrics from former slave camps and prisons, later also verses about sex and violence. The background of these new sounds were the gang wars in the ghettos that were supposedly playfully enacted in song form – instead of with weapons. It was at the beginning of the 1980s when Rapper's Delight from the Sugarhill Gang initiated the worldwide debut of hip hop.

ART IN NEW YORK

America, and Europe's fascination with it, was long defined by clichés in which the country's cultural efforts were of little importance. American fine arts tried to gain their independence from 1900 on, but attained this goal only after 1945 with **abstract expressionism**, an art movement that not only did away with the European influenced concept of a picture, but also took the leading role in artistic events in the Western world with New York as the centre. This autonomous development in art looks back on a long process of assimilating European influences. At the same time the interaction remained between progressive and conservative tendencies, the repression of the art and culture of North American Indians, the devaluation of the so-called secondary culture of the African Americans and the preference for the European-dominated art created by white artists. With about 150 **museums**, some among the best in the world, such as the Metropolitan Museum, the Museum of Modern

New York
and 20th-cen-
tury art

Art, the Guggenheim, the Frick Collection, the Brooklyn Museum and the American Museum of Natural History, as well as more than 400 art galleries and cultural institutes of European, Asian and African countries, New York is today one of the most important – if not the most important – **art centres of the Western world**.

From the beginning to the late 19th century

In the 17th century, mostly anonymous **folk art** was produced, whose character is often determined by a certain world view (for example Quaker) and is more rational and functional. In the 18th century artists in New York, as in other American cities, earned their living by painting **portraits** of wealthy citizens. As in English painting of the time the person portrayed was depicted in front of a landscape background. Along with artists living in New York, John Singleton Copley, who lived and painted here for a short time, is worthy of note as well as Charles Wilson Peale and Gilbert Stuart in the time after the Civil War, who both represented a romantic realism. Just like J. S. Copley, Benjamin West, who played a significant role in the emergence of the American history painting, went to Europe; he was successful in England and became the successor to J. Reynolds as president of the Royal Academy. After returning from France, John Vanderlyn settled in New York and with Ariadne created the first nude painting in America, which promptly provoked the resistance of the Puritans.

The invention of daguerreotype in around 1839 meant that portrait painting receded into the background in favour of animal and still life painting. Some New York painters (N. G. Wall, N. Calyo, among others) used **cityscapes** as motifs. The conquest of the country and the expansion to the west and south-west led to a stronger interest in **landscapes**. In the dramatically growing city, bankers, businessmen and railway directors promoted painters of the **Hudson River School**, for example Thomas Cole, Frederic E. Church and T. W. Whittredge; other Romantic landscape painters were Albert Bierstadt who took part in expeditions westward, George Catlin, a painter of Native American life, and G. C. Bingham. In part – as with Bingham – **land-scape and genre painting** pervade their work, whereby the genre was able to succeed as a form of its own from 1850 and artists who learned in London, Paris and Düsseldorf, such as J. G. Brown and Eastman Johnson, were able to combine European technique with American subjects. Thus Winslow Homer, whose pictures with their realistic painting of light are a high-point of the second half of the 19th century, found his subjects in the events of the Civil War. The painters George Inness and Morris Hunt, through contact with Corot and the Barbizon School, became important guides on the way from Romanticism to Realism and along with Thomas Eakins prepared the way for Pleinairism. However the realistic landscape and moralizing genre painting contradicted Impressionism, which had been imported from France, and the attitude of »art for art's sake« that accompanied it. To promote the new movements **Impressionism** and **Symbolism** the Society of American Artists was founded, which organized exhibitions with William Meritt Chase, Julian Alden Weir and John Singer Sargent among others. Other branches of the arts began to emerge: free and applied **graphics** became an important factor, and the **Arts and Crafts Initiative**, based on the English model, reformed artistic craftsmanship – above all in the production of glass and metal (L. C. **Tiffany**). Three main streams could be distinguished in the arts at the end of 19th century: the Romantic with Rader and R. Blakelock, the Impressionist with Chase and Childe Hassam, the academic neo-classical with Blashfield and Cox.

The basis for **American Realism** as the counterpoint to Impressionism and academic art was created by the group **The Eight** in New York under the leadership of Robert Henri – also called the Ashcan School by opponents – whose members exhibited in 1908 in the Macbeth Gallery. George Luks, William James Glackens, John Sloan, Everett Shinn, Arthur B. Davies, Ernest Lawson and Maurice Brazil Prendergast chose as their subjects the lives of simple people and the depiction of American urban life, while George Bellows produced socio-critical milieu studies and anti-militaristic pictures. Superficial, flattering and idealized forms are alien to them. The legendary **Armory Show**, with over 1,500 works of art, was held in 1913 in New York in order to bring modern art to North America. One third of the exhibits, among them pictures by Cézanne, Braque, Picasso, Matisse, Léger, Kandinsky and Duchamp, were of European origin and belonged to the avant-garde. But the Cubism, Constructivism and Dadaism movements of the 1920s were, despite vehement discussion, without great effect; even though »New York Dada« with Francis Picabia, Man Ray and Marcel Duchamp built the foundation for developments in art after 1945. Some painters carried orphean, futuristic tendencies further (for example Joseph Stella), others processed Cubist influences (Arthur Dove, Max Weber) or carried them out in a precisionist style that showed clear lines and reduced forms (Charles Demuth, Charles Sheeler, Niles Spencer).

20th century

In the 1930s the effort to suppress European avant-garde influences and to create **American painting** led to a retrospective of tradition-

1930s

al themes and forms, and to the school of the Regionalists Grant Wood, Charles Burchfield and Thomas Hart Benton. The realistic style of painting showed other variations as well: while Edward Hopper represented a completely unique, modern style of **new concreteness**, painters like Milton Avery, by withdrawing into a personal world, found their way to a **connection between realism and mysticism**. By contrast the Depression caused by »Black Friday« caused many artists in New York to become politically active. They organized themselves in the John Reed Club, published the Art Front and demanded **art by the people and for the people** with revolutionary zeal. Aaron Douglas and Charles Alston painted murals that combined African or African American ideas with modern techniques; Jacob Lawrence took his motifs from African American history. The New York sculptress Gertrude Vanderbilt Whitney promoted artists and gave them important opportunities to exhibit, eventually in 1930 founding the **Whitney Museum of American Art**.

WPA and foreign influences

During the worldwide Depression a programme was created for artists (WPA, Work Progress Administration). The work they carried out on public buildings was influenced by the murals of the Mexican artists José Clemente Orozco and Diego Rivera who lived in New York. Many artists who took part in the WPA project were European emigrants – Willem de Kooning from Holland, Arshile Gorky from Armenia, Mark Rothko from Russia, Hans Hofmann and Josef Hofmann, Lyonel Feininger from Germany, Piet Mondrian – and they brought the ideas of Bauhaus, Picasso and Surrealism to America.

Abstract art

Since the Museum of Modern Art's exhibitions in the 1930s and 1940s of abstract, cubist and surrealist art simply passed over American abstracts, it organized itself in the group American Abstract Artists, which declined in importance with the breakthrough of Abstract Expressionism. At the beginning of the 1940s the **surrealist movement** in New York was strengthened by the immigrant artists André Breton, Yves Tanguy, André Masson and Max Ernst as well by the exhibits of the gallery owner Peggy Guggenheim, who was married to Ernst. At about the same time in New York and Paris, around 1946/47, a style of painting developed called **l'art informel** or Tachism, which rejected geometric abstraction and promoted the total freedom of colour and form. The automatism of the surrealists – in America represented especially by Matta and Arshile Gorky – served as the source and the abstract-expressive style of Vassily Kandinsky. In contrast to Europe, **Action Painting** was predominant in the USA. Prominent representatives of the New York school of Abstract Expressionism were Jackson Pollock and Willem de Kooning, along with Arshile Gorky, Franz Kline, Robert Motherwell, Sam Francis

Ed Harris as Jackson Pollock in *Pollock*

and Cliffort Still. **Jackson Pollock** played the leading role as the master of the legendary »dripping«, the unconventional drop technique in which the artist apparently drips the runny colour on the canvas at random. A reaction to the emotionally charged Abstract Expressionism are the works of the painters who use »colour as colour«. Here, with the artists of the so-called **Colour Field Painting** and **Hard Edge** (simple geometric figures with clearly limited colour zones), the pure, homogeneously used colour can either become a space for meditation (Mark Rothko, Barnett Newman, Ad Reinhardt) or be used as an unemotional rational structure (Frank Stella, Kenneth Noland, Ellsworth Kelly, Jules Olitsky). A lyrical variation is represented by Helen Frankenthaler. This painting finds its equivalent in three dimensions in **Minimal Art**, in the geometric, sober sculptures – often lined up next to each other – of Carl André, Donald Judd, or Sol LeWitt of the 1960s.

The contraposition to abstract art grew into a new interest in depicting reality as with the New Realists like Robert Rauschenberg and Jasper Johns, who anticipated the later Pop Art. The methods of ac-

New Realists

quiring reality in readymade and objet trouvé, which had been developed from Dadaism, led to the forms of expression called combined painting, environment – represented by George Segal and Edward Kienholz – and object art; the Dadaist action and the action charged painting of Abstract Expressionism led to a new form of art, **Action Art** in the forms Happening (Alan Kaprow), Fluxus (George Macunias) and Performance.

Pop Art   In the mid-1950s in England and in the USA, Pop Art, which had urban culture, consumerism and mass media as its subjects, was taken up in New York by Richard Lindner, James Rosenquist, Roy Lichtenstein and Andy Warhol. The goal of the **photorealists** (for example Richard Estes) was to make people conscious of reality as a consequence of perception processes; as with pictures a corresponding over-sharpness can also be seen in the hyperrealistic sculptures of Duane Hanson. The realistic tendencies were continued in the work of Alex Kath and Janet Fish.

The multi-talented Robert Longo in his studio with Barbara Sukova

Growing wealth encouraged the formation of a market for contemporary art; in New York hundreds of galleries sprouted like mushrooms, and the city became the centre of the art trade. But the huge boom in art and the desire of the artists for their own programme created a split into many styles. More than ever before, gallerists and the market influenced aesthetic reception. That led to analyzing forms of art at the end of the 1960s, which left gesture and its effect completely to the material, in which the creative act or the idea gained more attention than the work of art. These include, along with the already mentioned Minimal Art, the **Land Art** of Walter de Maria, whose objects in remote areas can for the most part only be conveyed by the media, and **Conceptual Art**. This advocates »art in the head«, which will no longer be realized or which deals with everyday experiences. Conceptual tendencies are evident in the work of Lawrence Weiner, James Lee Byars, Jeff Koons, Joseph Kosuth, who uses art as a method of perception, Jenny Holzer, whose medium is language, and the process-oriented artists Eva Hesse and Don Graham. In three dimensions, Richard Serra represents a post-minimalist direction, John Chamberlain's objects work like painting that has been frozen in metal, and Dan Flavin's light installations – neon tubes which make the space perceivable as a space – are concrete minimalism. The answer to the reserved Minimal Art followed with massive vehemence and emotional energy with the **neoexpressionists** Susan Rothenberg, Julian Schnabel and Jean Michel Basquiat, the latter being close to the graffiti art of Keith Haring. The high value placed on **photo art** in New York is in the tradition of Alfred Stieglitz: in this context, Cindy Sherman and Robert Mapplethorpe should be mentioned, as well as the expansion to video art by Dan Graham and Gay Hill, while Action Art finds its echo with J. L. Byars and David Hammons. Within this pluralism of style Miriam Shapiro represented »Pattern and Decoration«, Nancy Spero and her husband Leon Golub took a socio-critical direction. With the arrival of post-modern culture in the 1980s, in the time of the **Trans-Avant-Garde** with artists like Jonathan Borofsky, Jeff Koons, Haim Steinbach and Robert Longo among others, a decentralization of the art trade appears. Increased mobility and improved communication make it easier for Europe to connect again and to become an equal partner in the art scene.

Famous People

WOODY ALLEN (BORN 1.12.1935)

There are neurotics in every city, but New York boasts the most famous neurotic of all: Woody Allen, producer and actor, whose films are almost all declarations of love to his home town on the Hudson River. Woody Allen was born Allen Stewart Ko-nigsberg on 1 December 1935 in the New York borough of Brooklyn. He earned his first wage as a joke writer for newspapers under the pseudonym Woody Allen, and then wrote gags for American films and television shows, eventually working in cabarets and nightclubs as an entertainer from 1961 on. In 1965 he had his first contact with films, as author of and actor in the comedy *What's New, Pussycat?*. At the latest since his film *Annie Hall* (1977), for which he received three Oscars, Allen has been regarded as the most important comedian of more recent American film, and is an idol of intellectual cinema audiences throughout the world. In further works like *Manhattan* (1978), *Hannah and Her Sisters* (1986) and *Mighty Aphrodite* (1995) he elected to expound on his city and on the lives of the better-off, often neurotic, bizarre New Yorkers – but never on the social problems of the city. Woody Allen lives on Fifth Avenue, in fact on fashionable Upper East Side. He plays clarinet almost every Monday in the Carlyle (about $135 admission, 35 East 76th Street, tel. 212-744-1600).

JOHN JACOB ASTOR (1763–1848)

Entrepreneur

John Jacob Astor, originally from Walldorf near Heidelberg in Germany, was one of the first great American entrepreneurial personalities. He came to New York at the age of 20 and was initially a dealer in musical instruments, but later traded the instruments for furs. In 1809 he started the American Fur Company, which was followed by two other fur companies in the following years, resulting in a near monopoly in the USA. The greatest part of his enormous wealth however came from real estate speculation, in which he bought countless plots of land, above all in Manhattan. When he died his estate was estimated at 25 million dollars, making him the richest man in America. Shortly before his death he founded the Astor Library in New York with a donation of 400,000 dollars, the first public library in America.

The dancer and choreographer Martha Graham as Judith, 1957

GEORGE GERSHWIN (1898–1937)

Composer George Gershwin was born Jacob Gershowitz on 26 September 1898 in Brooklyn, New York. The son of Russian-Jewish immigrants, he grew up with two brothers, Arthur and Ira, and a sister, Francis, on Manhattan's Lower East Side. It was in fact Ira who first wanted to study piano, but the young George took to the instrument immediately and began to play by ear, so his parents arranged lessons for him from the age of twelve. By the time he was fifteen, George was already setting out on a professional career in his first job as a pianist in Tin Pan Alley, the legendary 28th Street, home to New York's music publishers. Aspiring composers and songwriters would present new songs here in the hope of selling their tunes, and Gershwin, apparently able to identify what made a song successful, soon began composing himself. In 1919, at the age of 20, he wrote *La, La, Lucille*, his first complete Broadway musical. The following year, his song *Swanee* was a huge success for Al Jolson, and after that came a string of hits, usually with his brother Ira as lyricist. Gershwin was also a successful composer of music for the concert hall, in 1924 premiering *Rhapsody in Blue*. It is said that the piece was composed in three weeks, George having forgotten all about his promise to bandleader Paul Whiteman to write it until he read an advertisement in the press announcing an exciting new Gershwin composition. It became his most famous work. There followed *An American in Paris*, written in part on a trip to Europe, and the opera *Porgy and Bess* (1935), which centred on the lives and loves of the poor African American people of South Carolina. Though today the most successful opera ever written by an American, it only became a success after Gershwin's death in 1937 at the age of thirty-eight.

MARTHA GRAHAM (1894–1991)

Dancer and choreographer Martha Graham, who came from a doctor's family in Allegheny, Pennsylvania, is regarded as the leading figure of American Modern Dance. She grew up in Santa Barbara, California and was one of the early members of Denishawn, Ruth St. Denis' and Ted Shawn's school, which in Los Angeles was to play an important role in the development of modern American dance. At the age of 22 she made her debut in New York with her first solo programme; in 1917 she had already opened her own school, to this day internationally regarded as one of the most renowned establishments in its field. Martha Graham had a career as a dancer as well as choreographer and teacher. As almost no other teacher of dance in the 20th century she succeeded in developing a strictly codified system of teaching for non-classical dance, whose special technique rested on the contrast between tensing and relaxing the body. Her film A Dancer's World presents an impressive picture of her dance aesthetics.

ALEXANDER HAMILTON (1757–1804)

A close confidant of George Washington, Alexander Hamilton advocated the federal government assumption of debts accumulated during the War of Independence. As the first secretary of the treasury of the United States (1789–1793) he set important economic impulses by founding the Bank of New York and by playing a significant role in the establishment of the New York Stock Exchange. He was a major contributor to the constitution of the United States. It was mainly thanks to him that New York City was voted to be the first United States capital. His portrait is on the US ten dollar bank note.

Founding Father

EDWARD HOPPER (1882–1967)

The career of the painter and graphic artist Edward Hopper, who for decades had a studio on Washington Square in New York, started slowly. Hopper depended on his work as an illustrator to earn his living until the 1920s. The influence of his work on American art or on the formation of the nation's artistic identity was considered to be groundbreaking. He observed his environment as no other artist, creating paintings of the life of the city, its streets, its people and their isolation. His estate contained more than 2,000 oil paintings, aquarelles, drawings and graphics for the Whitney Museum of American Art, which held the first exhaustive retrospective in 1980.

Painter

ARCHER HUNTINGTON (1870–1955)

The adopted son of the railway magnate Collis P. Huntington, born in New York, wanted to found a museum when he was only twelve years old: specifically a miniature Spain in North America. He pursued this goal with enthusiasm and devotion. In 1904 he founded the Hispanic Society of America, whose aim was to disseminate and study Iberian language and culture. Four years later the society – half museum, half library – began its work. One of the most spectacular successes was the discovery of the »painter of light« from Valencia, Joaquín Sorolla Y Bastida (1863–1923), by whom the Hispanic Society has a large number of paintings. In addition works by Velázques, El Greco, Goya, Rivera, Murillo and modern Spanish painters as well as archaeological finds, gold objects and Islamic art can be seen.

Museum founder

LOUISE NEVELSON (1899–1988)

Artist   Alongside Georgia O'Keeffe, Louise Nevelson was one of the grand
dames of American art. Born in Kiev, she came to New York at the
age of six with her parents, where she studied art, religious studies

and philosophy from 1929 until 1931. After
studying for a while in Munich with the
painter Hans Hofmann she became the as-
sistant of Diego Rivera in Mexico City from
1932 to 1938. She found her own artistic
expression in the 1950s with her wood
sculptures, which she created from wooden
objects, table legs, off-cuts and driftwood
and painted monochrome black, white or
gold. Her mysterious, totem-like, even
threatening shrines and altars, often larger
than life, soon gained her entry into the
most important museums in the world. The
high point of Louise Nevelson's career was
three rooms which she conceived for the
American pavilion in the Biennale in 1962
and her work for the Documenta in Kassel,
Germany in 1964. Her works decorate
countless squares and buildings in New
York and all over America.

ADOLPH S. OCHS (1858–1935)

Publisher   The newspaper publisher Adolph S. Ochs was born in Knoxville,
Tennessee, the son of a German-Jewish immigrant. He began his career at the age of eleven as a newspaper boy in his home town and
was an apprentice typesetter until 1875. He then went to Chattanoo-
ga, Tennessee, where three years later, at the age of 20, he bought the
Times newspaper and in four years transformed it into a generally
respected newspaper. He landed his greatest coup in 1896, when he
bought the New York Times for 75,000 dollars. The paper had been
founded 45 years earlier and had survived only with difficulty
amongst the bitter competition of the New York press, but by the
time of his retirement in 1993 Ochs had made it the most important
newspaper in America, with its motto: »All the news that's fit to
print«. The newspaper, which has since grown into a corporation
with publishing house, paper factory, periodicals, radio and television stations, is now a stock corporation, but is still run by Adolph S.
Ochs' heirs: the present publisher, who took over in January 1992, is
Arthur Ochs Sulzberger jr., a great grandson of Adolph S. Ochs.

CORNELIUS VANDERBILT (1794–1877)

At only twelve years old, Vanderbilt would help his father to ferry **Entrepreneur** passengers and baggage from Staten Island to New York. Four years later he had his own boat, after eight years he became the executive of a steamship line, and after another ten years he founded his own steamship line, with which he brought gold diggers to California in 1849. He eventually entered into transatlantic traffic, but when the competition became too strong he changed to railway lines. In 1863 he bought his first railway company, the New York and Harlem Railway; others were added. When Vanderbilt died, the »Commodore«, as he was called, left a fortune of 105 million dollars, an inconceivable sum for his time. His son William Henry expanded the empire within eight years to 50 railway lines with 25,000km/15,000mi of track. The Vanderbilts were the richest family in the USA. For some, Cornelius Vanderbilt is the definitive American self-made man; for others he is a monster of capitalism, who gained his wealth through deception, exploitation, bribery and merciless competition – though it is said his competitors were no different.

ANDY WARHOL (1928–1987)

Probably the most famous representative of Pop Art was actually **Artist** called Andrew Warhola and was originally a graphic artist. At the beginning of the 1960s he painted his first pictures, and then turned more and more to screen printing, with which he reproduced photographs from mass media and printed them in series. As motifs he chose everyday items like dollar bills or soup cans (*200 Campbell's Soup Cans*) and mass idols like Elvis Presley, Elizabeth Taylor or Marilyn Monroe (*Marilyn Diptych*). The goal of his artistic work was the radical integration of art in the mechanical work process. From 1963 he turned to film (*Sleep, Blue Movie, Flesh*); only in the 1970s did he again produce prints (*Willy Brandt*). He created his works in a collective with the members of his living and working group, the »Factory«. With increasing fame Warhol himself became an idol and object of his own art. As well as possessing incontestable artistic talent, Warhol had a great ability to market himself; his concept of art extended so far that he declared the large number of objects and antiques that he acquired to have become part of his own existence through his act of purchasing them, and argued that they could thus themselves be viewed as art.

ENJOY
NEW YORK

Find the right restaurant for a good meal after a busy day of sightseeing. Round off the evening in a stylish or cosy bar. Get tickets for a musical or a high-class concert. Read on to find lots of suggestions!

Accommodation

A Never Sleeping City?

Even if, as Frank Sinatra sang, New York is the city that never sleeps, visitors do need a roof over their heads. This city is a noisy and expensive place to stay. In Manhattan a double room usually costs $ 200, and bargains are rare.

Bear in mind when looking at prices that sales tax (8.875 per cent), accommodation tax (14.25 per cent) and room tax ($2 per night) are added to the price – amounting to $46 extra on a net price of $200! The prices are per room, not per person, and in some hotels an opulent breakfast is included that would exceed the budget of most tourists if taken in a restaurant. It is highly advisable to book early, especially for trips in the high season, at Christmas and around American public holidays

Prices

A few tips: If you need a guarantee that your room will be kept free for late arrival (after 6pm), do not fail to make this clear when booking. Cash and valuables should be deposited in a hotel safe, either in the room or at reception. Apart from the usual options of twin beds, a queen-size or a king-size bed, a »rollaway« can often be provided for a third person in the room for a modest additional fee. Luggage porters expect a tip of $2 to $5, chamber maids $1 per day.

Rooms are generally well equipped, even in less expensive hotels: almost always a TV, telephone and internet connection are included, most bathrooms have a hairdryer, and higher-class hotels usually provide a mini-bar and room service.

The average price of a hotel room in New York in 2012 was $250. When booking, ask if any special price is available, as this can mean a saving of up to 50 per cent of the list price. At weekends and outside the main season attractive offers are made, and early booking helps to get a low price.

Savings

Rooms are cheapest between January and March, and again in July and August, most expensive in autumn and at Christmas. In Uptown and Downtown Manhattan, and in the other boroughs, accommodation is cheaper, although the subway journey to the centre of Manhattan takes only 30 minutes.

Online reservation is a further option for making savings, for example via: www.expedia.com, www.travelocity.com, www.hrs.com, www.trivago.com

The epitome of American luxury accommodation: the Waldorf-Astoria occupies a 42-storey Art Deco building on Park Avenue in Manhattan

For a longer stay in the USA it makes sense to stick with a hotel chain (e.g. Best Western or Holiday Inn) and to make savings by means of a loyalty card or bonus points. Among the reservation agencies that offer low-cost bookings, the best-known are Quikbook (tel. 1 212 779 7666, www.quikbook.com) and the hotel reservations network (www.hoteldiscount.com). Before booking through these channels, check with the hotel direct to see what rates you can get.

Bed & breakfast A good service for finding a bed & breakfast room is Manhattan Getaways (tel. 1 212 956 2010, http://manhattangetaways.com.

Recommended Hotels

PRICE CATEGORIES
per double room incl. breakfast (extra payment for breakfast is becoming more common)
$$$$: over $300
$$$: $250 to 300
$$: $180 to 250
$: up to $180

❶ etc. ▶maps p. 112 – 115 Entries without a number are not on the map.

LUXURY
❶ Carlyle $$$$
35 E 76th St.
(between Madison and Park Ave.)
Tel. 1 212-744-1600
www.thecarlyle.com
(180 rooms). Many critics consider the Carlyle to be the best-run hotel in New York. The five-star hotel has attracted famous guests since its opening in 1930. The staff, always present but unobtrusive, are so discreet that even two members of the Beatles, who stayed here after the group separated, did not know that the other was there. Only about 20% of the luxurious rooms are set aside for tourists and other travellers. The rest are leased long-term.

❷ Four Seasons $$$$
57 E 57th St.
(between Madison and Park Ave.)
Tel. 1 212-758-5700
www.fourseasons.com
(368 rooms). With 52 floors, the Four Seasons is New York's tallest hotel at 208m/681ft, and the rooms in Art Deco style are the biggest in the city. The bathtubs fill very quickly (in about 60 seconds).

❸ Pierre $$$$
61st St. / Fifth Ave.
Tel. 1 212-838-8000
www.tajhotels.com/pierre
(189 rooms) The painter Salvador Dalí felt at home in this hotel, which was opened in 1929 and still features old-fashioned luxury and elegant, European-style ambience. Madonna paid $2,900 per night for two suites – one for sleeping in and the other for her weights and fitness equipment.

❹ Mandarin Oriental $$$$
80 Columbus Circle
Tel. 1 212-805-8800
www.mandarinoriental.com
(248 rooms) Located between the 37th and 53rd floors of the Time

Warner Center, which was opened in 2004. The rooms offer guests spectacular views of Central Park, the Hudson or Manhattan's skyline.

❺ St Regis $$$$

2 E 55th St./Fifth Ave.
Tel. 1 212-753-4500
www.stregis.com
(229 rooms) The flagship of the luxury St Regis brand of Starwood Hotels, a former townhouse built from 1902 to 1904 by John Jacob Astor, who drowned in 1912 when the Titanic sank. The hotel impresses with its perfect service. The restaurant Adour by Alain Ducasse with its sophisticated cuisine is one of New York's foremost attractions for gourmets. Of course there has been no lack of big names at this hotel: these include Liza Minelli, Leonard Bernstein and Marlene Dietrich, who was a welcome guest in the King Cole Bar.

❻ Waldorf Astoria $$$$

301 Park Ave./50th St.
Tel. 1 212-355-3000
www.waldorf.com
(1,380 rooms). ►MARCO POLO Insight p.68

⓮ Mercer $$$$

147 Mercer St./Prince St.
Tel. 1 212-966-6060
www.mercerhotel.com
(75 rooms) The archetype of arty: André Balazs, a wealthy night-owl city celebrity, had an interesting mixture of atelier, café and living room built in the middle of trendy SoHo. The corridors are lit by changing pastel lights; star designer Christian Liaigre designed the rooms (often with a French balcony). Leonardo di Caprio relaxes here on a regular basis.

㉘ Gramercy Park Hotel $$$$

2 Lexington Avenue
(adjacent to Gramercy Park)
Gramercy Park, Manhattan
Tel. 1 212 920 3300
www.gramercyparkhotel.com
This legendary luxury hotel is known for its rich and colourful history. Since it was built in 1925, it has attracted many famous people. Humphrey Bogart got married here, the Kennedys lived here for several months, and it attracted famous actors, writers and artists, but mostly big-name musicians, such as the Beatles, Bob Marley, Bob Dylan, the Rolling Stones and David Bowie, to name a few. Hank Williams is said to have written one of his greatest hits »I am so lonesome I could cry« while staying at this hotel. World-famous artist Julian Schnabel designed the interior of the hotel. The hotel owns an impressive art collection, such as works of Julian Schnabel, Andy Warhol, Jean-Michel Basquiat, Damien Hirst, Richard Prince and Cy Twombly. The rooftop garden oasis is one of the most popular party locations of the rich and famous.

MID-RANGE TO EXPENSIVE
❼ Hotel Gansevoort $$$

18 Ninth Ave., near 13th St.
Tel. 1 212-206-6700

Who Sleeps Where...

Liz Taylor, the Dalai Lama, Prince Rainier and Princess Grace of Monaco – the list of prominent guests who have stayed at the Waldorf Astoria is endless. To this day, only the rich and famous stay here.

It was ever thus, ever since the hotel was opened in 1931. In 1893 the multimillionaire William Astor, a descendant of German immigrants from Waldorf, near Heidelberg, opened the **Hotel Waldorf** on Fifth Avenue. Another member of the family then opened the **Astoria Hotel** next door. Four years later the two hotels merged, but in 1929 they had to make room for the Empire State Building. In 1931 the hotel celebrated its re-opening on Park Avenue near 50th Street. With 42 floors and 1,380 rooms it was at that time the largest hotel in the world; it is still the most famous hotel in New York (and now sold to a Chinese investor). If the luxurious rooms and suites are too expensive, it is still possible to enjoy the atmosphere of the Art Deco hotel in the lobby, in the shops, bars and restaurants on the lower floors. But those looking for the elegance and exclusive atmosphere that a hotel like this one promises have to go to the top – and that applies to the prices, too. Waldorf Towers, between the 28th and 42nd floor, is run like a separate hotel – with 106 deluxe suites and 85 luxury rooms, where numerous permanent guests choose to stay, as the composer Cole Porter did in days past. Even the president stays here when he pays the city a visit to New York. The price for a night in the president's suite? $4,000.

The Chelsea

Ernest Hemingway, Arthur Miller, Sarah Bernhardt, Mark Twain, Bob Dylan, John Lennon, Andy Warhol, Jimi Hendrix – the Chelsea too has seen famous names. But crowned heads of state and statesmen did not and do not count among the guests of the ten-storey Victorian red brick house on 23rd Street. Erected in 1884 as an apartment building, at that time the Chelsea was the tallest building in Manhattan and gave the neighbourhood its name. In 1903 it was converted into a hotel. Stanley Bard, who took over in 1957, had soft spot for artists and castaways. He allowed them to pay with paintings, books, vinyl records and musical notes if they had no cash. This quickly attracted artists who lived here for months or even years, and who not uncommonly were inspired to produce masterpieces, like **Thomas Wolfe** who wrote *You Can't Go Home Again* here. Arthur Miller holed up here after his separation from Marilyn Monroe, Arthur C. Clarke wrote the screenplay for *2001 – A Space Odyssey* in the hotel, and in room 211 Bob Dylan wrote his 20-minute ballad *Sad-Eyed Lady of the Lowlands*. The saddest kind of fame came to room 100 where the punk musician **Sid Vicious** of the Sex Pistols stabbed his girlfriend.

Once the place where artists and art-lovers stayed: the Chelsea Hotel

In 2007, this area was redeveloped, and the luxury hotel was bulit here.

The Leo House

Illustrious names in the Leo House? Difficult question! But here, too, a part of the clientele comes from a certain segment of society. The hotel on 23rd St. is often frequented by **Catholic clergy**; the Leo House is a Roman Catholic establishment. But they won't ask for your religious affiliation when you reserve a room – every guest is welcome here. The Leo House originally stood in New York's Battery Park. The hotel was opened in 1899 by the St Raphael Society, a society of German clergy, who wanted to help German immigrants find work or relatives in the New World. At the end of the 19th century and the beginning of the 20th century the charitable society helped thousands of new arrivals to get started in the USA. In the mid-1920s the Leo House moved to 23rd Street where over 100 beds on eight floors are now available to guests: in single, double and so-called family rooms for up to six people. Even though the Leo House is still a »Christian guesthouse« for travelling Catholic clergy, these by no means make up the entire clientele anymore, and anyone can benefit from the **low prices** and the clean accommodation. A double room with toilet and sink (showers in the hall) costs little more than $100. The excellent breakfast buffet is also inexpensive – served daily except for Sunday, the Lord's Day.

Hotel Gansevoort is a hip place to stay in the trendy Meatpacking District

www.hotelgansevoort.com (187 rooms) An ultra-hip hotel in the middle of the trendy Meatpacking District. The roof area with a 15m/50ft glassed-in pool (with underwater music!) and the fantastic views cannot fail to impress; so too do the often very original room designs and the exquisite interior – marble dressing tables, bedding made of Egyptian linen, mobile phones and so on. There is a second, newer Gansevoort in Midtown at Park Ave./E 29th St.

㉙ The Standard $$$
848 Washington St/West 13th St
Tel. 1 212 645 4646
www.standardhotels. com
Straddling High Line in the Meatpacking District of Manhattan, this 18-storey luxury boutique hotel, with its sleek floor-to-ceiling and wall-to-wall windows in every room and suite, offers stunning views of the New York City skyline, the Hudson River and the Empire State Building. The rooms feel at once generous and open, glamourous and sexy and match

the vibrant nightlife of the Meat-packing District. You can watch the sunset over the Hudson River.

❾ Ameritania $$$

1701 Broadway, near 54th St.
Tel. 1 212-247-5000
www.ameritanianyc.com
The hotel's A-logo is futuristic, as is the entrance hall. But the rooms are furnished more traditionally in this 1930s building, located on Broadway right next to the Ed Sullivan Theater where the Late Show with David Letterman takes place. The hotel is an ideal base for guests who love theatre and musicals.

❿ Box Tree Inn $$$

250 E 49th St.
(between Second and Third Ave.)
Tel. 1 212-758-8320
Kitsch as kitsch can: there are canopy beds and fireplaces even in the standard rooms. As romantic as it gets. Robert De Niro and Barbra Streisand are among the stars who have stayed here.

The Franklin $$$ **Insider Tip**

164 E 87th St. (between Lexington and Third Ave.)
Tel. 1 212-369-1000
www.franklinhotel.com
(92 rooms). Very small rooms tastefully furnished, where you can enjoy luxury at an affordable price. Small breakfast and parking included in the price. This elegant hotel is near the Museum Mile, and the international boutiques on Madison Avenue as well as first-class restaurants are not far away. The Franklin is the preferred accommodation of fashion models.

⓱ Millennium Broadway $$$

145 West 44th St.
(near Sixth Avenue)
Tel. 1 212-768-4400
www.millenniumhotels.com
This cultivated Art Deco hotel is only two blocks away from Times Square and has numerous extras like larger beds, more comfortable covers and free internet access.

Best Western Bowery Hanbee $$$

231 Grand St.
Tel. 1 212-925-1177
www.bw-boweryhanbeehotel.com
Located in the middle of lively Chinatown, from where many sights can be reached on foot. New rooms with modern furnishings.

㉕ The Lucerne $$$

201 West 79th Street
(corner of Amsterdam Ave.)
Tel. 1 212-875-1000
www.newyorkhotel.com
The historic hotel was built already in 1903 as a dormitory for the university. But with elaborate remodelling in 1995 it was converted to a comfortable and European-style boutique hotel. It is surprisingly affordable for being on the Upper West Side. The rooms have wireless internet and numerous extras

MID-RANGE
❽ Algonquin $$

59 W 44th St.
(between Fifth and Sixth Ave.)
Tel. 1 212-840-6800
www.thealgonquin.net
Opened in 1902, the Algonquin hosted the famous round-table

meetings of Dorothy Parker, Robert Benchley and James Thurber among others in the 1920s and 1930s, where they pondered the decline of Western civilization. Today's hotel owners are Japanese and have restored it with great care. The rooms are tiny but nicely decorated, the panelled lobby has a living-room atmosphere.

⑫ Radisson Lexington $$
511 Lexington Ave./48th St.
Tel. 1 212-755-4400
www.lexingtonhotel.com
(712 rooms) Because of its central location – near Grand Central Terminal and the United Nations – the 27-floor hotel is especially popular among business travellers and shoppers. In addition to the in-house Chinese restaurant there is a sushi bar, a bistro, a coffee house and a night club.

⑮ Metro $$ **Insider Tip**
45 W 35th St.
(between Fifth and Sixth Ave.)
Tel. 1 212-947-2500
www.hotelmetronyc.com
(179 rooms) The hotel has small, tastefully furnished rooms and a nice rooftop terrace with a view of the Empire State Building. It is conveniently located, therefore also popular among business people. Breakfast is included and the Metro Grill restaurant was opened.

⑯ Paramount $$
235 W 46th St. (between Broadway and Eighth Ave.)

Tel. 1 212-764-5500
www.nycparamount.com
(610 rooms) This used to be a tourist hotel. After being completely remodelled by the French designer Philippe Starck it has become a popular place to go in the theatre district. The rooms are very small, but have all the necessities. The hotel has an elegant restaurant, a Dean and Deluca and two bars.

Hotel Wales $$
1295 Madison Ave
(near 92nd Street)
Tel. 1 212-876-6000
www.hotelwalesnyc.com
The rooms were furnished with care and everything fits to the last detail. The atmosphere is homely and the European bedding only makes it more comfortable. The fitness room and business centre are modern.

⑲ Salisbury Hotel $$
123 West 57th St.
Tel. 1 212-246-1300
www.nycsalisbury.com
This basic hotel is located opposite Carnegie Hall and only a few minutes from the shops on Fifth Avenue. The rooms are surprisingly big for a budget hotel. There are »corporate rooms« available with computer ports etc. for business travellers.

㉓ Milford Plaza $$
270 W 45th St./Eighth Ave.
Tel. 1 212-869-3600
www.milfordplaza.com

An unconventional and individual hotel: the Gershwin calls itself a »beautiful monster«

(1,310 rooms) This pre-war high rise is an easy walk from all of the Broadway theatres. The fitness room is available free for guests.

BUDGET
⑬ Belleclaire $
250 West 77th St
Tel. 1 212-362-7700
www.hotelbelleclaire.com
Almost posh, nevertheless affordable house – built in 1903 in Beaux Arts style, recently restored – on the Upper West Side. The cheapest rooms cost only a little more than $100 (without bathroom), but some run to over $400. Furnished very nicely and comfortably. There are many ethnic restaurants and trendy cafés nearby, or just go to Zabar's.

⑳ Gershwin $ Insider Tip
7 E 27th St.
Tel. 1 212-545-8000
www.gershwinhotel.com
(150 rooms) Somewhat crazy but very nice (recently renovated) hotel near Fifth Ave. and the Empire State Building. Rooms range from very cheap (with bunk beds) to family suite.

㉑ Leo House $ Insider Tip
332 W 23rd St.
(between Eighth and Ninth Ave.)
Tel. 1 212-929-1010
(100 beds) ▶MARCO POLO Insight p.68

㉒ Riverview Hotel $
113 Jane St.
(between 12th and 14th St.)
Tel. 1 212-929-0060
www.hotelriverview.com

(208 rooms) Low-budget hotel on the Hudson River in Greenwich with simple, clean rooms.

⑱ De Hirsch Residence $
1395 Lexington Ave./92nd St.
(between Seventh and Eighth Ave.)
Tel. 1 212-929-0060
www.92y.org
(2350 beds) Although this is a Young Men's/Young Women's Hebrew Association hostel, you don't have to be either young or Jewish to stay here. The rooms are spacious and there is a kitchen on every floor.

㉔ Seafarers and International House $
123 E 15th St./Irving Place
Tel. 1 212-677-4800
www.sihnyc.org
(84 rooms) First opened in 1873 as a home for poor sailors, today the hotel provides some of the cheapest accommodation in New York with small but clean rooms.

㉖ Vanderbilt YMCA $
224 E 47th Street
(between Second and Third Ave.)
Tel. 1 212-912-2500
www.amcanyc.org
(370 rooms) This centrally located former youth hostel has been converted into a low-price hotel. Some rooms are very small. A fitness room and two pools are available for the guests.

⑪ West Side YMCA $
5 W 63rd St. (between C. Park West and Broadway)
Tel. 1 212-787-4400
www.ymcanyc.org

(525 rooms) This youth hostel is located near the Lincoln Center and Central Park. The rooms are simple but clean.

㉗ East Village Bed & Coffee $
110 Avenue C
Tel. 917-816-0071
www.bedandcoffee.com
Ideal location but without breakfast! But the neighbourhood has enough on offer.

Regina's Bed & Breakfast $
16 Fort Green Place, Brooklyn
Tel. 1 718-834-9253
www.home.earthlink.net
Pretty rooms in a listed brownstone house.

BED & BREAKFAST · APARTMENTS · SUBLET
Private homes
Alternatives to hotels are in fashion, including bed & breakfast, apartments or flats or subletting. The price varies with the furnishings, number of rooms and location. Booking online is simplest:
www.urbanlivingny.com

www.newyork.craigslist.org
http://newyorkcity.sublet.com
www.airbnb.com

Others:

City Lights
Tel. 1 212-737-7049
www.citylightsbandb.com

Abode Bed & Breakfast
Tel. 1 212-472-2000
www.abodenyc.com

Bed & Breakfast Network of New York
Tel.1 813-265-2419
www.bedandbreakfastnetny.com

NY Apartment Petra Loewen LLC
Tel. 1 718-373-2226
www.aptpl.com

Affordable New York
Tel. 1 212-533-4001
www.affordablenewyorkcity.com

City Sonnet
Tel. 1 212-614-3034
www.citysonnet.com

Children in New York

No End to the Variety

The Big Apple has a lot to offer kids. There are parks with playgrounds, exciting hands-on museums like South Street Seaport and the Children's Museum, the world's biggest toy-shop FAO Schwartz and the Bronx Zoo. A full calendar of events and fast-food on every corner also add to the entertainment for children.

The Friday New York Times has a »For Children« page in the Weekend section with tips on where kids can have fun in New York over the whole week. Tips can also be found under »Children's Events« or »Activities for Children« in New York Magazine. Frommer's New York City with Kids, available in bookshops, also provides information. A few suggestions follow here; the ones marked with an arrow (▶) are described in the section ▶Sights from A to Z.

Activities with children

In ▶**Central Park** with its many playgrounds, children can play, ice skate, roller skate, ride bikes, etc. In the old harbour, the ▶South Street Seaport on the East River, there are historical sailing ships. Boat trips around Manhattan or to Staten Island, or city tours on double-decker buses are also fun.

Suggestions

The ▶**American Museum of Natural History** is considered to be the most popular museum in New York; among other things there are very impressive dinosaur skeletons here. In the **Brooklyn Children's Museum** children can touch, try out and play with all the exhibits (▶Brooklyn). In **FAO Schwartz** (767 Fifth Ave./59th St.), it is possible to buy anything a child's heart desires. Here, be prepared to spend lots of time – and money. The interesting space and sea travel museum, the **Intrepid Sea, Air & Space Museum**, is situated on a decommissioned aircraft carrier on the Hudson (▶p.136).

The ▶**Bronx Zoo** is one of the most beautiful zoos in the world with artificial jungles, huge open areas for animals, a children's zoo and a monorail. The Little Orchestra Society (»Happy Concerts for Young People«) in Avery Fisher Hall in the ▶Lincoln Center puts on **classical music** for children. When Handel's Water Music is played the conductor appears in a diving suit (every Saturday afternoon, times can vary). The **Big Apple Circus** performs in Damrosch Park next to the Metropolitan Opera from October to January (62nd St., between Columbus and Amsterdam Ave., tel. 1 888-541-3750, www.bigapplecircus.org).

A popular white-knuckle ride:
the wooden roller coaster on Coney Island

Hist for Kids

Information
www.gocitykids.com
www.mommypoppins.com
www.timeoutnewyorkkids.com

Creative play
Popular places to play are **Heck-scher Playground** in Central Park (daily from 7.30am); 62nd Street/ Central Park South), **Brooklyn Bridge Park** at pier 6 (Furman St./ Atlantic Ave.) with access to the beach and water games, **South Street Seaport Imagination Playground** (daily from 9am, Burlington Slip, John St. between Front and South St.) and **Union Square Park Playground** (daily from 8am, between E 14th and 17th St.).

Central Park Carousel

Insider Tip

A colourful carousel has been turning on this site ever since the first one was built in 1871. It is located in a round building, protected from wind and weather. Just as at the county fairs of the first half of the 20th century, children ride on large hand-carved wooden horses. Central Park near 64th Street, tel. 1 212-439-6900; summer daily from 10am until 6pm, winter until 4.30pm.

Blessing the animals in St John the Divine
Certainly a highlight for kids and other animal lovers: the annual blessing of the animals in the ►Cathedral of St John the Divine. On the first Sunday in October at 11am camels, elephants, donkeys, dogs, cats, birds and other representatives of the city's fauna gather to be blessed for the coming church year. Free tickets are available from 9am; come early, as the queue is long.

Children's Museum of Manhattan

Insider Tip

This museum invites children to join in: in an interactive computer department bikes learn to fly and robots to speak; children can draw, colour or scribble on various computer monitors. 212 W 83rd St., between Amsterdam Ave. and Broadway; tel. 1 212-721-1234; www.cmom.org; Tue–Sun 10am–5pm. Similar active museums: Snug Harbour (►Staten Island) and in ►Brooklyn.

Scott's Pizza Tours
Just the thing for pizza lovers: the NYC Pizza Bus Tour by Scott's Pizza Tours goes to four of the best pizzerias in New York. En route the history of the pizza is explained; watch pizzas being made in the pizzerias. Of course, there are also free samples and at the end a goody bag to take along. Spring Street, tel. 1 212-209-3370; www.scottspizzatours.com; Fri, Sat, Mon 11am–2pm, adults $55, children (aged 4–12) from $35.

New York Aquarium
In the New York Aquarium (►Brooklyn) children can admire hundreds of kinds of exotic fish – and hunt for Nemo, the little clownfish. The appearance of the family of beluga whales and the acrobatics of the sea lions are especially popular.

Coney Island – Back in Business

Nathan's sells the best hot dogs on the planet. This alone is a good enough reason to take the one-hour subway ride to Coney Island, which was the world's biggest playground in the 1920s.

For more than 75 years a legendary snack bar has stood at the subway exit at the corner of Surf Ave. and Stillwell Ave. It symbolizes the cult status of the peninsula at the southern tip of Brooklyn, and dyed-in-the-wool Islanders even maintain that the hot dog was invented at Nathan's. Whether true or not, Coney Island Hot Dog tastes so good that Nathan's has opened branches in Manhattan, where, of course, they taste different: connoisseurs say that the Coney Island Hot Dog is only at its best where it originated, on Coney Island.

Off to the Beach

The rest of Coney Island also has to be seen through nostalgia-tinted glasses, looking back as far as the time before the First World War, when the pleasure park on the Atlantic Ocean was a favourite day-trip destination for stressed, sun-starved residents of the city, who came here at weekends in hundreds of thousands. From 1893 a historic big wheel turned here: one of the original Ferris Wheels, an invention of George Washington Ferris. This giant with its blinking lights was a sensation in the park until the 1950s, and the miles of beach promenade were the haunt of countless pleasure-seekers and young couples.

After decades of decay, Coney Island's entertainment strip experienced a miraculous rebirth on Memorial Day 2010. Today the dilapidated amusement park has again become a worthwhile place for a day out – not only for children. Even the **Wonder Wheel** and the old **Cyclone**, an old-time, breathtakingly fast roller-coaster, are still there. The old Astroland was turned into Luna Park, commemorating the historic Luna Park that existed here from 1903 until 1940.

Today 19 more rides round off the attractions of Coney Island. The beach and the hot dog stand are only a stone's throw from the amusement park, and right next door lies the shell-shaped New York Aquarium (▶p.208).

Coney Island in 1902

Entertainment

The World Capital of Nightlife

New York is the world capital of nightlife. The selection is huge: music events, rock, pop and Latin concerts, both in halls and the open air, jazz clubs, pubs with live music, comedy shows, cinema, Broadway shows, clubs, dance, studio theatre – the offering ranges from magnificent entertainments that are broadcasted across the world by satellite to variety shows that hardly anyone outside the Village takes notice of.

Rituals of nightlife

The true nightlife of New York takes place during the week. Thursday, Friday and Saturday, the so-called »bridge and tunnel days«, belong to people who come in across or beneath the water from New Jersey, and to visitors who still believe in Saturday Night Fever. It is not always easy to get past the velvet rope that bouncers place in front of popular establishments. It is recommended to wear black, though khaki green may also do, to display a good deal of self-confidence and to be aware that a few dollars count for more at the door than belonging to an elite that does not necessarily mean hard cash for the management. The chances of getting past the doormen are higher if you arrive early, i.e. before 10pm, or late – after 3am. It is also a good idea to get on the guest list with an online booking.

Programmes

To get your bearings, first take a look at the daily newspapers and magazines: the *New York Times* (Fri, Sat), *New York Magazine* (Mon), *The New Yorker* (Mon). *Village Voice* has a good ear for what's trendy, especially when it comes to music, and the weekly *Time Out New York* is also well-informed. The gay and lesbian scene is covered by *Gay City News* and *Go!* For hip bars and lounges, take a look at www.sheckysnightlife.com. Listings of the latest plays and Broadway shows are at www.broadway.com, www.ilovenytheater.com and www.theatermania.com.

Further internet sources are www.nyc.go.com and www.flavorpill.com, the latter making interesting choices every Tuesday. For information on music and theatre, see Jazz Line (tel. 1 212-479-7888), Concert Hotline (tel. 1 212-777-1224), www.broadwayonline.com, www.broadway.org, www.broadway.com and www.nytheatre.com.

Times and costs

The clubs' programmes vary. There is music, live or mixed by DJs, theatre, cabaret and also poetry readings. The terms (entrance or minimum charge, reservations, time etc.) vary from programme to

Stars of the jazz world perform live at the annual Blue Note Jazz Festival – here Chris Potter of the Francisco Mela Quintet

programme. A (very rough) rule of thumb: the price of a live show with known stars is between $30 and $120 (or more), and a drink costs from $6.50. Live performances rarely begin before 9pm or 10pm, though there are exceptions including brunch sessions at jazz clubs at weekends. Dance clubs open at midnight, but things don't start to swing before the early hours. Information on individual clubs and bars is available at www.clubplanet.com. Links to the homepages of the clubs are found here as well, and they often offer special deals – in the form of coupons that have to be printed out.

Trendsetters' territory

The fact that few kids can be seen in Midtown has to do with the fact that the area north of 30th Street is considered to be forty-something territory, for the older and more well-behaved night-owls. Trendy areas lie south of 14th Street: the area around Tompkins Square Park or the Lower East Side and the Meatpacking District, the former meat market around Gansevoort Street. The **forefront of coolness**, however, has been shifting across the East River to **Brooklyn** since the late 1990s. The hippest neighbourhood is now considered to be **Williamsburg**, with its visionary live music clubs, nightclubs, bars, lofts and trendy shops around Bedford Avenue down to river. Once a working-class neighbourhood, this quaint but also hip neighbourhood draws especially young creative trendsetters and young professionals. Williamsburg is experiencing rapid, ongoing gentrification. The Brooklyn neighbourhoods Bushwick, Red Hook and Carroll Gardens are also experiencing a renaissance to some extent. It is said that New York's new cultural tones are set by the young and visionary creatives right here in these neighbourhoods of Brooklyn.

THEATRE, MUSIC BALLET AND CINEMA

Theatre

With more than 250 theatres, two opera houses, numerous orchestras, ballet and dance groups as well as an event calendar that's filled to bursting point, New York is a world capital of entertainment. There are almost 40 Broadway, 20 Off-Broadway and more than 200 Off-Off-Broadway theatres. While the elaborate musicals dominate the theatres on Broadway between 41st and 53rd Street, the Off and Off-Off-Broadway stages are more likely to be in Midtown or the Village. The most difficult part of going to a Broadway show is making your choice. Here it is helpful to take a look at who won the Tony Awards, the most prestigious in the business (www.broadway.com).

Visitors can dive into strange worlds in the Coral Room Club

Opera

Grand Opera is at home in the Metropolitan Opera. It is part of Lincoln Center (►Sights from A to Z, Lincoln Center for the Performing Arts). In addition there are a number of smaller opera companies that perform only occasionally.

Ballet

Ballet fans can chose from a unique selection in New York. The centre of the scene is the **Lincoln Center**, where from November until February and from the end of April until the beginning of June the New York City Ballet performs in the New York State Theater and the American Ballet Theater in the Metropolitan Opera House. Alongside the city ensembles there are regular guest appearances by companies from all over the United States and the rest of the world.

Concerts

In the main season (Oct–Apr) about 150 musical events take place in New York every week. Along with the concerts of the New York Philharmonic Orchestra four times a week (Tue, Thu, Fri, Sat) in the Avery Fisher Hall (►Sights from A to Z, Lincoln Center for the Performing Arts) there are guest appearances by American and foreign orchestras, choir concerts, chamber music, vocal music, jazz and rock concerts. Concerts of religious music are held in many New York churches, especially in the Christmas and Easter seasons (but by no means only then). They are listed in the Saturday edition of the New York Times. Free concerts and opera performances are held in the summer months by the New York Philharmonic Orchestra and the Metropolitan Opera in Central Park as well as in parks of the other four boroughs of New York (information: tel. 1 212-360-3456). ►Advance ticket sales

Late Show David Letterman is one of the best-known hosts of US talk shows. Prominent people from show business, sport and politics queue up to appear on his Late Show (Mon–Thu). Tickets for live shows are available, up to two tickets per request (tel. 1 212-247-6497, www.cbs.com/late-show, Mon–Fri 9.30am–12.30pm, Sat, Sun 10am–6pm, West 1697 Broadway, between 53rd and 54th St.; standby tickets on the day of recording at around 11am).

MARCO ◉ POLO TIP

For cinema lovers **Insider Tip**

The ►Lincoln Center is the site of the annual New York Film Festival. Foreign and independent productions can be seen at BAM Rose Cinemas in the Brooklyn Academy of Music, 30 Lafayette Ave., Brooklyn, tel. 1 718-636-4100, www.bam.org. The ultimate cinema venue in the summer is the Bryant Park Film Festival behind the Public Library on 42nd Street. For information: tel. 1 212-512-5700, or www.bryantpark.org.

Film premieres generally take place in the city cinemas (exceptions prove this rule). The **largest central cinemas** are in the area around Times Square, west of Broadway between 50th and 60th St. and east between 50th and 70th St., and on the Upper East Side on East 34th St. near Third Ave. The other large cinemas are in Greenwich Village. Smaller cinemas can be found all over town; some have specialized in certain types of films such as classics, cultural films or experimental films.

TICKETS

Plan in advance! In general, tickets can be purchased in person at the venue. Another possibility is to ask the hotel concierge who will try to obtain tickets, for a 20% surcharge. Since popular performances and shows are often sold out months in advance, it makes sense to order tickets before you travel to New York by telephone, either at a travel agency, from the theatre itself or – for a fee – from a ticket agency. This only applies to credit card purchases, and the number and expiration date must of course be provided.

It is much cheaper to call the theatre directly on the day of the performance (though this is not advisable during the Christmas season or at weekends). Tickets for matinees and previews will be cheaper than those for regular evening performances.

There are often cut-price tickets available on the day of the performance from TKTS – payable only in cash or with a traveller's cheque. But these are often the most expensive tickets for the show which the theatre isn't able to sell, so a bargain isn't always guaranteed.

Some adresses

❶ etc. ▶Maps p.112–115
No number: not on map

BARS, CLUBS & MUSIC
Bailey's Corner Pub
1607 York Ave.
(corner of 85th St.)
Tel. 1 212-650-1341
This pub has been a well known after-work address on the Upper East Side since 1951. The rustic bar comes from a 19th-century tavern. Real Guinness is served here, and of course the whiskey too is from the Emerald Isle.

❷ **Blue Bar/Algonquin**
59 W 44th St.
(between Fifth and Sixth Ave.)
Tel. 1 212-840-6800
Classic New York bar in the lounge of what was once a New York literary hotel. Works by the caricaturist Al Hirschfeld (1903–2003), who was a regular, adorn the walls.

❸ **bOb**
235 Eldrige St. (between Houston and Stanton St.)
Tel. 1 212-777-0588
Amusing, sparsely furnished lounge that feels like a terrarium and also serves as an art gallery. As well as hip hop, exotic world music is also played here.

❹ **Bubble Lounge** *Insider Tip*
228 W Broadway/
White St.
Tel. 1 212-431-3433
The only champagne bar in New York. Eric Benn and Eric Macaire serve over 250 types of sparkling wine and champagne. Until 4am classy snacks can be ordered, too.

❻ **230 Fifth**
230 Fifth Ave./27th St. *Insider Tip*
Tel. 1 212-725-4300
Huge roof terrace bar on Fifth Avenue with a view that includes the Empire State Building.

Flatiron Lounge
37 W 19th St.
(between 5th and 6th Ave.)
Tel. 1 212-477-0777
If you like the Golden Twenties, this is the place to come. F. Scott Fitzgerald would have loved the furnishings. Where this lounge really scores, however, is with its fantastic drinks – classic cocktails such as Manhattan and Martini, perfectly prepared. Definitely one of New York's best cocktail bars.

❽ **Kaña**
324 Spring St. (between Greenwich and Washington St.)
Tel. 1 212-343-8180
This tapas lounge is a good place to end the evening. Excellent Spanish, Chilean and Argentinean wines, but the sangria also tastes great. Shortly before midnight a DJ starts to play Spanish pop and rock.

❾ **Momofuku**
163 1st Ave./10th St.
Tel. 1 212-475-7899
Hip noodle bar in the East Village offering American-Asian dishes made from products supplied by small local farms

⑩ McSorley's Old Ale House
15 E 7th St.
(between Second and Third Ave.)
Tel. 1 212-473-9148
Earthy Irish pub from 1854 – the oldest in Manhattan. Good beer, but unfortunately mediocre food.

Saloon
1584 York Ave.
(near 84th St.)
Tel. 1 212-570-5454
Thirty-somethings and older are welcome – if they can dance. Guests whirl over a giant dance floor to top 40s tunes and the sound of (average) cover bands. The wrong place for under-30s

Insider Tip

South Street Seaport
19 Fulton St.
Tel. 1 212-732-8257

Pier 17 in front of the restaurants is a popular gathering place on warm summer evenings, with light bites and a historic sailing ship as a backdrop.

⑫ Webster Hall
125 E 11th St.
(between Third and Fourth Ave.)
Tel. 1 212-353-1600
Friendly, large club with three (unfortunately airless) dance floors. The music ranges from rock and pop to house.

⑬ Zum Schneider
E 7th St./Ave. C.
Tel. 1 212-598-1098
Whether German business people or just beer fans – here everyone feasts on genuine Bavarian food and twelve kinds of draught beer.

JAZZ

❶ (Le) Poisson Rouge
158 Bleecker St/Thomson St
Greenwich Village
Tel. 1 212 505 3474
www.lepoissonrouge.com
The programme at this nightclub ranges from performance art and cool jazz to folk music.

Apollo Theater
253 W 125th Street
Tel. 1 212-531-5300
Amateur nights, where beginners long to be discovered, are held on Wednesdays in this legendary club, in which the careers of many jazz musicians began.

Ginny's Supper Club
310 Lenox Ave, Harlem
Tel. 1 212 421 3821

At the heart of Harlem: Apollo, a legendary jazz club

www.ginnyssupperclub.com
You'll find big-name new Harlem
music and culture at this bustling
elegant underground club below
the Red Rooster in Harlem. Tickets
to shows are between $10-25.
Enjoy a live jazz performance at its
best, together with cocktails and
comfort food from the Red Rooster kitchen. Open until midnight.
On weekends, the tables are
cleared away, and the place turns
into a dance club.

Minton's
206 W 118th St, Harlem
Tel. 1 212 243 2222
www.mintonsharlem.com
Minton's is the reincarnation of
the legendary Minton's Playhouse
where Charlie Parker and Dizzy
Gillespie developed the BeBop
sound in the '50s. This is an elegant and fairly pricey supper club.
Great live jazz performances and
fine Southern Revival cuisine.

⑭ Birdland
315 W 44th St.
(between Eighth and Ninth Ave.)
Tel. 1 212-581-3080
The Upper West Side's answer to
the Village jazz scene: live jazz
and excellent cuisine, seven days a
week. Professional mainstream is
the programme here, often with
local artists.

Bill's Place
148 W 133rd St. (between Lenox
and A.C. Powell Jr. Blvd.)
Tel. 1 212-281-0707
Bill Saxton, the legendary saxo-
phone player, opens his basement
on Friday nights at 10pm. Reservations necessary!

⑮ Blue Note

131 W 3rd St. (between Sixth
Ave. and MacDougal St.)
Tel. 1 212-475-8592
One of the most famous jazz
clubs. Blue Note has been full to
bursting every weekend for years;
the very best mainstream jazz is
played here – from the greats of
jazz history to the stars of today.
Anyone who feels claustrophobic
might prefer the (more relaxed)
jazz brunch at weekends to a
night session.

⑯ Café Carlyle
781 Madison Ave. (near 76th St.,
in the Carlyle Hotel)
Tel. 1 212-744-1600
Woody Allen likes to play clarinet
here on Mondays, accompanied
by the Eddy Davis New Orleans
Jazz Band.

Cotton Club

656 W 125th Street / Broadway
This Harlem jazz club has hosted
music greats like Duke Ellington;
there is still a traditional programme with mainly African
American guests. The jazz brunch
at weekends is a favourite with
tourists.

⑰ Iridium Jazz Club
1650 Broadway / 51st St.
Tel. 1 212-582-2121
Since opening in 1994 the club has
brought some prominent jazz players to its stage and developed into
one of the best clubs of the city.
New jazz trends are created here.

Jazz at Lincoln Center
33 W 60th St./Broadway
Tel. 1 212-258-9829

www.jazzatlincolncenter.org
For decades the Lincoln Center has been putting on classic jazz of the very highest quality. The Frederick P. Rose Hall on the 5th to 7th floors of the Time Warner Center provides the perfect surroundings for this. Tip: from the Allen Room you have a great view across Central Park.

⓲ The Jazz Standard
116 E 27th St. (between Park and Lexington Ave.)
Tel. 1 212-576-2232
The guest bands or musicians cover the whole jazz spectrum. There is also good food.

⓳ Small's
183 W 10th St./Seventh Ave.
Tel. 1 212-929-7565
As the name says: small – but nice. Here the hard-core jazz fans meet, but things don't really get rolling until the early morning hours. Show begins at 10pm.

⓴ Sweet Rhythm
88 Seventh Ave.
(between Grove and Bleecker St.)
Tel. 1 212-255-3626 Sweet Rhythm – the former Sweet Basil – is one of the most venerable jazz domiciles in the West Village. What can be heard here is not meant to shock or challenge – it is the best mainstream jazz. Also a »supper club« with a jazz brunch on Saturday and Sunday afternoon, a very pleasant establishment, not too loud and even quite reasonably priced.

Insider Tip

㉑ Village Vanguard
178 Seventh Ave. South/Perry St.

Tel. 1 212-255-4037
Opened more than 50 years ago in a cellar in Greenwich Village; outstanding musicians such as Miles Davis and John Coltrane appeared here. Today, the best pieces and interpreters in mainstream jazz can be heard here. Still very popular: be sure to make a reservation in good time.

Barbès
376 9th St/6th Ave
Park Slope, Brooklyn
Tel. 1 347 422 0248
www.barbesbrooklyn.com/
The French owner of this legendary jazz club offers live concerts every evening at an admission of only $10. Focus: Avant-Garde Jazz and Afro Jazz.

ROCK · FOLK · FUNK & DANCE
㉒ Arlene Grocery
95 Stanton St.
(between Ludlow and Orchard St.)
Tel. 1 212-358-1633 Rock, folk and funk fans from the Lower East Side meet here.

㉓ CBGB
315 Bowery/Bleecker St.
Tel. 1 212-982-4052
The birthplace of American punk, with a dark interior. The bands that play here are mostly completely unknown, since the CBGB is an open stage for new groups in the punk and heavy metal scene.

㉔ Cielo
18 Little W 12th St. (between 9th Ave. and Washington St.)
Tel. 1 212-645-5700
With world-class DJs

㉕ Irving Plaza

17 Irving Place / 15th St.
Tel. 1 212-777-6800
The forum for independent bands
that have arrived, a New York institution. Unfortunately the drinks
are pricey.

❺ Marquee

289 Tenth Ave.
(near 26th St.)
Tel. 1 646-473-0202
Techno remixes blast from the
speakers and a giant chandelier
changes colours constantly. The
bouncers only let through people
who are stylishly dressed.

⑪ Secret Lounge

525 West 29th St.
(near Tenth Ave.)
Tel. 1 212-268-5580
Gays love this place. A chandelier
and many candelabras make for a
magical atmosphere. Music is
mainly European House. Vodka

and Red Bull is one of the favourite drinks.

㉖ The Living Room

154 Ludlow St. (between Stanton
and Rivington St.)
Tel. 1 212-533-7235
Popular club

㉗ The Knitting Factory

361 Metropolitan Ave. (Brooklyn)
Tel. 1 347-529-6696
Wide variety in a narrow space –
new trends in experimental jazz,
rock music and slam poetry.

⑳ The Mercury Lounge

Insider Tip

217 E Houston St.
(between Essex and Ludlow St.)
Tel. 1 212-260-4700
Great view of the stage from all
sides of the lounge; the acoustics
are excellent too. The club is in
the firm grip of earthy rock and
indie bands.

All the legends of jazz performed at Village Vanguard

㉙ Roseland and Ballroom

239 W 52nd St. (between Eighth
Ave. and Broadway)
Tel. 1 212-247-0200
Originally a ballroom. Today
avant-garde rock bands and other
unconventional artists appear
here.

㉛ S.O.B.'s

204 Varick St. / Houston St.
Tel. 1 212-243-4940
The name stands for »sounds of
Brazil«, but the repertoire has
passed far beyond that. Today
S.O.B.'s is the definitive world mu-
sic club.

Vudu Lounge

1487 First Ave. (near 78th St.)
Tel. 1 212-249-9540
Latin Thursdays are the liveliest
days, when Latino couples twirl
across the dance floor. Fridays are
for hip-hop and R&B, Saturdays
mainstream and dance music. The
dance floor with its giant crystal
ball recalls the 1970s. Scantily
dressed go-go girls dance on
stage. No admission charge.

COMEDY, CABARET

㉜ Carolines On Broadway   Insider Tip

1626 Broadway
(between 49th and 50th St.)
Tel. 1 212-757-4100
Everyone starts small – like the famous satirist Jerry Seinfeld, for example, in Carolines, which many
local people consider to be the
best cabaret club in the city.

㉝ Comic Strip Live   Insider Tip

1568 Second Ave.
(between 81st and 82nd St.)

Tel. 1 212-861-9386
A popular test stage for up-and-
coming comedians. There are several shows at weekends.

Gotham Comedy Club

208 W 23rd St. (between Seventh
and Eighth Ave.)
Tel. 1 212-367-9000
The best in stand-up comedy,
sometimes with performers known
from TV. Tuesday is the night for
new talent. Reservation necessary.

OPERA · CONCERTS
㉝ Metropolitan Opera House (Met)

Lincoln Center, 65th St./ Columbus Ave.
Tel. 1 212-362-6000
www.metoperafamily.org
Subway: 66th St./Lincoln Center
The season at the Met, one of the
most famous opera houses in the
world, runs from the end of September until April.

Bargemusic

Fulton Ferry Landing, Brooklyn
Tel.1 718 624 4924
www.bargemusic.org
Former concert violinist Olga
Bloom and fellow musicians welcome to chamber concerts at a
beautiful and unusual venue: on a
floating barge on the East River.
An unforgettable experience with
magnificent views of the Manhattan skyline in the background.

Alice Tully Hall

Lincoln Center (▶ above)
Tel. 1 212-875-5788
www.chambermusicsociety.org
Seat of the chamber orchestra of

Lincoln Center; concerts and song recitals.

Avery Fisher Hall
Lincoln Center (► above)
Tel. 1 212-875-5030
www.nyphilharmonic.org
The rehearsals of the New York Philharmonic on Thursday mornings are open to the public and cost much less than a concert.

Brooklyn Academy of Music (BAM)
30 Lafayette Ave. (Brooklyn)
Tel. 718-636-4198
www.bam.org
Subway: Atlantic Ave., Pacific or Fulton St.
The Brooklyn Academy of Music BAM, founded in 1859, has for years been the focal point in New York of international drama and music experimentation.

Carnegie Hall
154 W 57th St. / Seventh Ave.
Tel. 1 212-247-7800
www.carnegiehall.org
Subway: Seventh Ave. or 57th St.
Classical music as well as pop and rock concerts

92nd Street Y
1395 Lexington Ave. / 92nd St.
Tel. 1 212-415-5500
www.92y.org
Subway: 96th St.
Literature and music events

BALLET
New York City Ballet
Lincoln Center (► above)
Tel. 1 212-870-5570
www.nycballet.com

Season: May–beginning of July, Nov–Feb
The traditional dance company in the New York State Theater in the Lincoln Center is famous for its classical ballet.

Alvin Ailey American Dance Theater   **Insider Tip**
405 W 55th St. / Ninth Ave.
Tel. 1 212-405-9056
www.alvinailey.org
Subway: 57th St.
Season: first half of May and second half of November
The Alvin Ailey shows African American dance theatre at its very best. The theatre is the Mecca of modern dance and experimental performances.

Joyce Theater   **Insider Tip**
175 Eighth Ave. / 19th St.
Tel. 1 212-242-0800
www.joyce.org
Subway: 14th St., 18th St.
In this renovated cinema in Chelsea, expressive modern dance from all over the world is performed.

ROCK
Madison Square Garden
Seventh Ave.
(between 31st and 33rd St.)
Tel. 1 212-465-6741
www.thegarden.com
Subway: 34th St./Penn Station
Bob Dylan, Bruce Springsteen and Madonna have performed in this gigantic sports arena.

THEATRE
The following theatres are all in the Theater District between 44th and 55th street.

A Lively Theatre Scene

Broadway is alive and well, thriving as never before. Its revival is owed to big companies that have invested heavily in Times Square and the theatres round about.

The Lion King has good reason to roar. With a run lasting more than 14 years, this is the most durable musical of all time on Broadway. *The Phantom of the Opera*, *Mamma Mia* and *Chicago* are almost equally successful. Musicals are big money on Broadway, with over 12 billion dollars turnover per year, and audiences get plenty for their money, above all special effects that were once unimaginable in a theatre. Sometimes the story suffers from this, which prompted the New York Times to speak of the end of historic Broadway.

A stage for stars

Despite all the hype about musicals, the Theater District is still home to classic drama. This is partly due to Hollywood stars such as Al Pacino and Meryl Streep, who expose themselves to the critical theatre public for limited periods of time by treading the boards instead of acting in front of the camera.

New York has almost 40 Broadway, 20 Off-Broadway and 200 Off-Off-Broadway theatres. Broadway itself is synonymous with the bright lights and large auditoria for between 500 and 1500 spectators, which are the venue for more than 40 shows and plays at any one time. High-brow theatre is mainly played Off-Broadway, and experi-

mental drama is the realm of small to tiny houses Off-Off-Broadway, where the ticket prices are of course much lower.

Shakespeare for all *Insider Tip*

Shakespeare in the Park has become a huge event. This festival of open-air performances in Central Park, which started out in 1954 as the New York Shakespeare Festival, mainly stages the more popular pieces from the repertoire such as Romeo and Juliet. Tickets are free, though limited to two per person, sold on the day of the performance from 1pm at the **Delacorte Theater** in Central Park. In order to be sure of getting one of the coveted tickets, it is advisable to arrive early in the morning.

Theater District

The first professional theatre performance in New York, Shakespeare's Richard III, was staged at the New Theater in Nassau Street in 1750. In the 19th century, theatre was a means of escape for poor immigrants, usually performed in their native languages. Vaudeville shows were extremely popular in those days. In 1893 the well-known Empire Theater moved from Herald Square to the later Theater District on Broadway. Others followed, and by the 1930s the term »Broadway« had come to mean the area between 42nd and 53rd

The gigantic arena of the Delacorte Theater seats an audience of 1800 and is the home of an annual free festival: »Shakespeare in the Park«

Street where most theatres were to be found. The British journalist Nick Cohn, who lived in this district for several months, wrote »If you were to walk just one block along Broadway and open every door, you would discover a hundred different worlds.«

Sports venues

PRO SPORTS

There are professional teams in basketball, baseball, American football, hockey and soccer. Tickets are available at the following ticket agencies: ABC Tickets, tel. 1-800-355-5555 and Prestige Entertainment Tel. 800-243-8849; tickets for playoff games especially are difficult to get and expensive.

American Football

American football is especially popular, but its complicated rules are not easy for the uninitiated to understand. It developed from rugby and has nothing to do with European football, which is always referred to as soccer in the USA. New York has two pro teams, the **New York Giants** and the **New York Jets**. They play Sept–Dec in the new Meadowlands Stadium in East Rutherford, New Jersey, tel. 877-694-2010, www.giants.com (Giants) or tel. 800-469-JETS, www.newyorkjets.com (for the Jets). Directions: NJ Transit Meadowlands Sports Complex Bus from Port Authority Bus Terminal, Eighth Ave./42nd St.

Insider Tip

Baseball

Baseball, which developed from cricket, is the American sport (▶MARCO POLO Insight p.194). In New York there are even two pro teams: the **Yankees** and the **Mets**. The baseball season starts in April and ends in October. The Mets play in Citi Field in Queens, 12301 Roosevelt Ave., tel. 718-507-8499, www.mets. com; subway: Mets Willets Point-Station.
Yankee Stadium is on River Ave. in the Bronx, tel. 718-293-6000, www.yankees.com; subway: 161st St.-Yankee Stadium.

Basketball

New York's professional basketball team is the **New York Knicks** (Knickerbockers/Knicks). They play from October until June., Madison Square Garden, Seventh Ave., between 31st and 33rd St., Tel. 1 212-465-6073, www.nba. com/knicks; subway: 34th St./Penn Station
Brooklyn Nets, Barclay's Arena, 620 Atlantic Ave., Brooklyn, tel. 1 917-618-6700, www.nba. com/nets; subway: 2, 3, 4, 5, B, D, Q, N, R

Soccer

The only professional soccer team is the **Red Bulls**. They play in Red Bull Arena, 600 Cape May St., Harrison, New Jersey, tel. 877-RB-SOCCER.

Hockey (ice)

New Jersey Devils, Continental Airlines Arena, East Rutherford (▶above), tel. 973-757-6200, www.newjerseydevils.com
New York Rangers, Madison Square Garden, Seventh Ave., between 31st and 33rd St., Tel. 1 212-465-6000, www.newyorkrangers.com Subway: 34th St.-Penn Station

Horse racing

Aqueduct Race Track, 110th St./ Rockaway Blvd., Ozone Park

(Queens); tel. 718-641-4700,
www.nyra.com Belmont Park,
2150 Hempstead Turnpike, El-
mont (Long Island); tel. 718-641-
4700, www.nyra.com/belmont
Meadowlands Racetrack, East
Rutherford, Meadowlands
(New Jersey); tel. 201-843-2446,
www.thebigm.com

Tennis – U.S. Open
USTA National Tennis Center,
Flushing Meadows-Corona Park
(Queens); tel. 718-760-6200,
www.usopen.org (August/Sep-
tember; subway: Mets Willets
Point Station from Grand Central

SPORTS ACTIVITIES
New York Marathon
Since 1970, the world's largest
marathon has taken place on the
first Sunday in November. The or-
ganizer is the New York Road
Runners Club. The 42.2km/26.2mi
course starts on the Verrazano
Narrows Bridge (Staten Island),
goes through Brooklyn, Williamsburg, across the Pulaski Bridge to
Queens, across the Queensboro
Bridge to Manhattan, up to Harlem and finishes in Central Park
(information: New York Road Runners Club, 9 E 89th St. Tel. 1 212-
860-4455).

Ice skating
Lasker Rink, Central Park
(between 106th and 108th St.)

Nov–March daily
Rockefeller Center Ice Rink
Rockefeller Plaza – the most
famous skating rink in the world.
The nicest time to skate is in the
Christmas season.
Oct–Apr daily
Sky Rink, Chelsea Piers,
►MARCO POLO Insight p.220
Wollman Rink, Central Park,
62nd St.; end of Oct–March daily

**Bike riding • Bicycle sharing
system »Citi Bikes«**
Since June 2013, this privately-
owned bike sharing system has
been available to the residents
and visitors of New York City.
With thousands of bikes at hundreds of stations around Manhattan and Brooklyn, it is the largest
of its kind in the US. Citi Bikes are
available 24/7, 365 days a year,
and renting is very easy: Insert
your credit card into the touch-
screen kiosk at each station, you
will receive a ride code, enter it
into the keypad on the dock of
your bike of choice to release it,
and then you're ready to take off.
For information: www.citibikenyc.
com or via smartphone app of the
same name.
Bike rentals are also available at
Gotham Bikes (bike shop): downtown, 112 West Broadway
(between Duane and Reade St),
Tel. 1 212 732 2453,
www.toga bikes.com

Festivals · Holidays · Events

Highlights of the Year

There is a celebration in New York every few days. 50 parades are officially registered, and it is hardly possible to count the street parties. Every ethnic and religious group has brought its own festivals from its home country.

If you have enough time to plan a trip to New York in advance, get the **New York Visitors Bureau** (▶Information) to send you a **free calendar of events**.

Information

Those informations are also available online at **www.nycgo.com** Most events are also listed in the daily newspapers like *New York Times* (▶Media). The arts and leisure section of the *New York Times* on Fridays is especially informative.   On Thursdays the *Village Voice* publishes a lot of details of all important events.

Time Out is another good source. In addition bars have various what's-on guides and flyers listing events of a less official nature.

> **MARCO ⊕ POLO TIP**
>
> *Street parties*   **Insider Tip**
>
> Visit one of the New York street festivals that take place throughout the summer in the various parts of the city. This is typical weekend entertainment with food booths, stages and goods of all kinds on sale. Information on dates and places: www.nyctourist. com, click on Events.

Holidays

New Year's Day
(1 January)
Martin Luther King Day
(the Monday closest to
15 January)
Washington's Birthday
(third Monday in February)
Easter Sunday Memorial or
Decoration Day
(to remember the war dead;
last Monday in May)
Independence Day (4 July)
Labor Day
(first Monday in September)

Columbus Day
(12 October or second
Monday in October)
Veteranran's Day or Armistice Day
(11 November)
Thanksgiving Day
(last Thursday in November)
Christmas Day (25 December).

JEWISH HOLIDAYS
Rosh Hashanah (ten days before
Yom Kippur)
Yom Kippur (Day of Atonement,
September or October)

How New York likes to celebrate:
fireworks around the Statue of Liberty

Festival Calendar

JANUARY
Chinese New Year
Ten-day Chinese New Year festival, beginning on the first New Moon after 21 January; fireworks and giant dragons in Mott Street.

FEBRUARY
Annual Empire State Building Run Up
Who can run fastest up the 1,576 steps from the lobby to the 86th floor?

MARCO POLO INSIGHT

? *Did you know*

The pilgrims of the Mayflower only survived their first winter in the new world in 1621 because the Algonquin people showed them how to grow and store corn (maize). The settlers then celebrated the »First Thanksgiving« with the Native Americans – which didn't alter the fact that the following generation fought each other. In 1898 Thanksgiving became an official holiday in order to help foster a »common national identity« which had been missing until then.

MARCH
St Patrick's Day Parade and Greek Independence Day
Festivals and parades of the Irish (17 March) and the Greek Population (25 March) on Fifth Avenue

New Directors' *Insider Tip*
Film Festival
Film festival of new directors in the Museum of Modern Art.

APRIL
Opening of the *Insider Tip*
baseball season
A classic: Yankees versus Mets.

Easter Parade
Easter Parade on Fifth Ave. near St Patrick's Cathedral.

Ukrainian Festival
On E 7th St., with various music and dance groups (second weekend after Easter).

MAY
Black World Championship Rodeo
Rodeo championship in Harlem.

Bike NY
»Bike New York: the great five borough bike tour« runs 42 miles through the city.

Martin Luther King Parade
On Fifth Avenue (around 20 May)

Brooklyn Bridge Day Parade
Lots of activities and fun, with a parade across the legendary bridge (middle of the month).

Ninth Avenue International Food Festival
Big food fest (middle of the month).

JUNE
Puerto Rican Day Parade
Exuberant music and dance of the Puerto Ricans on Fifth and Third Ave. (first Sunday in June).

A highlight of the year: different ethnic groups parade along Fifth Avenue on St Patrick's Day

Gay and Lesbian Pride Day

Annual gay and lesbian parade from Columbus Circle via Fifth Avenue to Greenwich Village to remember the Stonewall Riot of 1969, when homosexuals for the first time resisted the police; Christopher Street Day (last Sunday of the month).

Mermaid Parade

Mermaids and sea gods on the Coney Island Boardwalk, Brooklyn (Saturday after 21 June).

Free performances

Insider Tip

of the Metropolitan Opera in the parks of all parts of town.

JuneFest

Staten Island celebrates the beginning of summer with concerts and many art exhibitions.

Long Island Motorcycle Fair

Popular meeting for bikers and their fans at Riverhead Raceway. Many stunt contests and shows. Concerts and open bars keep this event lively until late in the night.

Macy's Thanksgiving Day Parade

Macy's Thanksgiving Day Parade is known around the world thanks to the film Miracle on 34th Street, with Maureen O'Hara and John Payne in the leading roles.

In 1947 this movie was a box-office hit in American cinemas in the Christmas season. Its touching story and original footage of Macy's Thanksgiving Day Parade from the previous year enchanted children and their parents too, since when the parade has been broadcast live on television .

From a Family Celebration …

The first Thanksgiving Day Parade, in 1924, was more like a family event. The staff of Macy's department store, most of them immigrants from Europe, walked from Harlem to Herald Square wearing fancy dress to the sound of patriotic music to thank the United States and their employer for giving them a friendly welcome. Under the name Macy's Christmas Parade, it was the start of the pre-Christmas sales season. Three years later, the parade was already a major event, accompanied by well-known bands and for the first time by **enormous helium-filled balloons**. At the end of the route, the balloons, in the shape of clowns, animals and fantasy figures, soared into the air – but only half as high as the skyscrapers before they burst, raining to earth again as scraps of rubber. A year later, additional safety valves ensured that they stayed aloft for at least three days. A reward was given to those who found them and took them back to Macy's. In 1934 Macy's cooperated with Disney to send the first Mickey Mouse balloon on its six-mile trip through New York. From 1942 to 1944 the parade was cancelled, and the helium and rubber intended for the balloons was donated to the government for the war effort.

After the war, the celebrations sparkled more than ever before. More than two million spectators watched the parade live. A year later, NBC broadcast it on television for the first time. Today over three million people line the streets to watch the parade, and a TV audience of 44 million follow it at home.

… to a Major Event

A curious incident happened in 1957, when the parade took place during a deluge of rain. Water collected in the hat of the Popeye balloon and soaked spectators when the balloon tilted to one side. Comic figures are now an established part of the array of balloons – the most frequent participant has been Snoopy. In 1969 the parade went on its travels for the first time. The balloons are made in a former confectionery factory in Hoboken, New Jersey, dismantled before going through the Holland Tunnel and reassembled at the

Manhattan end. A permanent guest at the Thanksgiving Day Parade is Father Christmas – to the delight of all children, who have something to dream about for a few more weeks.

Fantasy characters in the shape of balloons.

Food and Drink

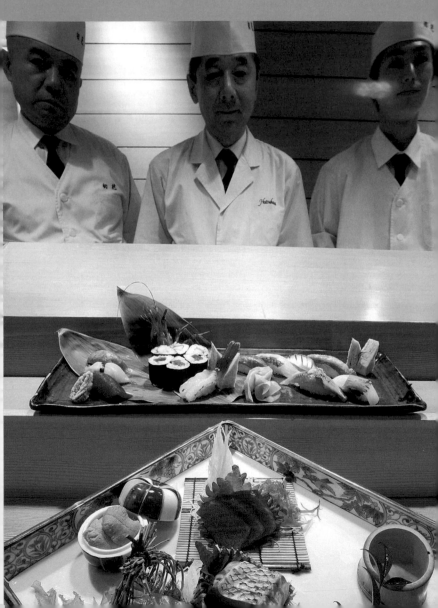

A Food Paradise
Not Only for Gourmets

No culinary wish remains unfulfilled in New York. The city's restaurants range from top addresses where the chefs enjoy global recognition to basic diners.

The total of 23,000 restaurants makes a powerful statement: New York offers its visitors gastronomic variety that is available nowhere else in the world. Countless immigrants brought recipes from their home countries and retained their cultural identity. This resulted in a restaurant scene that caters for every taste. At gourmet restaurants the likes of Joel Robuchon, the French chef of the century, and the Japanese sushi master Nobu Matsuhisa rule the kitchen. In ethnic restaurants guests are served all the dishes for which they would otherwise have to travel to exotic destinations, and even the mobile street stalls are now getting attention in the culinary magazines. New York is a Mecca for foodies. It may not be cheap, but what does that matter if the variety and quality are right?. There is no need to leave the city to take a journey around the cuisines of the world.

Starred cooking and world cuisine

There is no specific New York cuisine. The trend of recent years, in the wake of the global financial crisis, was a resurgence of cheap eateries such as pizzerias, while the gourmet restaurants with their fancy tasting menus had a difficult period. While there is no need to regret the demise of the Wall Street Burger Shoppe, which sold a Kobe burger with foie gras, black truffles and a little gold leaf for 175 dollars, it was unfortunate that first-class restaurants such as Chanterelle and Tavern on the Green had to close down.

Various trends

Some trends seem to last: steak houses such as Peter Luger remain popular, as does Asian food, especially Japanese – there is a plethora of sushi bars – and Indian. Organic food, sold in the restaurants run by the Whole Foods supermarket chain, and **fusion food**, a combination of often completely different cuisines of the world, for example Vietnamese and Italian, French and Russian, Cuban and Argentinean (»Nuevo Latino«). The motto is: creative, light, healthy and, above all, exotic. **Soul food** is the food of the Texas ranchers and cowboys: pork chops with beans, spicy honey fried chicken with fiery barbecue sauce and pancakes, juicy, sizzling spare-ribs, opulent and rich (also in calories – at Amy Ruth's the southern fried chicken is even served

Masters of presentation at work: sushi of the highest standard at Hatsuhana Restaurant

with waffles). New York's often strange-sounding dishes often come from **kosher cooking**, like knishes, fried pasties with a mashed potato filling, pretzels made of yeast dough or **bagels**, round sourdough rolls with a hole in the middle, often eaten with smoked salmon or cream cheese. **New York cheesecake** is also made according to a Jewish recipe – with cream cheese and cottage cheese.

? *Deli food*

A deli, short for delicatessen, was originally the word for a shop where Jewish immigrants sold kosher specialities such as blintzes, a kind of pancake filled with curd cheese, or fresh pastrami beef sandwiches, known as a reuben when served with sauerkraut. Today delis open round the clock and serve all kinds of food – ready-made sushi, pizza, Chinese dishes and other specialities from around the world

Donuts too have a hole in the middle, of course, and are on offer either plain or with various fillings and coverings. The famous hot dog is said to have been invented by Nathan Handwerker around the year 1900. The original hot dog is still sold on Coney Island, and they are on offer on every street corner in Manhattan, often with sauerkraut. For a cheap meal, there are coffee shops and of course the outlets of well-known fast-food chains.

As New York restaurants are often here today and gone tomorrow, it pays to keep up to date by finding recommendations on the internet, for example at www.nymag.com. The restaurant reviews of the New York Times can be found at www.mytoday.com, and cheaper eateries are reviewed at www.villagevoice.com. The best-known restaurant guide available in bookshops is called Zagat New York City. Tips and reviews are also available at www.zagat.com. The food critic Brian Hoffmann is always bang up to date, and blogs his discoveries at www.eatthisny.com. An inexhaustible forum for food lovers is the website www.chowhound.com.

Better value, but still stylish It can be done more cheaply, too – and still with style. The first **diners** were simple restaurants in old train cars or construction huts; they used to travel from factory to factory or construction site to construction site as mobile canteens and offer food to the workers, and a bit of that old charm still exists today. A must seems to be pastel colours, heavy plastic-covered benches and ochre-coloured plastic or glittery chrome tables – and of course typical Art Deco elements like the steel geometric trim that was considered chic in the 1930s. Simple, inexpensive meals are listed in the menus, often as a daily special served on a blue plate, the so-called »Blue Plate Special«. Incidentally: it is considered rude to sit at an already occupied table in diners, delis, fast-food restaurants or cafés in New York.

The love of good **coffee** only arrived in Manhattan at the end of the 20th century – but then all the more intensely. In the meantime even chains like Starbucks or Seattle Coffee Roasters serve Arabicas or Robustos of the best quality, whether from Brazil, Kenya or the highlands of Jamaica. All sorts of **drinks** are mixed in the many bars of the city; cocktails from Brazil such as the caipirinha are of course especially popular, and a fresh, cool beer, maybe even from a local brewery like the **Heartland Brewery**, is just as popular in New York as elsewhere. The fruit of the vine, from all over the world, is currently especially popular; **wine bars** are sprouting like mushrooms.

Drinks

In better restaurants the patrons are shown to their tables by a member of the staff, the host or hostess at the entrance, who also checks the reservation (which is almost always necessary). There may be a short wait – New Yorkers like to use this for a drink at the bar. Smart dress is desirable at better restaurants (suit/evening dress). If there is no stated **dress code**, men experienced in New York ways always have a tie in the pocket of their jacket just in case. As for women: well, in New York there's no such thing as a woman who's not well-dressed in the evening! **Smokers**, incidentally, suffer and at best can only indulge in the few remaining restaurants with a smoking area. One more thing: good times lead to more sophisticated manners. Nowadays requesting a doggy bag in a better-class restaurant is considered a faux pas.

Etiquette

Recommended Restaurants

❶ etc. ▶Maps p.112 – 115
No number: not on map

Price categories
For a main course
$$$$ over $30
$$$ between $20 and $30
$$ up to $20
$ up to $10

TOP RESTAURANTS
❶ **Adour Alain Ducasse at The St. Regis $$$$**
5 E 55th St./Fifth Ave.

Tel. 1 212-710-2277
www.adour-stregis.com
Subway: Fifth Ave./53rd St.
One of the best chefs in the world prepares (evenings only) the finest French cuisine here for stars and starlets and anyone else who can afford the prices (small prix fixe menu from $65, tasting menu $110).

❷ **Aureole $$$$**
135 W 42nd St.
(between Madison and Park Ave.)

What to Eat in New York

New York does not have its own specific cuisine, but in 23,000 restaurants recipes and flavours from all points of the compass can be tasted. Here are a few typical dishes.

New York cheesecake: Until 1969, when his Lindy's restaurant closed, Leo Lindemann jealously guarded the secret recipe for his original New York cheesecake. Countless variations on this classic cake are now on offer. The essential ingredients are cream cheese, sugar, eggs, vanilla and curd cheese on a base made from biscuits and butter. Fruity strawberry sauce is poured over the cake.

Bagels: In the early 20th century they were known only in New York's Jewish quarter, but now these flat yeast rolls with a hole in the middle have become part of the diet of Middle America. The purpose of the hole was originally to carry the bagels on a pole or string, but it also speeded up the process of baking. Bagels are made from wheat flour, water, yeast, malt and salt, and usually eaten with cream cheese.

Waldorf salad: This tasty salad is made from apples, celery and walnuts, mixed with mayonnaise and served on a bed of lettuce. It is said to have been invented between 1893 and 1896 by the chef at the Waldorf Hotel, one of the two predecessors of today's Waldorf Astoria Hotel. Modern versions of the salad are served with chicken or turkey, grapes or dried fruit, and yoghurt dressing can be served in place of the mayonnaise.

Hot dogs: Anton Ludwig Feuchtwanger from Bavaria is said to have sold sausages in bread rolls on the streets of St Louis as long ago as 1880 – the idea being that high-class people would not need to soil their white gloves while eating. In New York they were made popular by Nathan Handwerker on Coney Island. Street stalls in Manhattan sell hot dogs straight, or with sauerkraut or other toppings.

Reuben sandwich: This has been a classic New York bite for more than a century. Arnold Reuben, the owner of Reuben's Delicatessen, is said to have invented it in 1914 when a well-known actress came to his shop but almost nothing was left in his larder. The Reuben sandwich is usually made from dark rye bread, filled with corned beef or pastrami, Swiss cheese and sauerkraut.

Adresses · Midtown Manhattan

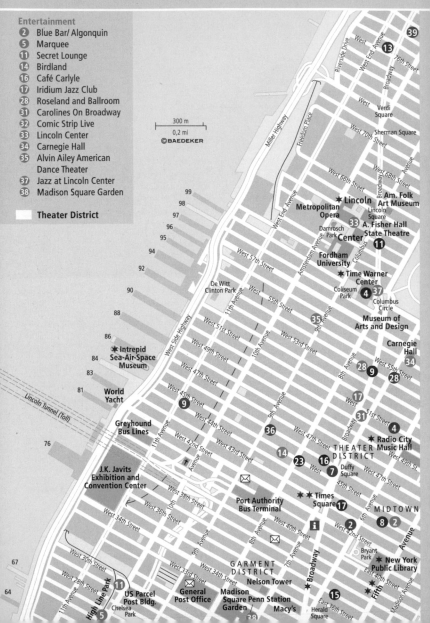

Entertainment

2 Blue Bar/ Algonquin
5 Marquee
11 Secret Lounge
14 Birdland
16 Café Carlyle
17 Iridium Jazz Club
28 Roseland and Ballroom
31 Carolines On Broadway
32 Comic Strip Live
33 Lincoln Center
34 Carnegie Hall
35 Alvin Ailey American
　 Dance Theater
37 Jazz at Lincoln Center
38 Madison Square Garden

　 Theater District

Where to eat
1. Adour Alain Ducasse at the St. Regis
2. Aureole
4. Le Bernardin
5. Tony's Di Napoli
6. Darbar Grill
7. The View Marriot Marquis
8. Mia Dona
9. Pom Pom Diner
10. Boathouse Café
11. Osteria del Circo
12. Hatsuhana Sushi Restaurant
13. Beyoglu
16. Oyster Bar & Restaurant
17. Brasserie
19. Cinema Cafe
23. Candle 79
24. Orsay
25. La Bonne Soupe
28. Carnegie Deli
32. Primola
36. Zen Palate
39. Kefi

Where to stay
1. Carlyle
2. Four Seasons
3. Pierre
4. Mandarin Orienta
5. St. Regis
6. Waldorf Astoria
8. Algonquin
9. Ameritania
10. Box Tree Inn
11. West Side YMCA
12. Radisson Lexington
13. Belleclaire
15. Metro
16. Paramount
17. Millennium Broadway
19. Salisbury Hotel
23. Milford Plaza
25. The Lucerne
26. Vanderbilt YMCA

Adresses · Downtown Manhattan

Entertainment

1 Le Poisson Rouge
3 bOb
4 Bubble Lounge
6 230 Fifth
7 Flatiron Lounge
8 Kaña
9 Momofuku Ko
10 Mc Sorley's Old Ale House
12 Webster Hall
13 Zum Schneider
15 Blue Note
18 The Jazz Standard
19 Small's
20 Sweet Rhythm
21 Village Vanguard
22 Arlene Grocery
23 Cielo
24 Irving Plaza
25 The Living Room
26 The Knitting Factory
27 The Mercury Lounge
29 Gotham Comedy Club
30 S.O.B.'s
36 Joyce Theater

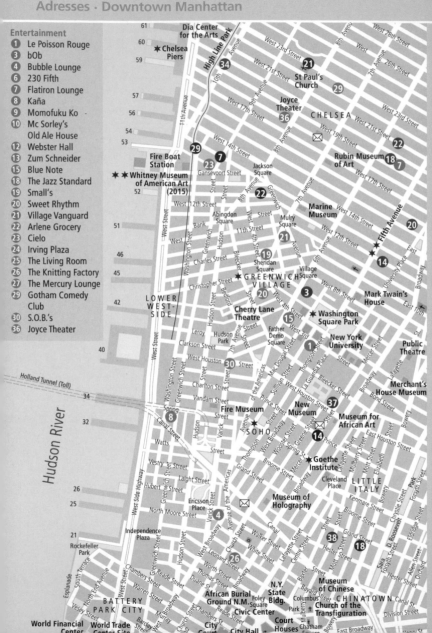

Where to eat

3 Babbo
14 Gotham Bar & Grill
15 11 Madison Park
18 Boqueria
20 Union Square Cafe
21 Prune
22 Justin's
26 The Breslin
27 Madras Mahal
29 Katz's
30 Ess-a-Bagel
31 Second Avenue Deli
33 Rai Rai Ken
34 The Park
35 Angelica Kitchen
37 Arturo's
38 Angelo
40 Wolfgang's Steakhouse

Where to stay

7 Gansevoort
14 Mercer
18 Best Western Bowery Hanbee Hotel
20 Gershwin
21 Leo House
22 Riverview Hotel
24 Seafarers and International House
27 East Village Bed & Coffee
28 Gramercy Park Hotel
29 The Standard

Tel. 1 212-319-1660
www.charliepalmer.com
Subway: Lexington Ave./63rd St.
or Lexington Ave./59th St.
Halibut filet on a bed of risotto
with asparagus sabayon, soba
noodles with tuna sashimi, triple
crème brûlée – Aureole, with
branches in Las Vegas, Sonoma,
Los Angeles and Washington, is a
classic purveyor of fusion cuisine,
which mixes food and spices from
various parts of the world. The
flower decorations, always fresh
and extravagant, are great.

❸ Babbo $$$$
110 Waverly Place
(between MacDougal St. and
Sixth Ave.)
Tel. 1 212-777-0303
www.babbonyc.com
Subway: Grand St. or W 4th St.
Mario Batali is king of the kitchen
here – and what he creates is simply
heavenly, be it light gnocchi on ox-
tail carpaccio, calamari à la minute
or fritelle di ricotta with caramel
bananas. Certainly one of the best
Italian restaurants in the city.

❹ Le Bernardin $$$$
155 W 51st St.
(between Sixth and Seventh Ave.)
Tel. 1 212-554-1515 (closed Sun)
Subway: Rockefeller Center
Master chef Eric Ripert gets his
fresh seafood from fishermen under contract to him and only fillets
them in his kitchen, of course. No
wonder they call him »King of the
Seas«.

Nobu $$$$
105 Hudson St.
(near Franklin St., TriBeCa)

Tel. 1 212-219-0500
Subway: Franklin St.
Can anything more be said about
Robert De Niro's legendary restaurant? For years now, chef Nobu-
uki Matsuhisa has served up the
best sushi, sashimi and miso soups
in the city along with tasty entrées
like tuna fish tartare with beluga
caviar, sprinkled with sake. The
dining room is a mixture of bistro,
cocktail bar and interior designer's
dream. Very trendy, chic clientele;
many celebrities can be seen here.

River Café $$$$
1 Water St./Old Fulton St.,
Dumbo (Brooklyn)
Tel. 718-522-5200
www.rivercafe.com
Subway: High St.
Not in a skyscraper but on a
freighter: an elegant restaurant
with exorbitant prices, offering a
wonderful panoramic view of the
skyline of Manhattan. Fish in particular is a speciality here.

❼ The View $$$$ Insider Tip
1535 Broadway
(between 45th and 46th St.)
Tel. 1 212-704-8900
www.theviewny.com
Subway: 42nd St., 42nd St./Times
Square
One of the finest gastronomic establishments of the city: a fascinat-
ing restaurant with a fantastic view.
Situated on the 48th floor of the
Marriott Marquis Hotel near Broadway and Times Square, the restaurant rotates 360° in one hour.

Water's Edge $$$$ Insider Tip
East River/44th Drive
Long Island City (Queens)

Tel. 718-482-0033 (closed Sun)
Subway: 23rd St./Ely Ave.
This exclusive restaurant serving
American cuisine is on the shore
of Queens The trip there is a
pleasure, too: at 6pm Mon–Sat
from the marina at 34th St. on
the East River the restaurant's own
water taxi transports guests.

Tribeca Grill $$$$
375 Greenwich St./Franklin St.
Tel. 1 212-941-3900
Subway: Franklin St.
American bistro cuisine, opened a
few years ago by the movie stars
Robert De Niro, Sean Penn, Bill
Murray and Christopher Walken
among others. Atmospheric, con-
genial, always crowded and loud.

Peter Luger $$$$ *Insider Tip*
178 Broadway/Driggs Ave.
Williamsburg (Brooklyn)
Tel. 718-387-7400
Subway: Marcy Ave.
Considered to be New York's best
steakhouse (▶MARCO POLO
Insight, p.118).

❿ Boathouse Café $$$$
Central Park Lake, Park Drive
North/East 72nd St. Tel. 1 212-
517-2233 Subway: 72nd St. Very
nice restaurant in Central Park on
the lakeshore with a great terrace
for dining. Fish dishes and American cuisine.

⓫ Osteria del Circo $$$$
120 W 55th St.
(between Seventh and Sixth Ave.)
Tel. 1 212-265-3636
Subway: 57th St.
One of the in-demand gourmet
restaurants of New York. Tuscan

cooking wonderful meals, both
light and more substantial.

⓮ Gotham Bar & Grill $$$$
12 E 12th St. (between Fifth Ave.
and University Place) Tel. 1 212-
620-4020 Subway: 14th St./Union
Square The gourmet address in
Greenwich Village. American
food, sophisticated preparation.

⓯ Eleven Madison Park $$$$
11 Madison Ave
Flatiron District in Manhattan
Tel. 1 212 889 0905
elevenmadisonpark.com
Subway: 23rd St
Swiss Chef Daniel Humm is a
shooting star of the culinary
scene. The restaurant's special
multi-course menu is $225 per
person is sure to be a unique experience. Please make reservations
at least a week ahead of time

Wolfgangs Steakhouse $$$$ *Insider Tip*
1 Park Ave., Murray Hill Tel. 1
212-889-3369 Subway: 33rd St.
In the former Vanderbilt Hotel
(with other branches), the best

Better than in the Wild West

Even Texans get enthusiastic at the sight of a New York steak. They are said to be better nowhere, Dallas or Chicago not excepted.

But you do have to leave Manhattan and cross the East River to Brooklyn, where the best steaks in the world are served at Peter Luger Steak House. It's not only the proprietors of this legendary restaurant who make this claim. It has regularly been voted New York's best steakhouse, and its 150 seats are booked out night after night – after all, it has been known as steak-lover's heaven since 1887. In that year a German immigrant founded Carl Luger's Café, Billiards and Bowling Alley. In the district of Williamsburg, then inhabited mainly by Germans, his steaks became extremely popular. It was not until 1950 that the family sold the restaurant to one Sol Forman, whose granddaughter is now responsible for purchasing the meat.

German Atmosphere

The **Peter Luger Steak House** has kept its excellent reputation. The plain surroundings, reminiscent of a German beer hall, and the surly waiters are all part of it. There is no point in asking for a menu. The only thing that is served is Porterhouse steak for two, three or four persons, along with creamy spinach and German (sautéed) potatoes. The steaks are served cut into strips on a plate that is so hot that the pieces on the edge continue to cook, and they are so tender that they almost melt in the mouth. The secret is dry-aged beef. The meat, usually Angus beef, is kept refrigerated for almost a month. During this time it becomes tender and develops its aroma, the juices evaporate, and it loses up to a third of its weight. If you want to try this treat, book at least three weeks in advance and bring cash – credit cards are not accepted.

The word »steak« comes from the **Old Norse »steik«** meaning »to roast« and »steikja«, »roast on a spit«. Scandinavian herdsmen, hunters and farmers stuck meat onto a spit, lance or spear and roasted it over an open fire. In northern Europe the word »steik« caught on for this, became »steak« in English, and arrived in America with emigrants. There it became the epitome of a high-class meal, and in the Wild West every cowboy who had a few dollars in this pocket ordered a juicy steak with beans. It had to be »big as a water-closet lid« and thoroughly cooked.

Order Like a Connoisseur

Tastes have changed today, and this doesn't only apply to cowboys. Steaks are ordered »rare«, »medium rare«, »medium« or »medium well«. »Well-done« is only for philistines, say true steak lovers. Americans have their **own special cuts of meat**. Steaks contain some bone and have a margin of fat, as well as a kind of tail, a strip of meat that gets thinner.

Well-known cuts include »chuck« and »brisket« (the upper and lower parts respectively behind the

These steaks on the grill at Peter Luger's are said to be the best in the world

neck), followed by »rib« and »plate«, and then come the prime cuts »short loin« and »tenderloin«. Next to that are »sirloin«, »top sirloin« and »bottom sirloin«, and finally »round« right at the back. The best-known cuts for ordering are sirloin, which is firm and very tender; strip steak, also from the sirloin and veined with fat; fillet steak from the sirloin, the tenderest piece of all; the extremely tasty rib-eye from the ribs; T-bone from the short loin (strip and tenderloin, the classic cowboy steak); and Porterhouse, also from the short loin. The last-named is cut from the rear end of the short loin, with tenderloin on one side of the bone and a strip steak on the other. The name comes from English pubs in which dark porter beer was on tap, where this kind of steak was served back in the 19th century.

One further mysterious name is the **Delmonico steak**, which was served in the New York restaurant of that name from 1827. Originally it was probably a boneless top sirloin, about 5cm/2inches thick. Today it is another name for New York strip steak from the short loin, but without bone or fat.

Peter Luger ▶p.117
Wolfgang's Steakhouse ▶p.117

Silvia's serves soul food – on Sundays with Gospel music

Samuelson moved to 125th and put Harlem back on the culinary map. Samuelson creates variations of traditional Harlem dishes. The prices for main courses are around $25, which is really not bad. Happy hour is quite the experience. Be sure to make reservations at least 10 days ahead of time; with a little luck you might even be able to get a table the same day.

㉒ Justin's $$$
31 W 21st St.
(between Fifth and Sixth Ave.)
Tel. 1 212-352-0599
Subway: 23rd St.
Yuppie venue for the Flatiron district – the later it gets, the more beautiful the guests! Maybe you'll get lucky and sit next to P. Diddy – one of the great New York hip-hop stars. Speciality of the house: fried chicken with fresh waffles.

㉓ Candle 79 **Insider Tip**
154 E 79th St.
(between Third and Lexington Ave.)
Tel. 1 212-537-7179
Very good vegetarian cooking. Sunday brunch from noon until 4pm.

㉔ Orsay $$$
1057 Lexington Ave.
(corner of 75th St.)
Tel. 1 212-517-6400
Subway: Lexington Ave./77th St.
Looks like an authentic French bistro. Mainly light dishes like lobster salad to tempt the palate.

㉖ The Breslin $$$
16 W 29th St
Chelsea , Manhattan
Tel. 1 212 679 1939
thebreslin.com
Subway: 28th St

British Chef April Bloomfield's restaurant The Breslin was awarded one Michelin star. It is located in the designer Ace hotel in Midtown Manhattan. Hipsters, especially from the design, fashion and .com world love to come here. This tavern-style restaurant is not only well-known for its delicious lamb burgers.

㉜ Primola $$$
1226 Second Ave.
(near 64th St.)
Tel. 1 212-758-1775
Subway: 68th St.
One of the most popular Italian restaurants on the Upper East Side. The fish and clam dishes are especially good. Atmosphere like a comfortable living room.

The Park $$$
2118 Tenth Ave./18th St.
Tel. 1 212-352-3313
Subway: 14th St.
Celebrities and artists show up here around midnight. The ideal place for a delicious snack and an exotic cocktail. The burgers and pizzas are excellent, and so is the finger food for sharing. With a garden, roof garden and view of the High Line.

❺ Tony's Di Napoli $$$
1081 Third Ave
(near 64th St)
Tel. 1 212 888 6333
www.tonys ny.com
Subway: 68th St
This cosy Italian restaurant is known for its fine selection of wines, pasta dishes, salads and antipasti.

MID-RANGE TO INEXPENSIVE
Amy's Restaurant
A recommendable soul food restaurant in Harlem. ►MARCO POLO Tip p.273

㉝ Angelica Kitchen $$ Insider Tip
300 E. 12th St.
(corner of Second Ave.)
Tel. 1 212-228-2909
Subway: Third Ave.
One of the few vegetarian restaurants in the city with creative cooking. The specialities include walnut-lentil pâté and Dragon Bowls, which are influenced by Asian and Latin American dishes.

㊴ Kefi $$
222 W 79th St.
(near Amsterdam Ave.)
Tel. 1 212-873-0200
Subway: 72nd St.
Good traditional Greek cooking on the Upper West Side.

㉝ Rai Rai Ken $$
214 E 10th St.
(near Second Ave.)
Tel. 1 212-477-7030
Subway: Astor Place
Soba, udon and ramen in all shapes and forms of the menu in this Japanese noodle bar. A successful alternative to the many sushi bars.

Jesus' Taco $$ Insider Tip
501 W 145th St./Amsterdam Ave.
Tel. 1 212-234-3330
Subway: 145th St.
Jeffry Chen and his crew offer the very best Tex Mex food around the clock. Only fresh ingredients are used.

Elaine's $$
1703 Second Ave.
(between 88th and 89th St.)
Tel. 1 212-534-8103
Subway: 86th St.
For three decades now (and because of that a bit out of fashion these days) this little restaurant on the Upper East Side has served excellent desserts. Scenes from the TV series Sex and the City were filmed here.

INEXPENSIVE
Lantern $
101 Montague St., Brooklyn Tel. 718-237-2594 Thai cooking with quick, cheap business lunch in a pretty interior.

The Diner $
85 Broadway/corner Berry St
Williamsburg, Brooklyn
Tel. 1 718 486 3077
dinernyc.com/
Subways: JMZ to Marcy Ave or L to Bedford Ave
This unique and charming diner in Williamsburg located underneath the Williamsburg Bridge is a classic. The official menu is mostly just decorative and contains the standard dishes such as hamburgers, but beyond that, the diner's menu with sophisticated New American cuisine changes daily.

⑲ Cinema Café $
45 E 60th St. near Madison Ave.
Tel. 1 212-750-7500, subway: Lexington Ave. Unique sandwiches and wraps, the crispy pizzas are good too. On the walls posters and photos of legendary film support the café's name.

⑨ Pom Pom Diner $ **Insider Tip**
610 Eleventh Ave. (near 45th St.)
Tel. 1 212-397-8395 Serving traditional American food such as cheeseburgers and club sandwiches since 1969.

㉕ La Bonne Soupe $
48 W 55th St.
(between Fifth and Sixth Ave.)
Tel. 1 212-586-7650.
The best soups in all of Manhattan are said to be served here. Congenial restaurant where diners have to queue up at lunchtime.

㉗ Madras Mahal $ **Insider Tip**
104 Lexington Ave.
(between 27th and 28th St.)
Tel. 1 212-684-4010
Subway: E 28th St.
This low-cost restaurant serving mainly vegetarian dishes is one of the best Indian restaurants in the city.

㉘ Carnegie Deli $
854 Seventh Ave.
(between 54th and 55th St.)
Tel. 1 212-757-2245
Subway: Seventh Ave.
Eastern Jewish cuisine with huge portions.

㉙ Katz's $
205 E Houston St./Ludlow St.
Tel. 1 212-254-2246
Subway: Lower East Side/Second Ave.
The chairs wobble, the rattle of dishes is constantly in the background, and it smells of meat, fried food, sauerkraut and beer. Politicians, film stars, sports heroes, Wall Street managers and

Jesus, that tastes good! Superb Tex-Mex food at Jesus' Taco

Museums and Galleries

New York, Capital of the Arts

The Museum of Modern Art, the Guggenheim Museum, the Metropolitan Museum, The Cloisters, the American Museum of Natural History, the International Center of Photography – in New York there is no lack of museums with a global reputation. The city also has many less-known collections and more than 400 galleries that show and sell art.

The museums in New York are privately owned and run, but many are subsidized. In a few museums there is no set entry fee; visitors pay what they can (»Pay what you wish«). On the »Museum Mile«, Fifth Ave. between 79th and 103rd Street, there is no admission charge at certain times (mostly Tue from 5pm). More information on reduced prices and discounts can be found in the chapter ▶Prices and Discounts. The museums marked with an arrow (▶) are described in detail in the section ▶Sights from A to Z.

Museums

There are more than 400 art galleries in New York. Contemporary art can be found above all in ▶SoHo and ▶Chelsea, established modern and older art on the ▶Upper East Side. An **overview** is provided by the monthly *Art Now Gallery Guide* and the website www.galleryguide.org. The guide can be bought in galleries, bookshops and at news stands.

MARCO ⊕ POLO TIP

Insider Tip

Don't miss

- American Museum of Natural History p.180
- Frick Collection p.257
- Guggenheim Museum p.286
- Metropolitan Museum p.289
- The Museum of Modern Art p.298
- Dia: Beacon p.175
- Intrepid Sea-Air-Space Museum p.136

New York's museums and galleries

ART · CULTURE · ARCHITECTURE
American Folk Art Museum
2 Lincoln Square
Tel. 1 212-595-9533
www.folkartmuseum.org
Subway: 66th St. (Lincoln Center)
Tue–Thu, Sat 11.30am–7pm, Sun noon–6pm
Admission free

Folk and applied art from America and other countries. Not limited to traditional techniques and subjects. Many exhibitions have a strong relationship to the contemporary art scene. The new building by architect Tod Williams and Billie Tsien (opposite Eero Saarinen's CBS headquarters) captivates above all with its dark shimmering metal fa-

**Contemporary by name and appearance:
the New Museum of Contemporary Art**

çade with 63 bronze panels (the irregular texture comes from a special casting process: the molten metal was poured onto a bed of coarse sand). There is a branch of the museum at the ▶Lincoln Center of the Performing Arts.

American Numismatic Society
▶Harlem, Audubon Terrace

Asia Society and Museum
725 Park Ave./70th St.
Tel. 1 212-327-9322
www.asiasociety.org
Subway: 68th St./Hunter College
Tue–Sun 11am–6pm, Sept.–June
Fri until 9pm, admission $12
John D. Rockefeller III (1906 to 1978), the oldest son of the great patron, founded the Asia Society in 1956 in order to further America's relationship with the Far East. One of the galleries shows his private collection, sculptures, bronzes, ceramics and pictures from China, Japan, India and Southeast Asia. In addition temporary exhibitions, dance shows, lectures, concerts and film viewings are offered. There is also a well-stocked bookshop. The seven-storey building in reddish granite and sandstone was built in 1981 according to plans by Edward Larrabee Barnes.

Bronx Museum of Arts
1040 Grand Concourse (Bronx)
Tel. 718-681-6000
www.bronxmuseum.org
Subway: 161st St.
Tue, Sat, Sun 10am–6pm, Fri until 8pm, admission free
Art exhibitions, especially New York artists

The Cloisters
▶p.228

Cooper-Hewitt National Design Museum
Fifth Ave./2E 91st St.
Tel. 1 212-849-8400
Subway: 96th St.
www.cooperhewitt.org
New York's best design museum belongs to the semi-private Smithsonian Institution, which has the world's largest collection of design and applied art, shown here in rotating exhibitions. The basis of the collection was compiled by the sisters Sarah, Eleanor and Amy Hewitt, the granddaughters of the steel magnate Andrew Cooper. The building itself is the extravagant town villa of the steel magnate Andrew Carnegie, built in 1901 in the neo-Renaissance style, where his family lived until 1946. The city also has him to thank for Carnegie Hall.

Dahesh Museum
580 Madison Ave.
(between 56th and 57th St.)
Tel. 1 212-759-0606
www.daheshmuseum.org
Subway: Lexington Ave./53rd St.
Tue–Sun 11am–6pm, first Thu of the month until 9pm
Sculptures, paintings and prints by academic artists of the 19th century from France and England.

Dia Art Foundation **Insider Tip**
www.diacenter.org
Tel. 1 212-989-5566
The Dia Art Foundation has an art museum in Beacon with art from the 1960s onwards (▶p.175).

Fashion Institute of Technology – Museum at FIT
Seventh Ave. / 27th St.
Tel. 1 212-217-5800
www.fitnyc.edu
Subway: 28th St.
Tue–Fri noon–8pm, Sat 10am–5pm, admission free
Rotating exhibitions on the subject of fashion and textiles.

Forbes Magazine Galleries
62 Fifth Ave., tel. 1 212-206-5548
Subway: 14th St.
Tue–Sat 10am–4pm
Admission free
Private collection of the deceased multimillionaire Malcolm Forbes.

Frick Collection
►p.257

Guggenheim Museum
►p.286

Hispanic Society of America
►Harlem, Audubon Terrace

Isamu Noguchi Museum
►Queens

Metropolitan Museum of Art
►p.289

Morgan Library Art & Museum
►p.297

Museo del Barrio
1230 Fifth Ave. / 104th St.
Tel. 1 212-831-7272
www.elmuseo.org
Subway: 103rd St.
Wed–Sun 11am–6pm
Admission $9

Mainly Puerto Ricans and other Spanish-speaking ethnic groups from the Caribbean, Central and South America live east of Fifth Ave., between 103rd and 125th Street. The museum shows Puerto Rican and Latin American art, folklore and historical crafts. Among the main attractions are the carved sacred figures called the Santos de Palo (saints of wood). There is also pre-Colombian art.

Museum of Arts and Design
2 Columbus Circle
Tel. 1 212-299-7777
www.madmuseum.org
Subway: Columbus Circle
Tue–Sun 10am–6pm, Thu, Fri until 9pm, admission $16
In 2008 the Museum of Arts and Design moved into the Chazen Building (originally Edward Durell Stone, 1964), which has been completely remodelled by Brad Cloepfil of Allied Works. Along with temporary exhibitions there are crafts made of ceramics, textiles, glass, wood, paper, silver and metal, quilts and furniture dating from 1900 to the present day on display.

Museum of African Art
Corner of Fifth Ave./
East 110th St.
www.africanart.org
Subway: 110th St.
The Museum of African Art (architect. Robert A.M. Stern) displays historic and modern African art; lectures and events.

Museum of Modern Art MoMA
►p.298

Museum of the Performing Arts
►Lincoln Center for the Performing Arts

Staten Island Museum
75 Stuyvesant Place
(Staten Island)
Tel. 718-727-1135
www.statenislandmuseum.org
Ship: Staten Island Ferry, from Battery Park
Open: Mon–Fri 11am–5pm, Sat from 10am Sun from noon
Exhibitions on natural history and fine arts.

National Academy of Design
1083 Fifth Ave./89th St.
Tel. 1 212-369-4880
www.nationalacademy.org
Subway: 86th St.
Wed–Sun 11am–6pm, Sun noon–6pm
American and European design, architecture, art.

Neue Galerie
►p.303

Newhouse Center for Contemporary Art
►Staten Island

What will inspire you today? – this is the fitting slogan at the Museum of Arts and Design.

New Museum of Contemporary Art
235 Bowery/Prince St.
Tel. 1 212-219-1222
www.newmuseum.org
Subway: Prince St.
Wed, Fri–Sun 11am–6pm, Thu until 9pm, admission $16
The New Museum of Contemporary Art is a mixture of art museum and gallery. The newest art movements are shown in changing exhibitions. Along with the presentation of internationally known stars, the intention is to promote young artists here – as also in P. S. 1 (▶Queens) – and help them to a breakthrough. The museum is worth visiting for the architecture of its new building alone, a work by the Japanese duo Kazuyo Sejima and Ryue Nishizawa and their office SANAA

P. S. 1 Contemporary Art Center
▶Queens

Queens Museum of Art
▶Queens

Rubin Museum of Art
150 W 17th St./Seventh Ave.
Tel. 1 212-620-5000
www.rmanyc.org
Subway: 18th St.
Mon 11am–5pm, Wed until 9pm, Fri until 10pm, Sat, Sun until 6pm
Admission $15
Painting from Tibet and the Himalayas.

Schomburg Center for Research in Black Culture
▶Harlem

Skyscraper Museum
39 Battery Place
Tel. 1 212-968-1961
www.skycraper.org
Subway: South Ferry, Bowling Green
Wed–Sun noon–6pm
Lots of valuable information about New York's high-rise architecture.

Studio Museum in Harlem
▶Harlem

Tibetan Museum
▶Staten Island, Jacques Marchais Center of Tibetan Art

Whitney Museum of American Art
▶p.347t

PHOTOGRAPHY
International Center of Photography – ICP
1133 Sixth Ave./43rd St.
Tel. 1 212-857-0000
www.icp.org
Subway: 42nd St.
Tue–Thu, Sat, Sun 10am–6pm, Fri until 8pm, admission $14
The only museum in New York solely devoted to photography was founded in 1974 by Cornell Capa, the brother of the famous photojournalist Robert Capa. The collection includes photographs by Werner Bischof, Robert Capa, David Seymour and Dan Weiner, who were all killed while photographing, as well as works by Ansel Adams and Henri Cartier-Bresson, shown in rotating exhibitions.

Alice Austen House Museum
▶Staten Island

Aperture Foundation Gallery
547 West 27th St., 4th floor
(between 10th and 11th Ave.)
Tel. 1 212-505-5555
www.aperture.org
Subway: 23rd St.
Tue–Sat 10am–6pm, admission free
The exhibition in an historical
brownstone house gives an overview of artistic photography in the
20th century.

FILM · TELEVISION
Museum of the Moving Image
▶Queens

**Paley Center for Media
(formerly MT&R)**
25 W 52nd St.
(between Fifth and Sixth Ave.)
Tel. 1 212-505-5555
www.paleycenter.org
Subway: 47–50th St./Rockefeller
Center
Wed, Fri–Sun noon–6pm
Admission $10
This museum built by Philip Johnson and John Burgee is dedicated
to the history of radio and television. The imposing entrance hall
leads to the Steven Spielberg Gallery, devoted to temporary exhibitions. The two cinemas and smaller viewing rooms show, in
rotation, films from the museum's
archive, which contains more than
100,000 TV and radio pro-
grammes and commercials. On
the third floor visitors can put together their own viewing programme at one of the computers
using the museum catalogue.

MUSEUMS FOR CHILDREN
Brooklyn Children's Museum
▶Brooklyn

**Children's Museum of
Manhattan**
▶Children in New York

**Staten Island Children's
Museum**
▶Staten Island, Snug Harbor
Cultural Center

HISTORY ·
CULTURAL HISTORY
**Museum of Bronx History
Valentine-Varian House**
3266 Bainbridge Ave. / E 208th
St. Tel. 718-889-8900
www.bronxhistoricalsociety.org
Subway: 205th St.
Sat 10am–4pm, Sun 1pm–5pm
Admission $5
The history of the Bronx is exhibited
in a farmhouse dating from 1758.

**Mount Vernon Hotel
Museum and Garden**
421 E 61st St.
(between 1st and York Ave.)
Tel. 1 212-838-6878
www.mvhm.org
Subway: Lexington Ave./59th St.
Tue–Sun 11am–4pm, admission $8
Colonial-style house with garden
from the year 1799.

Bowne House
▶Queens

Brooklyn Historic Museum
▶Brooklyn

Chinatown History
▶Chinatown

**Dyckman Farmhouse
Museum**
Broadway / 204th St.
Tel. 1 212-304-9422

www.dyckmanfarmhouse.org
Subway: 207th St./Dyckman Street
Fri–Sun 11am–5pm, admission $1
The only remaining farmhouse in
Manhattan in the so-called colonial style, from 1783. The furniture is from the 18th century; in
the garden is one of the cherry
trees for which the Dyckman Farm
was famous years ago.

**Ellis Island Immigration
Museum**
►Ellis Island

Fraunces' Tavern Museum
►Financial District

**Hall of Fame for Great
Americans**
►Bronx

Historic Richmond Town
►Staten Island

**Lower East Side Tenement
Museum**
►Lower East Side

Merchant's House Museum
►East Village

Morris-Jumel Mansion
►Harlem

**Museum for American Finan-
cial History**
►Financial District

**Museum of the City of
New York**
1220 Fifth Ave. / 103rd St.
Tel. 1 212-534-1672
www.mcny.org
Tue–Sun 10am–5pm
Admission $10

With over 500,000 objects the
300-year history of the city of
New York is displayed, from the
discovery of the island by Verrazano, on to the settlement Nieuw
Amsterdam, through the colonial
period and the American Revolution, and up to the present day.
The theatre collection is famous,
and the collection of doll's houses
and toys from days gone by is especially popular.

New York Historical Society
170 Central Park West/77th St.
Tel. 1 212-873-3400
www.nyhistory.org
Subway: 81st St./American Museum of Natural History
Tue–Sat 10am–6pm, Fri until 8pm,
Sun 11am–5.45pm, admission $15
The New York Historical Society,
founded in 1809, is one of the
oldest scholarly and research institutions of the city. The museum,
the oldest in New York State, has
been in the same building since
1908, often renovated and expanded, next to the ►American
Museum of Natural History. The
society organizes rotating exhibitions all year on the city's history
and has a comprehensive library
on the history of the city and
country. The museum's treasures
include lamps from the workshop
of Louis Comfort Tiffany (1848–
1933) and watercolours by the
bird painter John James Audubon
(1785–1851).

NYC Fire Museum
258 Spring St.
(between Hudson and Varick St.)
Tel. 1 212-691-1303
www.nycfiremuseum.org

Subway: Spring St. or Houston St.
Daily 10am–5pm
Admission $8
History of the New York City Fire
Department, with a special sec-
tion on 11 September 2001.

**Queens County Farm
Museum**
73-50 Little Neck Parkway, Floral
Park (Queens)
Tel. 1 718-347-3276
www.queensfarm.org Subway:
Kew Gardens, then bus Q 46 to
Little Neck Parkway Daily 10am–
5pm History of agriculture in New
York, presented in an old farm.

Snug Harbor Cultural Center
▶Staten Island

**Staten Island Historical
Museum**
▶Staten Island

**Theodore Roosevelt
Birthplace**
▶Flatiron District

**Van Cortlandt House
Museum**
▶Bronx

NATURE · TECHNOLOGY
**American Museum of
Natural History**
▶p.180

**Intrepid Sea-Air-
Space Museum**   Insider
Pier 86 Hudson River   Tip
Tel. 1 212-245-0072
Subway: 42nd St./Port Authority,
then bus 42 to Twelfth Ave.
www.intrepidmuseum.org
Apr–Oct Mon–Fri 10am–5pm, Sat,

Sun 10am–6pm Nov–March daily
10am–5pm, admission $31
This impressive naval museum tells
you all you need to know about
the US Navy. The main attraction
is the USS Intrepid itself, which
served in the Pacific during the
Second World War. The aircraft
carrier was bombed seven times,
five Kamikaze pilots dived at her
and a torpedo broke through her
side. Along with viewing historical
and modern aeroplanes including
a Lockheed A-12 (SR-71) and a
Concorde, a submarine, a destroy-
er and other ships as well as air,
sea and space technology can be
seen including teh space shuttle
Enterprise As well as trying a flight
simulator that places would-be
pilots into the cockpit of an F/A
18 fighter jet, visitors can test
their stomachs in a g-force simulator. (Neither attraction is included
in the entry fee.)

New York Aquarium
▶Brooklyn, Coney Island

New York Hall of Science
▶Queens

New York Transit Museum
▶Brooklyn

**South Street Seaport
Museum**
▶South Street Seaport

ETHNOLOGY
Americas Society
680 Park Ave.
Tel. 1 212-249-8950
www.americas-society.org
Subway: 68th St.
Wed–Sat noon–6pm

The US Navy and Air Force: to find out about their past and present, visit the Intrepid Sea-Air-Space Museum

Exhibitions on Central and South America, Canada and the Caribbean.

Japan Society
333 E 47th St.
Tel. 1 212-832-1155
www.japansociety.org
Subway: Lexington Ave. / 53rd St.
Tue–Thu 11am–6pm, Fri until 9pm, Sat, Sun until 5pm
Admission $12
The Japan Society, situated somewhat northwest of the ►United Nations Headquarters, was founded in 1907 to promote understanding between the USA and Japan. The black building was built in 1971 according to the plans of Junzo Yoshimura and George Shimamoto in Japanese style. Rotating exhibitions of Japanese crafts are shown here. In addition there is a Japanese garden,

a lecture hall in which Japanese films and theatre productions are shown as well as lectures held, a language centre and a library.

Jewish Museum
►p.279

Museum of the American Indian
1 Bowling Green
Tel. 1 212-514-3700
www.si.edu
Subway: Bowling Green
Daily 10am–5pm, Thu until 8pm
Admission free
Since 1994 what used to be the US Custom House (►p.188) has been a branch of the National Museum of the American Indian, which is split over several sites. The core of the collection was gathered by the banker George D. Heye, who undertook several

journeys of exploration in North and South America from 1897. The museums are now headquartered in Washington and run by the Smithsonian Institution. The New York branch puts on temporary exhibitions about the culture and history of Native Americans, as well as showing contemporary works.

Museum of Jewish Heritage
▶Battery Park

Ukrainian Museum
▶East Village

OTHER MUSEUMS
Edgar Allan Poe Cottage
▶Bronx

Madame Tussaud's New York
234 W 42nd St.
(between Seventh and Eighth Ave.)
Tel. 800-246-8872
www.madame-tussauds.com
Subway: 42nd St./Times Square
Daily 10am–10pm, admission $39
Along with famous names in world history, local greats like actors Woody Allen, Whoopi Goldberg, Barbra Streisand, Brad Pitt, former mayor Rudolph Giuliani and the real estate magnate Donald Trump have been immortalized in wax.

Museum of Sex
233 Fifth Ave./27th St.
Tel. 1 212-689-6337
www.museumofsex.com
Subway: 28th St.
Sun–Fri 11am–6.30pm, Sat until 8pm, admission $17.50

Find out about various aspects of human sexuality, from the murder of the prostitute Helen Jewett in 1830 to the great clean-up under Mayor Giuliani, in the rotating exhibitions at the »MoSex«.

Museum of Comic and Cartoon Art (MoCCA)
594 Broadway, Suite 401
(between Houston and Prince)
Tel. 1 212-254-3511
www.moccany.org
Tue 10am–8pm, Wed–Fri until 5pm, Sat noon–6pm, admission $10

Louis Armstrong House Museum
34–56 107th St., Corona, Queens
Tel. 1 718-478-8274
www.louisarmstronghouse.org
Subway: 103rd St./Corona Plaza
Tue–Fri 10am–5pm, Sat, Sun noon–5pm, admission $10
This modest dwelling was the home of the legendary jazz trumpeter Louis »Satchmo« Armstrong from 1943 to 1971. It was furnished by his wife Lucille and turned into a museum shortly after his death. The 40-minute tour provides interesting insights into the way they lived.

SELECTED ART GALLERIES
Aquavella
18 E 79th Street
Tel. 1 212-734-6300
www.aquavellagalleries.com
Impressionist and post-Impressionist French masters.

Mary Boone
745 Fifth Ave. and
541 W 24th St.

Tel. 1 212-752-2929
www.maryboonegallery.com
She assisted Julian Schnabel, Eric
Fischl and David Salle among others to achieve their breakthroughs.

Barbara Mathes
22 E 80th St.
Tel. 1 212-570-4190
www.barbaramathesgallery.com
Modern paintings and sculptures
by young artists in a setting full of
atmosphere.

Leo Castelli Gallery
18 E 77th St.
Tel. 1 212-249-4470
www.castellagallery.com
American artists like Jasper Johns,

Claes Oldenburg and James
Rosenquist.

Paula Cooper Gallery
534 W 21st St.
Tel. 1 212-255-1105
http://paulacoopergallery.com
Works by Carl Andre and Robert
Wilson, among others.

Larry Gagosian
980 Madison / Fifth Ave.,
555 West 24th St. and
522 West 21st St.
Tel. 1 212-744-2313
www.gagosian.com
Presently probably the internationally most prominent dealer in
modern and contemporary art.

Once the magnificent seat of the US Customs, now the Museum of the American Indian

Barbara Gladstone
515 W 24th St. and 530 W 21st St.
Tel. 1 212-206-9300
www.gladstonegallery.com
Promotes new artists.

Marian Goodman Gallery
24 W 57th St.
Tel. 1 212-977-7160
www.mariangoodman.com
Considered to be one of the best establishments in the field of installations, also represents painters such as John Baldessari, Maurizio Cattelan, Lawrence Weiner.

Marlborough
40 W 57th St.
Tel. 1 212-541-4900
www.marlboroughgallery.com
Works by artists such as Bacon, Botero etc.

Mathew Marks
523 W 24th St.
Tel. 1 212-243-0200
www.mathewmarks.com
Ellsworth Kelly, Bryce Marden, as well as American newcomers.

John McEnroe
42 Greene St.
Tel. 1 212-219-0395
www.johnmcenroegallery.com
The former tennis champion now serves up modern art, above all figurative painting.

Metro Pictures
519 W 24th St.
Tel. 1 212-206-7100
www.metropicturesgallery.com
Contemporary art.

Pierogi
167 N 9th St., Williamsburg

Tel. 1 212-599-2144
www.pierogi2000.com
Traditional gallery in Brooklyn.

Andrea Rosen
525 W 24th St.
Tel. 1 212-627-6000
www.andrearosengallery.com
One of the best noses for new talent.

Tony Shafrazi Gallery
544 W 26th St.
Tel. 1 212-274-9300
www.tonyshafrazigallery.com
He made Keith Haring and his stick figures famous, among others.

Sonnabend Gallery
536 W 22nd St.
Tel. 1 212-627-1018
www.sonnabendgallery.com
Modern classics, young artists – pop art, minimal art, conceptual art, including Gilbert & George, Bernd & Hilla Becher.

Sperone Westwater
257 Bowery
Tel. 1 212-999-7337
www.speronewestwater.com
Presents work by e.g. Alighiero Boeti, Lucio Fontana, Richard Long and Bruce Naumann in a building by Norman Foster.

Michael Werner
4 E 77th St.
Tel. 1 212-988-1623
www.michaelwerner.com
Modern and contemporary artists from Europe and the USA, including James Lee Byers, Marcel Broodthaers, Sigmar Polke, Francis Picabia, Ernst Ludwig Kirchner and Peter Doig.

Most galleries in Chelsea are situated between 20th and 26th Street

The Pace Gallery
534 W 25th St. and
545 W 22nd St.
Tel. 1 212-929-7000
thepacegallery.com
Old masters and French Impressionists.

David Zwirner
525 W 19th St.
(between Tenth and Eleventh Ave.)
www.davidzwirner.com
Tel. 1 212-727-2070
Contemporary art, e.g. Donald
Judd, Dan Flavin, Neo Rauch and
Luc Tuymans.

PHOTO GALLERIES
Janet Borden
560 Broadway
Tel. 1 212-431-0166
www.janetbordeninc.com
Includes pictures by Martin Parr of
England's money aristocracy.

Pace/McGill
32 E 57th St.
Tel. 1 212-759-7999
www.pacemacgill.com
Photos that imitate paintings by
old masters and classical works.

Staley-Wise
560 Broadway
Tel. 1 212-966-6223
www.staleywise.com
Fashion photos in particular are
shown here.

Grey Art Gallery
100 Washington Square East
Tel. 1 212-998-6780
www.nyu.edu/greyart/
Exhibitions gathered from the collections of well-known museums,
retrospectives of the works of unjustly neglected artists.

Shopping

Shop Till You Drop

The world's largest department store is in New York. Where else? Macy's occupies two buildings and displays its wares on ten storeys with a total area of 200,000 sq m/2,150,000 sq ft. What more could you ask? In New York it is not difficult to take literally the slogan »shop till you drop«.

New York is the American consumer paradise. Its department stores, superstores, exclusive boutiques and quirky little shops hold everything the heart desires, from stunningly expensive designer wear to cheap T-shirts.

In the face of this excess, you need to plan. Specific retail branches are based in certain districts. The following is intended to provide some orientation, from south to north.

Orchard Street on Lower East Side is the main street of the Jewish community, where **Orchard Street Market** takes place on Sundays. Clothes and fabrics are very cheap here. In the little corner shops of **Chinatown**, exotic spices and vegetables are on sale. On **Broadway in SoHo**, brand-name fashion is widely available. **Greenwich Village** is known for its weird and wonderful shops, where the wild 1960s have still not come to an end. It is the ideal place to find rare books and records, or all kinds of esoteric knick-knacks, and has stores that appeal to the gay and lesbian community. The **East Village** is famed for its originality – for example, a shop that sells nothing but kimonos. It is also a good place to look for stylish furniture. **Chelsea** is an area of big chain stores, but also unusual retailers. There is a lot going on at Herald Square, where brand-name stores and discount markets have sprung up in the shadow of Macy's. **Fifth Avenue** is known for its design stores – Tiffany, Prada and Versace, for example. Jewellery is made and sold in the **Diamond District**, between 40th and 50th Street. Bargains can be found here. Top designers from the USA and Europe have outlets on 57th Street. The **Upper West Side** is the best area for bookshops, and the **Upper East Side** has a concentration of fashion and antiques.

> **?** MARCO ●POLO INSIGHT
>
> *Did you know*
>
> No city in the world makes it easier for visitors to part with their money. As a bonus there is no city tax on clothing and shoes, provided the value of the goods does not exceed 110 dollars.

A seductive city: shopping is not a chore in New York but a way of life

Not only clothes and CDs, but also hi-fi and camera equipment is cheaper here than at home. The selection is huge – from exclusive fashion and jewellery shops on Fifth Avenue (►Sights from A to Z, Fifth Avenue) to exotic items from Asia (►Sights from A to Z, Chinatown), to trashy goods on 42nd Street. The city also offers shopping opportunities for the most unique tastes. Countless shops are concentrated in malls and markets.

Sales tax

Price tags usually show pre-tax prices. Except for books, periodicals and groceries as well as clothing and shoes under $110 (starting April 2012), a **sales tax**, currently set at 8.875%, is charged on all items.

Opening hours

Opening hours are not set by law. Most shops are open from 10am to 7pm from Monday to Saturday and from 12 noon to 6pm on Sundays. Exceptions are the rule, and in the two weeks before Christmas, Macy's stays open until midnight.

Guide to shopping paradise

A century ago, a »white sale« applied only to cut-price bed sheets, which were always white in those days. Nowadays it denotes a sale for any goods for a fixed period. **Bargains** like this can be found on the shopping pages of Time Out New York, or online at www.mymag.com

Shopping

MARKETS
Chelsea Market
75 Ninth Ave. (between 15th/16th St.) City block with numerous shops and small restaurants including the excellent Fat Witch Bakery and Hale and Hearty Soups.

Farmers' Markets
There are more than 20 farmers' markets in the city. The best-known takes place at Union Square, between 16th and 17th St. Mon, Wed, Fri, Sat 8am–6pm Cheese from small producers, flowers, herbs, honey, fruit and vegetables.

Chinese Market
Canal St.

Saturdays Fruit, vegetables and all sorts of odds and ends.

FLEA MARKETS
Information
www.fleausa.com

Hell's Kitchen Flea Market
West 39th/Ninth Ave.
Sat, Sun from sunrise to sunset The largest and most frequented flea market in the city; right next door: Indoor Antiques Fair (122 W 26th St.) and The Grand Bazaar.

PS 44 Flea Market
Columbus Ave.
(between 76th and 77th St.)
Sun 10am–5pm
All sorts of bric-a-brac of greatly varying quality.

The Garage

112 W 25th St.
Sat, Sun 7am–5pm
Indoor flea market – ideal for a visit on rainy weekends, affordable antiques.

DEPARTMENT STORES

Barney's

660 Madison Ave./61st St. and Seventh Ave./17th St. (branch)
www.barneys.com
One of the most exclusive department stores in the city and the largest men's store in the world.

Bergdorf Goodman

754 Fifth Ave./58th St.
www.bergdorfgoodman.com
Very formal, very expensive; exquisite fashion by various couturiers.

Bloomingdale's

Lexington Ave./59th St.

www.bloomingdales.com
»Bloomies« is one of the leading department stores in the city; designer fashion, cosmetics etc., fashionable, elegant and yet affordable.

Lord & Taylor

4245 Fifth Ave./38th St.
www.lordandtaylor.com
Classic, conservative style with a casual touch at affordable prices.

Macy's

Broadway/34th St.
www.macys.com
A New York institution, partly because of the annual Thanksgiving Day Parade. Almost anything is available here; the gourmet department in the basement is definitely worth a visit.

Farmer's Market: the countryside comes to the city

Fifth Avenue – a Street for Exclusive Shopping

Fifth Avenue was originally planned to be just one more street like the others, when in 1811 the decision was taken to extend Manhattan on the basis of a grid street pattern.

This Commissioners' Plan was drawn up according to the ideals of the young American democracy, with a view to avoiding magnificent boulevards and luxury districts. In 1862 this idea was consigned to the scrapyard when the rich Astors built a luxurious mansion at the corner of Fifth Avenue and 34th Street. They were followed by the Vanderbilts, Carnegies and Rockefellers, whose magnificent »estates« lined the broad sidewalks of the avenue and gave it the name Millionaires' Row.

A Street for the Wealthy

In the late 19th century, as New York spread ever further north, Fifth Avenue was suddenly at the centre of Manhattan. Its over-indulged residents found the traffic noise a nuisance and moved north, at the latest following the opening of the **Waldorf Astoria Hotel** in 1893. They found the peace and quiet that they desired on either side of Central Park. The Astors' residence was replaced by the Astoria Hotel, which was itself demolished and then gloriously resurrected in a different location as the Waldorf Astoria. Between 1930 and 1931 the Empire State Building, then the world's tallest building, was constructed on this site.

Luxurious Hotels, High-class Shops and the Museum Mile

Fifth Avenue, still New York's most prestigious boulevard, starts at Washington Square in Greenwich Village, then passes through Midtown and along Central Park to the Upper East Side and the Harlem River on 142nd Street. On what was once an avenue of mansions, luxurious hotels and exclusive shops were built after the departure of the millionaires' families. In 1907 the **Plaza Hotel** opened. It is still one of the finest in the city, although most of the hotel rooms have now been converted into apartments. The Plaza has accommodated many celebrated guests, including numerous US presidents, Ernest Hemingway and the Beatles. The hotel plays a leading role in Alfred Hitchcock's film *North by Northwest*.

A Fleet of Flagship Stores

The world-famous shopping strip lies between 34th Street and 59th Street. Bergdorf-Goodman, Louis Vuitton, Prada, Gucci, Versace and many other well-known brands have flagship stores here, and in-

Tiffany: jewellery designed by a legendary company

ternationally renowned jewellers such as Harry Winston, Cartier, Fortunoff and Tiffany's, made into a tourist attraction by the film Breakfast at Tiffany's, try to outdo each other with the splendour of their window displays.

FAO Schwarz, one of the world's biggest toy shops, is paradise for children – especially before Christmas, of course. Disney and Apple have also chosen Fifth Avenue as the location for prestigious store. There are several well-known buildings on Fifth Avenue. The Empire State Building, which was con-structed in an astonishingly short time in 1931, remained the world's tallest building until 1972. St Patrick's Cathedral, dating from 1878, overshadowed its neighbours when it was completed. Other notable edifices on the avenue are the New York Public Library, opened in 1911, the Rockefeller Center, built between 1931 and 1940, the Trump Tower, commissioned by the eponymous billionaire and completed in 1983, and world-famous museums such as the Guggenheim and the Metropolitan Museum of Art.

Saks Fifth Avenue
611 Fifth Ave /50th St.
www.saksfifthavenue.com
Typical American fashion, exclusive perfume department, accessories.

Takashimaya
693 Fifth Ave.
Branch of the largest Japanese department store, a Mecca of good taste.

SHOPPING MALLS
South Street Seaport and Pier 17
Boutiques, bookshops and galleries ►Sights from A to Z, South Street Seaport.

Rockefeller Center
►p.317

Trump Tower
►Fifth Avenue

Manhattan Mall
Sixth Ave./33rd St.
Pleasant, covered shopping street with good restaurants.

ELECTRONICS
Apple Store
767 Fifth Ave.
Open almost around the clock. I-Macs, iPads, iPods and more.

B&H Photo – Video-Pro Audio Superstore   **Insider Tip**
420 Ninth Ave.
This camera department store carries everything that the photographer's heart desires at attractive prices.

J & R Music & Computer World
9176 Park Row and Broadway (opposite City Hall)
Supermarket for cameras, computers and CDs.

Nintendo World Store
24 West 48th St.
Interactive paradise.

MUSIC AND BOOKS
Bleeker Music Inc. Store
188 West 4th St.
An overwhelming selection of old vinyl records and rare CDs, well-informed staff.

Westsider Records
233 W 72nd St.
Classical and jazz records and cassettes, some of which are long since »out of print«.

Jazz Record Center
236 W 26th St , 8th floor
Tue–Sat
Jazz specialist.

Barnes & Noble
1972 Broadway
Huge »book department store« with not just bestsellers. Book prices are reduced just a few weeks after coming on the market. A café allows relaxed browsing in books and periodicals. Numerous branches.

St. Mark's Comics
148 Montague St.
Inexhaustible selection of comics, also plastic figures, t-shirts, jackets and bags with comic-book figures.

Think big: Macy's presentation is not meant to be modest

Fast Food with a Touch of Gourmet

Yissir has to park his food truck at the corner of Water Street and Old Slip by 8am at the latest. If he is later, he gets stuck in the traffic and someone else might grab his spot. Space is precious in the business district around Wall Street. Every vendor tries to park his truck as close to the action as possible, as hungry finance traders are good customers.

Yissir, who comes from Morocco, serves North African specialities such as lamb kebabs, lamb burgers – this is America, after all – and Mediterranean vegetables. All of these is cut into convenient-sized pieces and placed in plastic trays so that customers can eat on the hoof. Yissir, who used to own a restaurant, has been taking his food truck to Manhattan for two years now, and serves from 11am to 2pm on weekdays. He realized that New Yorkers are not only keen on hot dogs, hamburgers and pretzels, and gave them a pleasant surprise by preparing lighter meals. »A food truck is harder work than a restaurant, but it is fun.«

Food carts are in fashion in Manhattan. They are dishing up not merely fast food, but gourmet fast food from all around the world, imaginative competition for the likes of McDonalds, Starbucks and all the hot dog and pretzel carts that throng the streets of the city. In the Finance District, where food carts are particularly thick on the ground, Urban Oyster organizes its Food Cart Tours. Brian Hoffman, an experienced restaurant critic, food expert and food blogger, takes his guests to the best food carts in the Finance District or Midtown, where they are treated to interesting and unexpected stories about New York's latest food craze and, of course, some samples. »No-one has ever been hungry at the end of the tour,« says Hoffman.

The origins of food carts

There were food carts 100 years ago. Immigrants from Europe pushed their wooden hand-carts through the Lower East Side, selling meat, fruit and vegetables. Modern food carts are made of metal, are resistant to heat and rain, and look nothing like their forebears. In order to run a mobile snack stall, it is necessary to have one of the 2,800 mobile food vendor permits which are issued in New York. These permits can only be obtained on the black market, and cost around 10,000 dollars. The queue to get one is as long as for a ticket to watch the New York Jets. Often these coveted permits are passed on among members of a family.

Some recommendations

Adel from Egypt rules the roost at the corner of Front Street and Maiden Lane. At Adel's Best Halal he cooks up lamb and chicken dishes with yoghurt sauce – red (hellishly hot) or white. Joe Jianetto, an Italian from Staten Island, produces »grandma's pizza« with thin, crispy dough and lots of mozzarella, tomato and basil. Gillian Bennett-Reide from Jamaica is known for her spicy chicken on rice and infectious good humour. Her truck is at the corner of Bridge Street and Broadway, where no-one can resist the broad smile and delicious chicken of »Jamaica Mama«.

The rock-and-rollers among the food-cart owners are the young Asians of Korilla BBQ. Edward Song, James the cook and their team rock Manhattan with three trucks that are easily recognizable thanks to their striking leopard-skin pattern and their famous Korean tacos and burritos. The fillings, consisting of beef, chicken, kimchi (pickled vegetables), cheese, bacon and hot sauces and spices, are so popular in New York that long queues form at the Korean stands every lunch-time. The name Korilla derives from »Korea« and »grill«. This BBQ offering earned the team, once a group of high school kids, the »Rookie of the Year Award«.

Now it's time for dessert. For example at Wafels and Dinges at the corner of Water Street and William Street. Warm waffles, made in a trice by Paul and Jerry, served with witty quips and delicious, thick, sweet sauces, taste so good that no-one stops to count the calories. They just taste »wafelish«, as Paul and Jerry say.

Of course you can go in search of these food stalls without a guided tour, but they change their locations often. Urban Oyster knows where to find them:

Insider Tip

Urban Oyster
Tel. 1 347-618-8687
www.urbanoyster.com

Business lunch to go – some excellent alternatives to hamburger chains

Hop-on-hop-off tours on a double-decker

www.bigonion.com
Wide selection of guided tours through the city, e.g. historic Harlem, multi-ethnic eating tour, Greenwich Village.

New York City Cultural Walking Tours
Tel. 1 212-979-2388
www.nycwalk.com
Guided tours through Manhattan's architectural and cultural history.

Municipal Art Society Tours
457 Madison Ave.
Tel. 1 212-935-3960
www.mas.org
Architectural tours

Harlem Heritage Tours
104 Malcolm X Blvd.
Tel. 1 212-280-7888

www.harlemheritage.com
Harlem Heritage dedicates itself by bus or on foot to the Harlem Renaissance, the soul of Harlem and Harlem's nightlife.

Harlem Spiritual Inc.
690 Eighth Ave.
(between 43rd and 44th Street)
Tel. 1 212-391-0900
www.harlemspirituals.com
A variety of tours through Harlem with gospel concerts in churches.

On Location Tours
Tel. 1 212-209-3370
www.screentours.com
In the footsteps of famous TV series and cinema films such as Sopranos and Sex and the City.

Inside/Out
Tel. 718-644-8205

www.insideouttours.com
Unique tours, for example behind the scenes of the New York fashion industry.

By horse-drawn carriage

A tour through Central Park in a horse-drawn carriage. Starting point is the former Plaza Hotel on Fifth Ave./59th St.

Bike the Big Apple

Tel. 1 347-878-9809
www.bikethebigapple.com
A bike ride from Harlem, via Manhattan and Queens to Coney Island.

Central Park Bike Tours

Bite of the Apple Tours
Tel. 1 212-541-8759
www.centralparkbiketours.com
Two hours by bike through Central Park, starting at the New York Visitors Bureau, 2 Columbus Circle, corner of West 59th Street/Broadway.

Circle Line Cruises

Pier 83/42nd St., or Pier 16 on South Street Seaport
Tel. 1 212 563 3200
www.circleline42.com

The half-hour to three-hour boat tours go around the southern point or the whole of Manhattan and are great for photographing the skyline.

NY Waterway

Pier 78, 38th St. / West Side Highway
Tel. 1 800-533-3779
www.nywaterway.com
Boat tours around the southern point or circumnavigating the whole of Manhattan.

Travelling in a limo

NYC Limousine
http://nyclimousine.com
Discover Manhattan like a VIP in a stretch limo.

Liberty Helicopter Tours

VIP Heliport
West Side Highway/30th St. and Pier 6 (between Broad Stand Old Slip)
Tel. 1 212-967-6464, 1 800-542-9933
www.libertyhelicopters.com
Breathtaking views; flights up to 20 minutes, as well as charter flights and flights to the airport are available.

TOURS

If you are wondering where to start your visit to New York, these tours will give you a few suggestions for getting to know the city, and for making excursions in the surroundings of New York.

The tour starts and finishes at the ❶**Grand Central Terminal**. A ceiling painted like the sky and magnificent chandelier transform the imposing Beaux Arts style building into a work of art. Leaving the station and heading towards 42nd Street, on the left hand side you see the ❷**Chrysler Building,** reaching to the sky with its stainless steel point. Walk west along 42nd Street to Fifth Avenue to the ❸*New York Public Library**, the second-largest library in the USA. In good weather the steps to the entrance are a popular place for lunch with the people who work in the surrounding offices. The most opulent street, **Fifth Avenue**, gets its nickname »Boulevard of Golden Credit Cards« from luxury shops like Tiffany and Cartier, all of which are between 49th and 59th Street. Eight blocks to the south at 34th Street/Fifth Avenue, what is probably the most beautiful skyscraper in the world rises into the heavens: the ❹**Empire State Building**, built between 1929 and 1931. Its lookout decks on the 86th and 102nd floors are among the quietest places in midtown Manhattan. Follow

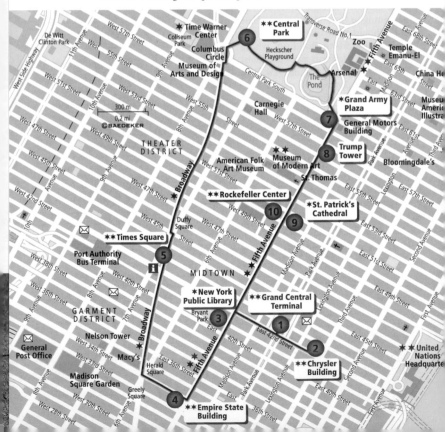

34th Street west for one block to reach **Herald Square**, and turn onto **Broadway**, the famous entertainment district. Eight blocks to the north is ❺**Times Square**, which pulsates with life both day and night. A visit is particularly worthwhile at dusk when the advertising lights bring a touch of Las Vegas to the heart of Manhattan.

It slowly gets quieter further north on Broadway up to **Columbus Circle**, where the new **Time Warner Center** towers with its luxury shops, hotels and restaurants, and where there is an entrance to ❻**Central Park**, Manhattan's »green oasis«. Head east across the park, which is a nature reserve, on a route of your own choosing. ❼**Grand Army Plaza** is the site of the Pulitzer Fountain and a stopping place for horse-drawn carriages, which offer a relaxed ride through Central Park. Opposite is the Plaza Hotel, built in 1907 in French chateau style. Walk back along Fifth Avenue, this time south, past the black ❽ **Trump Tower**, where a spectacular atrium houses a two-storey shopping mall, to ❾**St. Patrick's Cathedral**, the seat of the archbishop of New York. Directly opposite the cathedral is the ❿**Rockefeller Center**, a city within a city with its 19 interconnected high-rises. In the winter, when a Christmas tree with around 30,000 coloured electrical lights illuminates Rockefeller Plaza, a famous skating rink attracts thousands of ice skaters. Follow Fifth Avenue now to 42nd Street and turn left to get back to the start and finish of the tour, **Grand Central Terminal**. Here, the lower floor restaurants and bars are an inviting place to take a well-earned break.

From the Rockefeller Center to Grand Central Terminal

MARCO POLO INSIGHT

? *Did you know*

Times Square at the intersection of Broadway and Seventh Avenue is the centre of the theatre district. It takes its name from the building of the *New York Times* newspaper, T.S.1., and is known for its brightly flashing advertising. The monthly rent for 2,813 sq m/ 3,364 sq yd is more than $150,000. The average lifespan of a neon light here is, incidentally, 2.5 years.

Downtown: Where it All Began   Tour 2

Start and finish: Civic Center – South Street Seaport
Duration: 4 hours

The rise of New York from a Native American village to a world-famous metropolis began in southern Manhattan. The Statue of Liberty, the Brooklyn Bridge and the largest stock exchange in the world are visible signs of the unbending will that made the city into one of the most important centres of the Western world. But Ground Zero is here too, evidence of the biggest terrorist attack in the United States of America.

The bronze bull by the Custom House is the symbol of Wall Street

From the Civic Center to the south tip of Manhattan

The tour's starting point is the ❶ **Civic Center**, a city in the city, where over 300,000 employees of various city offices and departments work. Walk south along **Broadway** to reach the seat of the mayor and the city council, ❷ ***City Hall**. Opposite is the **Woolworth Building**, built in 1913; with its copper dome it was the tallest building in the world for 17 years and began the era of skyscrapers. A little further along Broadway is Park Row; turn right here into **Vesey Street**, on which the site of the ❸ ****World Trade Center** with **Ground Zero** is located. Follow West Street south and make a detour to **Battery Park City**. The high-rises were built in the 1980s on ground artificially created from the material excavated during construction of the World Trade Center. 30% of south Manhattan stands on reclaimed land.

From Broadway to Wall Street

Take a stroll on the ❹ ***Esplanade** along the **Hudson River** and enjoy the spacious green areas. At the end are ❺ ***Battery Park** with **Castle Clinton**, the **East Coast War Memorial**, dedicated to the missing soldiers of the Second World War, and the ❻ **ferry terminals**. Tickets for the ferry to ***Ellis Island** are available here as well as to the ****Statue of Liberty**, though the stairs to the crown are

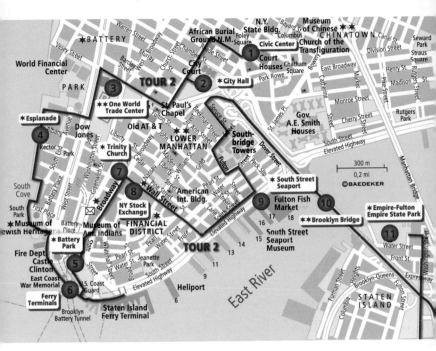

accessible with a special »crown ticket«, which has to be reserved ahead of time (www.statecruises.com). Just as good (almost) and above all cheaper – in fact it's free – is a ride on the **Staten Island Ferry**. The route passes relatively close to the Statue of Liberty and offers a beautiful view of the skyline of downtown Manhattan. Leaving the park and heading north leads to the beginning of **Broadway**, and it is a short walk up to ❼**Trinity Church**. The church with New York's oldest cemetery provides a strong contrast to the money-mania that otherwise predominates here in the world of bankers and brokers. ***Wall Street**, the legendary financial street, begins directly opposite the church. Where once a massive wall protected Dutch Nieuw Amsterdam from the Native Americans and the English, there now stands the largest and most important stock exchange in the world today, the ❽**New York Stock Exchange** (NYSE). At the end of Wall Street are the docks on the **East River**; follow the river north to the ❾***South Street Seaport** at the end, a popular spot after work with its shopping mall, restaurants and bars. Walkers who still have the energy will find the entrance to the ❿****Brooklyn Bridge** in Park Row near the Civic Center – the starting point of this tour. Those who are feeling tired can take the subway to Brooklyn.

On the other side of the East River, the ⑪ **Empire-Fulton Ferry State Park** is a wonderful place to relax, especially in the evening. It lies at the foot of the Brooklyn Bridge and offers a wonderful view of Manhattan.

Tour 3 From West to East – a Cable Car in New York

Start and finish: 72nd St./Central Park – United Nations
Duration: 2 hours

Cable cars are not only found in the Alps: New York has one too. It doesn't go up mountains but it does take passengers across the East River and delivers them to Roosevelt Island – with dry feet.

Before getting into the cable car, why not take a walk through **Central Park**. Enter the park from 72nd Street West and go into ❶ **Strawberry Fields**, a garden with a mosaic which John Lennon's widow Yoko Ono commissioned in memory of the Beatles' singer. Take whatever route you wish across the park but it is well worthwhile to make a detour to ❷ **Bethesda Fountain** on **The Lake** – with its boats in the summer – and to ❸ **The Mall**, an avenue of elm trees with sculptures by various artists. Leave the park at ❹* **Grand Army Plaza** to get to **Fifth Avenue**. Follow 59th Street further east past the towering 215m/705ft-high ❺ **General Motors**

Crossing the river in a cable car

Building on the right, one of the most beautiful buildings in New York. Further up 59th Street on the corner of Lexington Avenue is ❻ **Bloomingdale's**, one of the city's famous retail palaces. Two blocks further, on the corner of 60th Street/Second Avenue, is the entrance to the ❼ **aerial tramway** to ❽ **Roosevelt Island**. In good weather the view of Manhattan from the cable car (the trip costs as much as a subway ticket: $2.25) is very pleasant and a little different from the usual aerial views. There is not much to see on the former hospital island, so decide for yourself whether to take the cable car

or the subway back. A walk further along First Avenue, which runs parallel to the East River, leads to an extra-territorial enclave 15 blocks to the south: neither the USA nor the City of New York calls the shots here, as this is the headquarters of the ❾**United Nations** – and the end of this tour. Numerous works of art and the UN souvenir shop are found in the entrance hall, which is open to the public.

Tour 4 Culture Tour: Museum Mile

Start and finish: Radio City Music Hall – American Museum of Natural History
Duration: varies

World-famous museums like the MoMA, Guggenheim or MET lure art lovers from all over the world to New York. It takes days just to get a rough overview – making the right choices is an art in itself.

Start:
Rockefeller Center

At the start of the culture tour it's worth taking a look inside ❶* **Radio City Music Hall** to see the largest theatre auditorium in the world. Only three blocks to the north on ❷**53rd Street**, between Fifth Avenue and the Avenue of the Americas, there are two notable museums, the **Museum of American Folk Art** and the **Museum of Modern Art (MoMA)**. Now follow ❸**Fifth Avenue** north to reach 70th Street between Fifth and Madison Avenue and the former home of the industrialist Frick with the ❹**Frick Collection**, which he accumulated himself. It contains masterpieces by Rembrandt, Titian and Goya among others. Five blocks to the north on the corner of Madison Avenue/75th Street is the ❺**Whitney Museum of American Art**, which specializes in American art of the 20th and 21st centuries. The ❻**Metropolitan Museum of Art (MET)**, on Fifth Avenue/82nd Street, the probably best-known art museum in the world has with constantly changing exhibitions and a unique art collection.

Austrian specialities

Not far away, on 86th Street between Fifth and Madison Avenue, Café Sabarsky in the ❼**Neue Galerie New York** offers Austrian specialities. After this well-earned refreshment, visitors can take a look at the carefully restored house with German and Austrian art from the early 20th century. On Fifth Avenue, between 88th and 89th Street, the unusual exterior of the ❽**Guggenheim Museum** attracts all the attention. The great collection contains paintings by Picasso, Kan-

dinsky and Klee. New York's only design museum, the **⑨ *Cooper-Hewitt Design Museum,** is only two blocks further north. The corner of Fifth Avenue/92nd Street with the **⑩ Jewish Museum,** devoted to over 4,000 years of Jewish history, is at the end of the walk along Fifth Avenue. Those who can still take anything in may enjoy the walk through the upper part of Central Park to the first-class

⓫**American Museum of Natural History, where the 15 billion year history of evolution is on display – marking the end of the »culture tour«.

Tour 5 Chelsea, a Neighbourhood on the Upswing

Start and finish: Madison Square Garden – Chelsea Piers
Duration: approx. 2 hours

Chelsea in New York and Chelsea in London actually don't have anything to do with each other, but there are some parallels. Just as in London, New York's Chelsea developed into a »place to be«, as in the last years more and more artists and gallery owners as well as unusual shops have moved here.

From the concrete bowl to the Empire State Building

❶ Madison Square Garden, the starting point of the walk and home of the Knicks and the New York Rangers, holds more than 20,000 people. A tour through the concrete bowl is worthwhile for sports fans, and on days when no event is taking place visitors can even go into the arena's holy of holies, the teams' locker rooms. Across from the »Garden« on Eighth Avenue is the **❷ General Post Office** with its Corinthian pillars. Since the old Penn Station was torn down in 1963 the building seems a bit out of proportion. On 34th Street going west between Seventh Avenue and the Avenue of the Americas is the largest department store in the world, **Macy's**, while a little to the east looms what was once New York's tallest building, the **❹**Empire State Building**.

Across Fifth Avenue to the Hudson

Follow ****Fifth Avenue** south, and the surroundings become less well-to-do. But it is precisely here, on the intersection of Broadway, Fifth Avenue and 23rd Street, that New York's first steel skeleton skyscraper stands, known as the **❺ Flatiron Building** because of its triangular shape. The famous **❻ Chelsea Hotel** on 23rd Street, between Seventh and Eighth Avenue, was once the favourite hotel of the beat and rock scene. Jack Kerouac wrote his cult novel *On the Road* here, and Thomas Wolfe and Dylan Thomas were regulars. **West Chelsea** lies west of Ninth Avenue; this former industrial area is one of the trendiest neighbourhoods in New York. Here, particularly between West 22nd and West 29th Street in so-called Gallery Row, countless young artists and gallerists have set up shop. Follow 22nd Street to the Hudson, reaching the recreation area known as **❽ Chelsea Piers**.

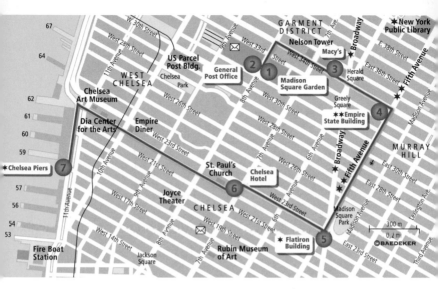

The site where ocean liners and freighters once docked has been converted into one of the largest sports facilities in the world with golf courses, ice rinks, walking and jogging paths (►MARCO POLO Insight p.220). For those not interested in sport, the piers also have attractive bars and restaurants, and are a nice finish to the tour.

New York by Subway

Tour 6

Start and finish: Times Square
Duration: 30 min travelling time

A trip on line 7 of the New York subway between Times Square in Manhattan and Main Street in the borough of Queens gives you an insight into the ethnic diversity of the city.

Cross several continents by subway — line 7 of New York's IRT (Interborough Rapid Transit) does exactly that. Especially along Roosevelt Avenue in Queens, where the ethnic mix is extremely diverse, it takes passengers to districts that have kept their own character to this day. This is why the line is known as the »International Express«. The journey starts at ❶ **Times Square** in Manhattan, the heart of New York. Below ground you will encounter many buskers, who find a big

Start: Times
Square

audience for their music in this large station. The Times Square Visitors Center provides information and a New York city plan. At the computer terminals you can check e-mails free of charge and even send electronic postcards (1560 Broadway, between 46th and 47th Street, Mon–Fri 9am–8pm, Sat, Sun 8am–8pm, tel. 1 212-869-1890).

Queens

The first three stops are in Manhattan, and then the train passes under the East River to Queens, a borough in the west of Long Island that was incorporated into the city in 1898. In the early 20th century immigrants were already taking the subway to their new home, having built the subway line themselves. Along the tracks of line 7, which becomes an overhead railway in Queens, people from several continents made their homes and opened shops, small businesses and markets. ❷ **Sunnyside** was originally rural. After the construction of the Queensboro Bridge in 1909 it became a dormitory town for people who work in

46th St./Bliss St. subway

Manhattan. The multi-storey apartment blocks date from the 1920s and 1930s. Sunnyside Gardens, the first planned residential area in the USA with private gardens (between Queens Blvd., 43rd and 52nd Street, Barnett and Skillman Avenue), is now protected heritage. In Sunnyside there are many Rumanian, Latin American and Asian restaurants and food shops, while Jackson Heights is inhabited by a large number of Indians, and Flushing is home to the Chinatown of Queens, which is now almost as large as the Chinese enclave in Manhattan.

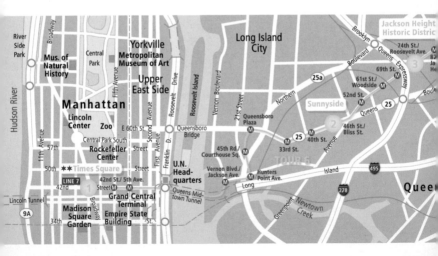

The ❸ **station** is one of New York's first »green« subway stations: it generates most of the energy it requires from solar collectors. The Jackson Heights Historic District consists of over 2,000 historic buildings between 93rd and 69th Street, Northern Blvd. and Roosevelt Avenue. The biggest concentration of Indian restaurants and shops is on 74th Street.

74th St./ Roosevelt Ave. subway

In order to show the diversity of its residents in art, the Queens Council of the Arts holds the annual Queens Art Xpress, with concerts, exhibitions and events (www.queenscouncilarts.org).

Excursions

Just outside New York City lie two of the most beautiful destinations in the north-east of the USA: the Hudson Valley, where art and nature combine to form a romantic landscape, and the Hamptons, where the rich and famous come to rest and relax on wonderful beaches. Some destinations can be reached with public transport, but a hire car is necessary for those who want to explore further.

★★Hudson Valley

A few miles upriver from New York the Hudson becomes a mighty river. The graceful countryside of the Hudson Valley stretches from both banks with villages such as **Sleepy Hollow** and art colonies like **Sugarloaf**. The most famous military academy of the USA (Visitor Center, Highland Falls, www.usma.edu; guided tours only possible with passport or driving licence) is located in **West Point** on the west bank of the Hudson. The **Storm King Art Center**, where sculptures by Alexander Calder, Henry Moore, Louise Nevelson and others enliven the lawns, is an accomplished combination of art and nature (Old Pleasant Hill Road, Mountainville, www.stormking.org).

The town Beacon on the opposite bank of the Hudson has a spectacular museum for contemporary art, known as Dia:Beacon. In the halls of a former paper factory, as large as football fields, works by 24 artists representing avant-garde and conceptual art of the 1970s, including Judd, Heizer, Serra, Darboven, Warhol and Palermo, are exhibited (3 Beekman St., Beacon, www.diacenter.org; directions: Metro-North Railroad from Grand Central Terminal to Poughkeepsie, 90 minutes travel time; five minutes' walk from Beacon station). Around the little town of Hyde Park, the magnificent 19th-century mansions of

Insider Tip

? MARCO ⊕ POLO INSIGHT

Bear Mountain State Park

Bear Mountain rises 400m/1300ft above the river, close to West Point. From a distance it looks like a reclining bear. The open woods and the large lake are very popular among New Yorkers (Palisades Parkway/Route 9W). On the way back to New York City, drive onto I287 East south of Nyack to pass the Palisades Center, the tenth-largest mall in the USA.

Dia Beacon: Richard Serra's steel sculptures weigh many tons

industrial magnates line the east bank of the Hudson. It is possible to visit them and walk in the wonderful parkland on the Hudson (www. hud sonriver.com/estates.htm). It is worth visiting the Vanderbilt Mansion National Historic Site, the smaller Wilderstein estate and the Home of Franklin Roosevelt, four times American president (information: www.nps.gov/vama, www.wilderstein.org and www.nps. gov/hofr).

**Long Island

Long Island is a narrow strip of land that stretches 200km/130mi into the Atlantic from Manhattan. In pretty villages reminiscent of New England, New York society cools down on the hottest days of the year.

Getting there: with a hire car the journey via Long Island Expressway and route 27 takes approx. 2 hrs; the Hampton Jitney bus goes to Southampton from Manhattan hourly all year round (corner of 3rd Ave and 40th St.; www.hamptonjitney.com). From the end of May until early or mid-September the Long Island Railroad (LIRR) connects Penn Station (Manhattan) and Flatbush Avenue (Brooklyn) with Long Island City (Queens); www.lirr.org. To explore Long Island further, you need a car. For information about what's on: www.hamp-

tons.com; there is a list of shops, restaurants and activities at www.
easthamptonchamber.com and www.southamptonchamber.com; see
also Long Island Convention & Visitors Bureau: www.discoverlong-
island.com.

At first glance it is not obvious in the Hamptons that the rich and famous come here to recuperate from their tough lives. The motto is
understatement. Manhattan society wants for nothing here, as pure
luxury is concealed behind the façade of simplicity.

White wine is grown on **North Fork**, to the east of the northern
point. Most vineyards are found along Route 25 (www.liwines.com).
In **Sag Harbor**, one of the oldest villages on Long Island, there is a
small whaling museum. **Montauk**, where a lighthouse marks the
easternmost end of the island, is one of the best surfing areas on the
east coast, and less exclusive than the Hamptons. The abstract Ex-
pressionist Jackson Pollock and his wife Lee Krasner lived and
worked in East Hampton; their house and studio are open to visitors
(www.pkhouse.org).

There are wonderful beaches for swimming on Long Island. One of
them, overcrowded at weekends, is Jones Beach, which extends
10km/6mi along the Atlantic Ocean and has all kinds of entertainments for visitors; a quieter place in the far north-east is Shelter Island, reached by ferry. The 50km/30mi-long Strand Fire Island, part
of a narrow chain of islands to the south of Long Island, is a good
place for angling, swimming and walking (www.fireislandferries.
com, www.islanderstravel.com, www.sayvilleferry.com).

SIGHTS FROM A TO Z

New York: capital of art and entertainment, shopping paradise, non-stop rush-hour, infectious rhythms, colourful and trendy neighbourhoods – and four multifaceted boroughs in addition to Manhattan

** American Museum of Natural History

✦ E 8

Location: Central Park West, 79th St.
Subway: 81st Street
❶ Daily 10am–5.45pm

Tours of the main sights daily and hourly
10.15am–3.15pm
Admission: $22
www.amnh.org

Founded in 1869, this is the oldest museum in New York. With more than 35 million exhibits it is the largest museum of natural history in the world.

The museum is housed in a building complex built in 1874–99 by Calvert Vaux and J. Wrey Mould in the monumental Roman triumphal style; its façade, which faces Central Park, is by John Russel Pope. The meeting point for guided tours to the main attractions is on the second floor between the Theodore Roosevelt Memorial Hall and the Hall of African Mammals. Since the end of the 1990s the separate departments have been gradually transformed away from the dusty charm of the late 19th century and brought up to the latest standards. Especially recommended are the **Hall of Biodiversity** with its life-size diorama of a rainforest, the **Hall of Planet Earth**, which is concerned among other things with the interior of the earth, the recently converted **Hall of Ocean Life** and the **dinosaur department** – in the foyer **Barosaurus lentus**, the tallest dinosaur in the world, amazes visitors. The Rose Center for Earth and Space is connected to the museum (▶p.183).

> **?** *Did you know*
>
> **MARCO ⊕ POLOINSIGHT**
>
> A good rule of thumb for getting around in Manhattan is: one minute for the north-south blocks between Uptown and Downtown, five minutes for the cross-town blocks going east to west.

First floor The collection is primarily dedicated to human and animal biology and the natural history of the North American continent. Along with flora and fauna, the life of the American Indians of the Pacific Northwest and the Inuit is documented. Every department features numerous life-size models; the model of the blue whale in the **Hall of Ocean Life** is especially impressive. The significant collection of precious stones and minerals includes the Star of India, the largest cut sapphire at 63 carats, and a 100-carat ruby along with various replicas. Since 1985, the museum has been in possession of the largest cut

American Museum of Natural History

Third Floor

1 Pacific peoples
2 Eastern woodlands and plains Indians
3 Primates
4 North American birds
5 New York State mammals
6 New York City birds
7 African mammals
8 Hayden Planetarium Space Theater
9 Reptiles and Amphibians

Fourth Floor

1 Vertebrate origins
2,3 Dinosaurs, special exhibition gallery
4 Advanced mammals
5 Primitive mammals

First Floor

1 Meteorites
2 Gemstones and Minerals
3 Human origins
4 Environment in New York State
5 North American forests
6 Northwest coast Indians
7 Ocean life
8 Biodiversity
9 Small mammals
10 North American mammals
11 Rose Center for Earth and Space
a Rose Gallery
b Planet Earth

Second Floor

1 South American peoples
2 Mexico and Central America
3 Birds of the world
4 African peoples
5 Asian peoples
6 Asian mammals
7 African mammals
8 Rose Center for Earth and Space
a Cosmic pathway
b Big bang
c Scales of universe
9 Butterfly conservatory

An impressive welcome to the American Museum of Natural History

gemstone in the world, the Brazilian Princess, a light blue topaz which weighs 21,327 carats (4.3kg/9.5lb) donated by an anonymous patron. Meteorites are on display in the next room, among them Ahnighito, the largest meteorite ever to fall on Earth, which was discovered in 1897.

Second floor   Exhibits on ethnic groups and animals of Africa, Asia, Central and South America and the world of birds are the main attractions on the second floor.

Third floor   The third floor shows exhibits on the history and life of North American Indians in the forests of the East Coast and the Great Plains as well as the Native American nations of the Pacific region. Further departments cover the birds of North America, mammals of New York State, African mammals, reptiles, amphibians and primates.

The rooms here have exhibits on natural history, early and recent mammals, the world famous dinosaur collection of the early and late periods with skeletons and reconstructions, as well as a collection of fossilized fish.

More than 200 scientists work behind the scenes at the museum, which has its own research laboratories. The museum also sends scientists on expeditions all over the world. New finds are constantly added to the museum's collection. Scientific films and multimedia shows are often shown on a giant screen.

MARCO POLO TIP

! *Halloween Parade* **Insider Tip**

On the last Sunday in October the Avenue of the Americas is transformed into »Magical Sixth Avenue«. Already in early evening costumed New Yorkers mingle with artists, clowns, jugglers and bands on the broad avenue between Spring and 15th Street. Anyone wearing a costume may join in! The Halloween Parade has a different motto every year. For more information, see the website www.halloween-nyc.com.

** ROSE CENTER FOR EARTH AND SPACE

The new Rose Center for Earth and Space, which also contains the Hayden Planetarium, explores the origins of the universe based on the latest scientific discoveries with the help of the most modern technology: from the Big Bang to the entire evolutionary process. Special attractions are the 15.5-ton »Williamette« meteorite, the **Cosmic Collisions** show in the Space Theater, narrated by Robert Redford, in which visitors are taken on a journey through the universe and through time, and the **Sonic Vision** show which makes music visible by means of computer animation.

* Battery Park

✦ A 19

Location: southern tip of Manhattan
Subway: South Ferry, Bowling Green

The park on the southern tip of Manhattan is named after the battery of guns that used to defend the harbour. It offers a great view of Liberty Island with the Statue of Liberty (▶Statue of Liberty), ▶Ellis Island, Governor Island, the harbour with the docks and the Verrazano Bridge. Boats to the Statue of Liberty and Ellis Island leave from here. At the southern end of the park is the Staten Island Ferry Terminal, with its round-the-clock ferries to Staten Island.

Sculptures and monuments in Battery Park

There are numerous sculptures and monuments in the park. At the entrance a monument commemorates Giovanni da Verrazano, who discovered New York Bay in 1524 (by Ettore Ximenes, 1909). In front of Castle Clinton *The Immigrants*, a monument by Luis Sanguino, portrays the ethnic and social diversity of New York. Another monument honours Emma Lazarus (1849–87), from whose poem *The New Colossus* the lines at the base of the Statue of Liberty come. At the nearby ferry dock the East Coast War Memorial (Albino Manca, 1963) bears the names of the Navy servicemen lost in the Atlantic during the Second World War. **The Sphere** (Fritz König) originally stood on the plaza between the Twin Towers of the World Trade Center and now commemorates the victims of the terrorist attack of 11 September 2001. Behind the memorial – outside the park – towers the striking semicircular glass office building 17 State Street (Emery Roth & Sons, 1989), built on the site of the birthplace of Herman Melville, author of the novel *Moby Dick*. In the bar of the posh restaurant **Battery Gardens** (in the park, near 17 State St.) there is a nice view of the Hudson River.

❶ Daily 11.30am–10pm, Sun only until 4pm, tel. 1 212-809-5508

Castle Clinton

Castle Clinton was built in 1811 about 90m/100yd from the coast, but only used for a short time for military purposes. As early as 1824 the city opened a place of entertainment in the fortress, and 20 years later it was covered and converted into a concert hall. In 1850 the »Swedish nightingale« Jenny Lind performed here before 6,000 people. From 1855 the building served as a port of immigration and from 1896 as a popular aquarium, which was moved to Coney Island in 1941. Today the history of New York is displayed here in dioramas; the tickets for the ferry to the ►Statue of Liberty and ►Ellis Island are sold here.

Fire station

There is a beautiful promenade along the bank of the Hudson northwards to Battery Park City. It passes the fire station at Pier A, which reaches far out into the water; it was built in 1886 and is the former headquarters of the New York harbour police.

*Museum of Jewish Heritage

Behind it is the striking building of the Museum of Jewish Heritage, A Living Memorial to the Holocaust: a three-storey, six-sided granite building with a six-step roof pyramid (architect: Kevin Roche). The number six refers to the six points of the Star of David and the six million murdered Jews; but six times three equals 18 – and this number stands for the Hebrew word »chaim« = life. The core exhibition focuses on three themes: Jewish Life a Century Ago, The War Against the Jews and Jewish Renewal. The tour of the museum ends – symbolically – in a room flooded with light with a view of the Statue of Liberty. The arrestingly displayed documents exhibit items from

Inside the Museum of Jewish Heritage

many survivors of the Holocaust, video films and computer games give a living impression of Jewish history and present day life. In 2003 the museum was expanded, and recently the Garden of Stones was opened. The 18 blocks of stone, which the London land art artist **Andy Goldsworthy** collected from various regions in the north-eastern United States, and on which short varieties of oak trees grow, symbolize hope, transformation and survival in adverse conditions.

❶ Sun–Tue, Thu 10am–5.45pm, Wed until 8pm, Fri until 3pm, in summer until 5pm, admission $12, www.mjhnyc.org

Ferries leave around the clock for Staten Island from the Staten Island Ferry Terminal at the southern end of Whitehall Street, one of the few free tourist attractions in New York. A one-way trip takes 30 minutes, and the view of the Manhattan skyline and the Statue of Liberty is unique. Note: passengers can only go on deck on the »old« boats.

Staten Island Ferry Terminal

* Battery Park City

✳ A 17–19

Location: south western tip of Manhattan
Subway: Cortland St., Rector St., Chambers St., World Trade Center

The most important construction project of the 1980s in New York City was Battery Park City. It is located on reclaimed land – using material excavated to build the ▶World Trade Center (WTC), which was destroyed in a terrorist attack in 2001 – in the waters of the Hudson in Lower Manhattan, between West Street and the Hudson River.

Battery Park City

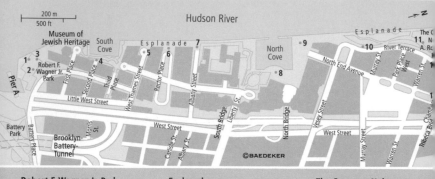

Robert F. Wagner Jr. Park

1   Louise Bourgeois
    The Welcoming Hands
2   Tony Cragg
    Resonating Bodies
3   Jim Dine
    Ape & Cat
    At The Dance

South Cove

4   Mary Miss, Stanton Eckstut
    & Susan Child
    South Cove

Esplanade

5   Richard Artschwager
    Sitting/ Stance
6   R.M. Fischer
    Rector Gate
7   Ned Smyth
    The Upper Room

North Cove

8   Siah Armajani, Scott Burton,
    Cesar Pelli, M. Paul Friedberg
    World Financial Plaza
9   Martin Puryear
    Pylons

The Governor Nelson A. Rockefeller Park

10 Inscribed Writings
    The Lily Pool
11 Demetri Porphyrios
    The Pavilion
12 Tom Otterness
    The Real World
13 Kristin Jones & Andrew Ginze
    Mnemonics
14 Michelle Stuart
    Tabula
15 Inscribed Writings
    Stuyvesant Plaza

The head architect was the Argentinean Cesar Pelli. The office and residential area for 60,000 people is composed of more than 30 buildings, among them the World Financial Center, and the extensive plaza with cafés, a marina, adjoining parks and a beautiful riverbank promenade – a popular and lively venue.

World Financial Center (WFC)   The heart and commercial centre of Battery Park City are the four glass and granite towers of the World Financial Center, cleverly staggered and of different heights, their roofs decorated with stylized domes and pyramids. The headquarters of American Express, the publishing house Dow Jones, and Merrill Lynch, the largest dealers in stocks in the world, are located here. Between the towers Pelli constructed a **winter garden**, a 38m/124ft-high and 61m/70yd-long roofed inner courtyard the size of Grand Central Terminal, in which giant palm trees grow. It is the reception area of the WFC, a kind of piazza with restaurants and shops, where concerts and other events take place here. Stairs, corridors and lifts access the various office towers from here.

A 2 km/1.3mi-long promenade runs along the bank of the Hudson ***Esplanade** River, from Chambers Street in the north to the small Robert F. Wagner Jr. Park at the southern tip of Manhattan. From here the ▶Statue of Liberty is visible as well as the Colgate-Palmolive clock erected on the opposite bank in New Jersey in 1924. All in all 50% of Battery Park City is open space with numerous lawns, sports areas and playgrounds, something very untypical of older Manhattan; families with dogs and children, joggers, roller-skaters and bikers come here. The park is decorated with the sculptures of contemporary artists, among others the New Yorker Tom Otterness in the North Park. His sculpture garden Real World

> **!** *New Yorkers on the waterfront* **Insider Tip**
>
> **MARCO ⊕ POLO TIP**
>
> The New Yorkers have rediscovered their shoreline. Particularly in the summer at midday, smartly dressed office workers populate the steps of the plaza, families picnic with children, tourists doze In the benches on the esplanade with a view of the Hudson and the Statue of Liberty, and the athletic jog and skate along the promenade.

deals with the subject of money, whose key role in the Financial District cannot be overlooked. Next to the sculpture garden, near Chambers Street, the newly built Stuyvesant High School can be seen. There are plans to extend the Esplanade from Chambers St. up to 57th St.

Bowling Green

✳ **A 19**

Location: southern tip of Manhattan
Subway: Bowling Green

Bowling Green, the small park at the southern tip of Manhattan, is the oldest park in the city.

The monument to King George III that originally stood here was toppled in 1776 in celebration of the Declaration of Independence. At the northern end of Bowling Green stands the famous **Charging Bull** sculpture by Arturo di Modica (photo p.166), the symbol of Wall Street. The bronze bull »guards« the entrance to the Standard Oil Building, which was built between 1920 and 1928 for John D. Rockefeller.

Custom House	The US Custom House, a fine granite palace, was built in 1907 in neo-classical style by Cass Gilbert, who was also the architect of the Woolworth Building. Chester French sculpted the groups on the door, with figures representing America, Asia, Africa and Europe. Since 1994 the former Custom House has been home to a branch of the National Museum of the American Indian (▶p.137).
Cunard Building	A little way to the north of the museum, one the city's most attractive post offices is housed in the Cunard Building, constructed in neo-Renaissance style in 1921 by Benjamin W. Morris for the Cunard shipping line (25 Broadway). The large counter hall decorated with mosaics is especially impressive.
James Watson House	The James Watson House, south of the museum, was built by 1793 John McComb in the Federal Style. The veranda with columns was added in 1806. From 1801 until 1803 this was the **home of Elizabeth Ann Seton** (1774–1821), who in 1975 became the first person born in America to be canonized by the Catholic Church.

❶ 7 State St., between Pearl and Whitehall St.; Mon– Fri 8am –5pm, Sat before and after Mass at 12.15, Sun before and after Mass at 9am and noon; www.setonshrine.com

Bowery

✦ C 16–18

Location: Between Chinatown and Greenwich Village

The 1.6km/1mi-long Bowery is New York's second-oldest street after Broadway. It starts at Catham Square in ▶Chinatown and runs northwards to Cooper Square (▶Greenwich Village).

A Native American trail ran along here originally. In the 17th century the Dutch called the path »Bouwerie« (= farmer), since it ran through farmland. In 1651 the last Dutch governor Peter Stuyvesant bought the land; the Bouwerie became the access road to his estate. Until 1800 the Bowery lay outside the city limits, forming part of the main road to Boston. As the city expanded the Bowery developed in the 19th century to become a preferred residential area of rich New Yorkers. Both the railway magnate and philanthropist Peter Cooper and the fur dealer Jacob Astor had their residences built here. In 1826 the Great Bowery Theater opened, and other places of entertainment and restaurants followed. But at the end of the Civil War the district began to decline. Slowly but surely the Bowery lost entertainment businesses to Broadway and shops to

Fifth Ave. Those who could afford it moved away and establishments offering cheap entertainment moved in. Until a few years ago the Bowery was a street with one of the worst reputations in the city. Today the process of gentrification has taken hold, with old building stock redeveloped and rented as apartments costing more than $ 20,000 per month in some cases. The most cynical example of this trend is regarded as the residential building at 40 Bond St., built by the Basel architects Herzog & de Meuron for the hotel owner Schrager – a kind of graffiti sculpture has been installed here as a fence against sprayed protests.

In 2007 the city's most eye-catching new museum architecture was completed here: the New Museum of Contemporary Art (235 Bowery, www.newmuseum.org;; architects: Kazuyo Sejima and Ryue Nishizawa, SANAA, Tokyo,).
The **Bowery Savings Bank** (130 Bowery/Grand St.), built in 1895 in neo-classical style, is the work of McKim, Mead & White architects. On 6th St., between First Avenue and Bowery, many good, cheap **Indian restaurants** can be found.

Insider Tip

Bridges in New York

New York's geographical location on the East and Hudson Rivers makes it a city of bridges, of which there are officially 2,027; 76 of them cross bodies of water – 18 connect Manhattan with the other boroughs and with New Jersey. The first bridge was King's Bridge, built in 1693 between Manhattan and Spuyten Duyvil Creek (today Bronx); it was torn down in 1917. The oldest remaining bridge is High Bridge (►below).

► Brooklyn Bridge

Brooklyn Bridge

This suspension bridge, which was completed in 1931 according to plans by Cass Gilbert and Othmar A. Amman as the Hudson River Bridge (West 179th St.), is carried by two pylons, each 194m/212yd high. With a total length of 2,650m/2,898yd (largest span 1,065m/1,165yd) and with one pedestrian walkway and roadways on two levels (14 lanes) – the lower one was added in 1959–62 – it connects Manhattan's west side with Fort Lee in New Jersey. The bridge, which is simply called GWB, offers an especially nice view of Manhattan at dusk.

George Washington Bridge

This iron arched bridge from the year 1917 stretches from Queens to Ward's Island in the East River.

Hell Gate Bridge

The famous »Queen Mary« passing the Verrazano Narrows Bridge

High Bridge   Built in 1837–48 to span the Croton Aqueduct, this construction with 13 arches over the Harlem River is the oldest Manhattan bridge. Today it is reserved for pedestrians (West 174th/175th St.).

Manhattan Bridge   Gustav Lindenthal designed the bridge, which was opened in 1909 and connects Manhattan (Confucius Plaza) and the new up-and-coming area DUMBO in ▶Brooklyn. Since 2001 pedestrians have been able to cross the bridge again.

Queensboro Bridge   This bridge was also completed in 1909 (length 2,271m/2,484yd) and in a broad arch spans the long and narrow Roosevelt Island (Second Avenue/East 60th St.). The view from the bridge inspired F. Scott Fitzgerald. In *The Great Gatsby* he has Nick Carraway rhapso-dize: »The city seen from the Queensboro Bridge is always the city seen for the first time, in its first wild promise of all the mystery and the beauty in the world.« The bridge itself is rather ugly; »It looks like a scrapheap,« the architect is supposed to have groaned when it was done. The 3km/ 1.8mi-long and only 250m/275yd-wide. **Roosevelt Island** was the site of a prison and several hospitals until the mid-1950s. At the end of the 1970s a residential quarter (architects: Philip Johnson, John Burgee) for about 10,000 people was built.

Over Randall's Island or Ward's Island the broad, sweeping, multi-section construction (1936; total length 5km/3mi, with access roads and ramps 23km/14mi) connects Manhattan (Harlem; Franklin D. Roosevelt Drive/East 125th St.) with Queens and the Bronx. There is an especially good view of the bridge from Carl Schurz Park (East End Avenue; ►Gracie Mansion).

Cable car in New York **Insider Tip**

MARCO ⊕ POLO TIP

! It has appeared in countless films: the Roosevelt Island Tram between Manhattan and Roosevelt Island. The tram leaves Manhattan at the intersection 60th Street/Second Ave. and floats the 956m/1045yd across to the island at a height of 43m/141ft above the East River. The cable car offers a spectacular view of the Manhattan skyline (tel. 1 212-832-4555, www.rioc.com).

Triborough Bridge

The bridge was completed in 1964 to plans by Othmar A. Amman and connects Brooklyn and Staten Island. It crosses the Narrows, the strait that marks the entrance to New York's natural harbour. Giovanni da Verrazano, the first European to enter New York Bay, dropped anchor here in 1524. With an entire length of 4,176m/4,567yd (largest span 1,298m/1,417yd) it is one of the longest suspension bridges in the world. The monument at the bridgehead consists of stones from Verrazano Castle in Tuscany as well as from the beach of the French city of Dieppe, from where Verrazano set sail.

*Verrazano Narrows Bridge,

This suspension bridge was built in 1903; its largest span is 488m/534yd; it connects Manhattan's Lower East Side (Delancey St.) with Williamsburg in Brooklyn.

Williamsburg Bridge

* **Broadway**

✳ **A 19–H 1**

Location: Runs from the Battery in the south through the Bronx northwards

The streets and avenues of Manhattan are laid out in a rectangular grid pattern. Broadway is the only exception.

It begins at the Battery in the south, meanders north-west through all of Manhattan (about 20km/12.5mi) and the Bronx (another 6km/3.5mi), then leaves New York and continues north past Yonkers, Westchester County and Albany. Broadway was originally a Native

American trail which was also used as a trading route from early times and then developed into an important connecting road between the harbour and the hinterland. It has completely different faces on its long course: at first with Wall Street it represents the heart of the ▶Financial District, later the art trade and the new shops in ▶SoHo.

It is most often referred to in connection with the theatre district. Around 1730 one of the first theatres of the city did indeed open on Broadway, between Beaver St. and Exchange. Later hundreds of theatres, musical and opera houses followed, as well as cinemas. In the 1920s they moved to the area north of ▶Times Square, which with the exception of London's West End has the highest concentration of theatres in the world today.

Bronx

—————————— ✳ **Outside the city centre**

Location: North of Manhattan

The 106 sq km/41 sq mi Bronx is the northernmost part of New York. It is separated from Manhattan by the Harlem River and is the only part of New York that lies on the mainland. About 1.2 million people live here: one third are African American, the rest are primarily Puerto Rican and white. Belmont, the neighbourhood near the ▶Bronx Zoo, is a large Italian community and there are more Italian restaurants and grocery shops on and around Arthur Ave. than in Little Italy.

Above all the South Bronx used to be considered to be the epitome of urban neglect. That was not always the case. »The invisible hand of the almighty Father must have guided me here, in this land full of untouched forests and unlimited possibilities«, wrote the Swedish seafarer Johan Bronck in 1639. He was the first European to settle on the peninsula that is now named after him. Even when the Bronx was connected to the subway network in 1904 it retained its reputation as a preferred residential area. Beautiful brick homes with pretty front gardens, wide avenues, the Grand Concourse as the main boulevard with New York's most impressive ensemble of Art Deco houses, the famous Bronx Zoo and the Botanical Garden were built. The decline began in the 1930s. In the 1950s white people in particular left the area and went nort‚h while slum clearing in Manhattan forced African Americans and Puerto Ricans into the Bronx. At the same time New York lost over 600,000 jobs in industry. Unemployment and poverty changed the social climate and the »beautiful Bronx« decayed. At the end of the 1980s the vision of the new Bronx

Bronx

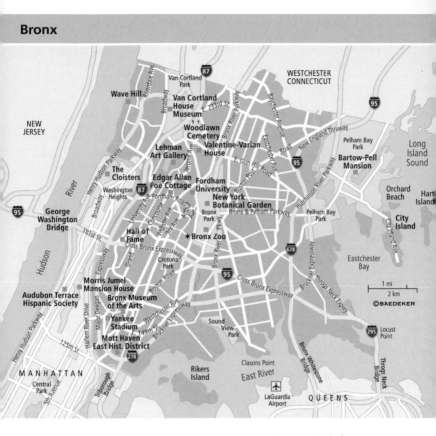

was born. Thanks to an energetic city government thousands of affordable flats were built, old houses restored and the unemployment rate reduced. Thus the situation in the once notorious South Bronx has become stable and the northern Bronx has even become a tourist destination.

SIGHTS IN THE BRONX

There are other attractions in the north Bronx in addition to the two main sights, the ►New York Botanical Garden and the ►Bronx Zoo. Get there either by taxi, hire car or subway, which emerges from underground in the South Bronx and becomes an elevated train.

A Man's World

»Baseball is America« and America is baseball. As the great American poet Walt Whitman (1819–92) put it: »I see great things in baseball. It›s our game – the American game. It will take our people out-of-doors, fill them with oxygen, give them a larger physical stoicism. Tend to relieve us from being a nervous, dyspeptic set. Repair these losses, and be a blessing to us.« But what would baseball be without New York?

Opinions are divided on how, when and where baseball came to be. We can assume that the game developed from English cricket and German-Austrian »Schlagball« or »Kaiserball«. At any rate, New York had the first baseball team: the »Knickerbocker Club of New York« founded by Alexander Cartwright in 1845. It was also Cartwright who set the first rules for the **New York game** in 1846, which are still valid today, with the exception of a few changes. On 19 June 1846 in Hoboken, New Jersey the first official baseball match was held: between the »Knickerbockers«, and the »New York Nine«. In the following 15 years 60 baseball clubs were started in and around New York. When Cartwright followed the gold rush of 1849 to California, he introduced San Francisco to baseball, too. The soldiers of the American Civil War (1861 until 1865) spread the game after the war through the whole country. Soon baseball was the most popular sport in the USA.

Trailblazer New York

And New York was the trailblazer. In 1876 the National League of Professional Baseball Clubs was founded here; and it was here that fans sang for the first time the official **baseball song** *Take Me Out to the Ballgame* (1908), composed by two New Yorkers. New York has the best baseball team in the New York Yankees, and the two baseball legends **Babe Ruth** and **Joe Di-Maggio** played here. The national popularity of baseball was of course also caused by the media: television, which broadcast a match for the first time in 1939 – from New York, naturally – and the press, which always had its headquarters in this city. A pitcher in the baseball film Bull Durham describes the most American of sports like this: »Baseball is a very simple game: you throw the ball, you catch the ball, you hit the ball. Sometimes you win, sometimes you lose. Sometimes it rains.«

Rules

Baseball is a game that differs from every other sport in one way: It is not the position of the ball which decides whether points are awarded, but the players' completion of a circuit around the course of bases. In baseball the player runs in a circle from base to base.

Two teams of nine players play against each other. The field has an area of 175 x 125m (194 x 136yd) at

The Yankee Stadium in the Bronx

the most; balls, bats and leather gloves are the required equipment. The ball has a circumference of 23cm/9in and weighs 150g/5.25oz; it is made of cork or synthetic material wrapped in a thin layer of string and covered with white leather, which is sewn together. The club-shaped bat is made of wood or lightweight metal and may be no longer than 107cm/42in and have a diameter of no more than 7cm/2.8in. The team at bat is the offensive team, and the team in the field is the defensive team. A baseball match gener- ally runs for **nine innings**. In each one the teams are each once in the defensive and once in the offensive position. Only the batting team can score points.

Scoring Points

The **batter** stands between the **pitcher** and the **catcher** of the opposing team and must try to hit the ball, delivered by the pitcher, into the field in such a way that the defensive players in the field cannot easily catch it and he can run unhindered around the course of four bases – three running bases and **home plate** – touching each of them. If he succeeds, the team gets a point. The goal of the team in the field is to get the batter out of the game. A batting player is out when a fielder catches the ball without it bouncing, throws the ball to a base before the runner reaches it, or, holding the ball, touches a base before the runner reaches it. The batter is only safe when he is touching a base. If he gets on base, the next batter from the offensive team goes in to bat. If he in turn runs, the previous runner must advance so that the base is free, since only one runner can be on any one base at a time. The defensive team tries to get three offensive players out in this way in order to come up to bat itself. Errors by the batter can also lead to an out: if the batter swings at three balls and misses, he goes back to the bench. The team with the highest number of completed runs by batters around the field to home plate wins. There are no ties, innings are added until one team has more points than the other.

Dangerous Game

Baseball can be dangerous. The batter wears a helmet for a good reason reason, the catcher wears a face mask, and stomach, knee and shin protectors. The ball thrown by the pitcher reaches speeds over 100 km/h (60mph). It can **break bones** when it hits unprotected parts of the body. Clearly, baseball is seen as a real man's sport. In 1931 there was a woman professional player, but in 1952 women were banned from the sport: baseball is indeed a man's game. But

the game is not dangerous for the spectator: fans of opposing teams sit together in the grandstands of baseball stadiums. There is rarely even quarrelling, let alone the riots which occur in European football stadiums. Tickets for a two to three hour game are not expensive, even though the professional players are highly paid.

Fair-weather Sport

If it begins to rain, the head umpire decides whether the game should be stopped or not. Rain quickly soaks into the balls and leather mitts. If a game is stopped or rescheduled because of rain the watchers get a »rain check«, a ticket for the continuation of the interrupted game or the repeat game. In New York there are two professional clubs, the Mets and the Yankees.

Immediately east of the Harlem River is Yankee Stadium, home of the New York Yankees baseball team (►MARCO POLO Insight p.194). The stadium was built in 1923 and holds 54,000 people. Two of the greatest players of all times played here, the legendary Babe Ruth, which is why the stadium is also known as »the house that Babe Ruth built«, and Joe DiMaggio, who was married to Marilyn Monroe. The architecture of the new stadium is based on that of the old one, from which the roof decoration was re-used.

Yankee Stadium

❶ 161st St./River Ave.; subway: B, D, 4 to 161st St.; tickets: tel. 1 718-293-4300, www.yankees.com

From the Yankee Stadium, get onto Grand Concourse (6.5km/4mi long and built in the 1909), which will take you quickly to the nearby Bronx Museum of the Arts. The museum has contemporary art collections and exhibits that enhance cross-cultural dialogue. These are works of contemporary artists of African, Asian, and Latin American descent as well as works by artists with a direct connection with the Bronx. In the summer, the salsa parties held in the museum are very popular.

Grand Concourse

❶ 1040 Grand Concourse, Thu – Sun 11.00am –6.00pm, Fr. until 8.00pm, free admission, www.bronxmuseum.org

The simple farmhouse built in 1812 is the last home of the first American poet to become world famous. Poe, who was not comfortable in overcrowded Manhattan, rented the house in 1846 in Fordham, then a village, for $100 per year. The notorious alcoholic died in Baltimore on his way home from a lecture tour in 1849. The rooms in which he wrote some of his best-known poems, like Annabel Lee, Ulalume and Eureka, are furnished as they were during his lifetime.

Edgar Allan Poe Cottage

❶ 2640 Grand Concourse/192nd St.; subway: B, D, 4 to Kingsbridge Rd.; Mon–Fri 9am–5pm, admission $5; tel. 1 718-881-8900

Around 1900 the architects McKim, Mead & White built a branch of New York University (today Bronx Community College; 441 East Fordham Rd.) on a hill above the Harlem River. Part of this site is the American **Hall of Fame**, a colonnade designed by Stanford White, in which the busts of about 100 famous Americans are displayed.

Fordham University

❶ 181st St., Morris Heights, subway: 183rd St., daily 10am–5pm, free admission

In the north-west Bronx lies Van Cortlandt Park, where cricket, golf, tennis and other sports are played. The colonial-style country estate of Frederick Van Cortlandt, built in 1748, is also located here. The house is furnished with original furniture and gives a picture of the life of its former occupants. The dining room is supposed to have been George Washington's headquarters during the Revolutionary War.

Van Cortlandt House Museum

❶ Subway: 242nd St., Van Cortlandt Park; Tue–Fri 10am–3pm, Sat, Sun 11am–4pm), admission $5

Fordham Road in the Bronx

Woodlawn Cemetery Many prominent and wealthy New Yorkers are buried in the 130-year-old cemetery, among them F. W. Woolworth, who rests in a kind of Egyptian palace; Herman Armour, a meat dealer; Fiorello LaGuardia, mayor of New York (1932–44); Roland Macy, founder of the department store of the same name; the writer Herman Melville; and the jazz musician Duke Ellington. A map of the cemetery showing the most interesting graves is available from the cemetery office.
❶ Jerome and Banbridge Ave.; subway: Woodlawn; daily 8.30am–4.30pm; tel. 1 212-920-0500

Wave Hill in Riverdale This English-style manor house, built in 1843 and extended several times, lies directly on the banks of the Hudson in Riverdale in the north-west Bronx, probably the most exclusive rural part of New York. The beautifully designed 11ha/27ac garden is especially attractive, and offers a grand view of **The Palisades**, the cliffs on the opposite bank of the Hudson in New Jersey. The original owner William Lewis Morris lived here, as well as Theodore Roosevelt, Mark Twain, Arturo Toscanini, George Perkins and others. The house and garden are open to the public and a venue for concerts, film viewings, lectures and art exhibits. The concerts mostly take place in Armor Hall, built in 1928.

❶ West 249th St./Independence Ave., Riverdale; subway: 1 to 231st St. or 9 to 231st St., transfer to buses 7 or 10 to 252nd St.; tel. 1 718-549-3200. Tue–Sun 9am–5.30pm, mid-Oct until mid-May only until 4.30pm; admission $8, free admission Tue and Sat until noon

Pelham Bay is a small peninsula in the extreme north-east of the Bronx. In the park you can play golf, bike, ride horses, play ball and fish (subway: 6 to Pelham Bay Park, transfer to buses 12 to Orchard Beach or 29 to City Island). **Bartow-Pell Mansion**, which was built in 1842, is located in the park, today a historical museum. **Orchard Beach**, which is most popular on weekends, lies on the mainland directly before **City Island.** A bridge connects Pelham with City Island, a scant 2.5km/1.5mi long and only 800m/900yd wide. Today the former fishing village is a popular venue for New Yorkers, with numerous sailing boats in the harbour and excellent fish restaurants. The **North Wind Undersea Institute Museum** has an interesting exhibition on the history of whaling (610 City Island Ave., currently closed).

Pelham Bay Park

❶ Bartow-Pell Mansion Wed, Sat, Sun noon–4pm, Mon–Fri 10am–5pm, Sat, Sun noon–5pm, admission $5

✳ Bronx Zoo

✳ **Outside the city centre**

Location: Fordham Rd., between Southern Boulevard and 185th St. (Bronx)
Subway: Pelham Parkway, East 180th St.

❶ Mon–Fri 10am–5pm Sat, Sun, holidays until 5.30pm, Nov–Mar only until 4.30pm
Admission: $29.95

Those needing a change from the concrete jungle of Manhattan should try a visit to the Bronx Zoo. With 107ha/264ac it is the largest of New York's five zoological gardens (the others are Central Park in Manhattan, Prospect Park in Brooklyn, Flushing Meadows in Queens and Barrett Park on Staten Island). The zoo was built in 1899 and is, like the ▶New York Botanical Garden, part of the Bronx Park. In a landscape of forests, streams and parks live more than 4,000 animals mostly in generously sized open-air enclosures; there are also modern houses for birds, monkeys, large animals, aquatic birds, reptiles, penguins and gorillas. Look out for **Jungle World**, a newly built house for the animal world of tropical Asia, the architecturally interesting **World of Birds**, the **World of Darkness**, where you can see nocturnal animals during the daytime, and **Wild Asia**, where the Bengali Express, a small train, runs through Asiatic forests and meadows. For the best overview, take the 25-minute ride on the Skyfari cable car. Children will enjoy a visit to the children's zoo.

Brooklyn

✦ C–J 15–19

Location: South-east of Manhattan, on the western tip of Long Island

Until the boroughs were incorporated into New York in 1898, Brooklyn was the fourth-largest city in the USA. It was named after the Dutch community Breuckelen. There is a fantastic view of Manhattan from here, as well as the Brooklyn Museum, the second-largest museum in New York.

With about 2.6 million residents (**Brooklynites**) in 2013, Brooklyn is the most populous of New York City's burroughs. It was named after a town that Dutch settlers had founded, namely Breuckelen, and is like Manhattan, Queens and Staten Island situated on an island. Breuckelen was an independent town and grew to a sizeable city so that, in 1898, it was consolidated with New York City by a majority of a mere 277 votes. The ▶Brooklyn Bridge, built in 1883, was the first permanent structure to connect Brooklyn to Manhattan. In 1905, Brooklyn was also linked to Manhattan's subway system. The burrough continued to grow steadily in the 1960s, but during New York City's economic crisis in the 1970s, many people lost their job because large factories shut down. Today, the service sector is the strongest industry in Brooklyn.

Diner *Insider Tip*

The diner in Williamsburg, serving the best French fries in Brooklyn, has been standing firmly at the foot of the Williamsburg Bridge since the 1940s. The menu changes daily and offers a wide variety of dishes (85 Broadway/Berry St., tel. 1 718-486-3077).

MARCO ✦ POLO TIP

Many Brooklyn neighbourhoods are working-class neighbourhoods or neighbourhoods in which a particular culture or nationality is predominate or are multi-ethnic. These neighbourhoods are however becoming increasingly mixed. Young people, especially musicians and other artists, have long been drawn to the less expensive Brooklyn neighbourhoods for many years, melting Brooklyn's cultural boundaries to a certain extent. The onset of gentrification in many of the neighbourhoods is further attracting waves of young creative trendsetters as well as young professionals to Brooklyn's neighbourhoods, such as Williamsburg, Brooklyn Heights and Park Slope, thereby changing Brooklyn's landscape yet again. Rents are going up, affordable housing becoming scarce, often resulting in the displacement of lower-income people.

Brooklyn today Brooklyn is roughly divided into two by Flatbush Avenue (15km/9mi long). To the northeast lie **Bedford-Stuyvesant**, **Bushwick** and **Brownsville**, once poor ethnic neighbourhoods, where

Brooklyn

NEW
JERSEY

MANHATTAN

QUEENS

Queens Boulevard

Long Island Expressway

Greenpoint

Queens Expressway

Grand Avenue

Metropolitan Avenue

Elliott Avenue

Central Avenue

Myrtle Avenue

Forest
Park

Jamaica Avenue

Hudson River

Holland Tunnel

West Side Highway

Canal Street

Broadway

East River Drive

East River

Manhattan

Williamsburg Bridge

Berry Street

Humboldt Avenue

Brooklyn Avenue

Flushing Avenue

Myrtle

Bedford Avenue

Buswick Avenue

Broadway

Cooper Street

Jackie Robinson Parkway

★★ Brooklyn Bridge
Fulton Ferry Landing **DUMBO**

Liberty
State Park

Ellis
Island

★ Brooklyn Heights Promenade

Myrtle Avenue

Brooklyn Historical Society
N. Y. Transit Museum

Lafayette

Avenue

Stuyvesant Heights Historic District

Statue of
Liberty

Brooklyn-Battery Tunnel

Cobble Hill Historic District

Brooklyn Academy of Music

Fulton Street

Atlantic

Fulton Street

Atlantic Avenue

Atlantic Avenue

Liberty Avenue

Conduit Boulevard

RED HOOK

9th

4th

Street

Clinton Hill Historic District

Old Stone House

★ Brooklyn Children's Museum

Eastern Parkway

New York Ave

Granville Payne Avenue

New Lots Avenue

Linden Boulevard

Rockaway Parkway

Pennsylvania Ave (Belt Parkway)

Upper
New York
Bay

Gowanus Expressway

3rd Avenue

Prospect Expressway

Prospect
Park

Brooklyn Museum of Art ★★
★ Brooklyn Botanic Garden

Empire Blvd.

Utica Avenue

Remsen Avenue

Flatlands Avenue

Ralphs Avenue

Prospect Park Zoo

Lefferts Homestead

Linden Boulevard
Church Avenue

Greenwood Cemetery ✝✝✝
✝✝✝

Sunset
Park

39th Street

Litchfield Villa

Coney

Ocean

McDonald Avenue

Dahlia Avenue

Clarendon Road

Foster Avenue

★ Jamaica Bay Wildlife Refuge Center

7th Avenue

Hamilton Parkway

65th Street

Fort Hamilton Parkway

Island Avenue

Ocean Avenue

Nostrand Avenue

Flatbush Avenue

Avenue J

Floyd
Bennett Field

★ Verrazano-Narrows Bridge

Shore Parkway (Leif Ericon Drive)

4th Avenue

Bay Ridge Parkway

65th Street

New Utrecht Avenue

14th Avenue

18th Avenue

Bay Parkway

BENSONHURST

86th

Street

Kings

Highway

Avenue P

Avenue U

Ocean Avenue

Gerritsen Avenue

Marine
Park

Shore Parkway (Belt Parkway)

Marine Parkway Bridge

Shore Parkway (Belt Parkway)

278

Dyker
Beach Park

Stillwell Avenue

Flatbush Avenue

Lower
New York
Bay

Dreirer-Offerman-
Park

Shore Parkway (Belt Parkway)

Neptune Avenue

New York Aquarium

BRIGHTON BEACH

Emmons Avenue

Sheepshead
Bay

Rockaway Inlet

Channel Drive

Beach

Boardwalk

Surf Avenue

Coney Island

| 1 mi |
| 2 km |

© BAEDEKER

MARCO ◉ POLO INSIGHT

Insider Tip

A water taxi to Brooklyn Bridge

With a hop-on-hop-off ticket from New York Water Taxis ($25 for unlimited trips on one day) you see New York from a different angle. The yellow boats stop at various piers, e.g. South Street Seaport and Fulton Ferry Landing, and chug past Manhattan with a superb view of the skyline. The evening trip to Brooklyn Bridge is especially recommended, as sunset over Manhattan is an incomparable sight (www.nywatertaxi.com).

more and more young people had settled in. **Brooklyn Heights** and **Park Slope** in southwestern part of the avenue have always been wealthy residential areas with tree-lined streets and the classic brownstone homes (»brownstones«, as New Yorkers call them). A top-notch restaurant scene that equals Manhattan's has developed in Park Slope over the past few years. With its many live music clubs, **Williamsburg** is now the centre of New York's music scene. Once however this neighbourhood was known for its large Jewish community. When affordable housing was no longer available in SoHo and East Village, more and more painters, sculptors, filmmakers and performers moved here. Meanwhile, rents have skyrocketed and are almost as high as in Manhattan. With its many shops, restaurants and cafés, Bedford Avenue is where most of the action is in Williamsburg. **Flatbush** has a distinct Caribbean flair, while **Bensonhurst** is very Italian, but, just as in Manhattan, Brooklyn's so-called Little Italy is shrinking, giving way to Brooklyn's rapidly growing Chinatown. In the south, young people have converted the former warehouses into residential and commercial spaces in **Red Hook**, the old port of Brooklyn.

A visit to New York is not complete without experiencing Brooklyn. Today's generation of artists, musicians and writers continue the tradition of this district's cultural independence, which began with such famous writers as Walt Whitman, Norman Mailer, Paul Auster, Jonathan Franzen and most recently Jonathan Safran Foer. Filmmakers such as Woody Allen and Spike Lee have their roots in Brooklyn, the most vibrant district of New York. Only recently American actor Alec Baldwin said, »New York's soul lives in Brooklyn«.

BROOKLYN HEIGHTS AND DUMBO

Walking
across
Brooklyn
Bridge

Those who enjoy a stroll should take the 45-minute walk from Manhattan across ▶Brooklyn Bridge. The walkway is one level above the busy roadway. At the ramp of the bridge stands the headquarters of the Jehovah's Witnesses, founded in 1872, on whose façade giant letters proclaim »The Watchtower«, the name of their well-known periodical (Furman St.).

Borough Hall in Brooklyn

Brooklyn Heights (subway: High St.) lies at the mouth of the East River, between Brooklyn Bridge and Atlantic Avenue. This neighbourhood, which has been protected heritage since 1965, has a charm all its own: narrow tree-lined streets, some still with cobblestones, and many pretty sandstone or brick houses, some of them from before 1860 with small front gardens. Number 24 Middagh St. is said to be the oldest house, built in 1824. Truman Capote wrote *Breakfast at Tiffany's* and other works in the basement of 70 Willow Street; Arthur Miller lived at number 155. Along the East River is the romantic Brooklyn Promenade, also called the **Esplanade**. The Brooklyn-Queens-Expressway runs under the small strip between Orange and Remsen Street. The **** view** from here across the river to Manhattan is spectacular – particularly in the afternoon and early evening – and has been photographed and filmed thousands of times. The southern end of the promenade leads to Montague Street, the neighbourhood's main street with numerous shops and restaurants. The **Brooklyn Historical Society** explains the history of the area, including an account of the sale of the Dodgers, the legendary baseball team, to Los Angeles in 1957. Built in 1848 by Gamaliel King in the Greek Revival Style, **Borough Hall** (209 Joralemon St., subway: Jay St., Borough Hall) was once the city hall. Every Tuesday and Saturday there is a farmers' market here. The **New York Transit Museum**, located in the decommissioned subway station, is devoted to the history of New York's urban public transportation. A few blocks outside of Brooklyn is the **Brooklyn Academy of Music** (BAM), a major performing arts venue that has been presenting performances for over 150 years. This cutting-edge urban arts centre offers world-renowned programming in theatre, dance, music, opera, film, and much more (30 Lafayette Ave; www.bam.org). There are many shops and eateries on **Montague Street**, the main street in Brooklyn Heights. **Atlantic Avenue** is the southern boundary of the Heights and has long been known for its antique shops, delicatessen shops and restaurants.

Brooklyn Historical Society: 128 Pierrepont St. / Clinton St.; Wed–Sat noon–5pm, Fri until 8pm, Sun noon–5pm, admission $6; www.brooklynhistory.org
New York Transit Museum: entrance on Boerum Place and Schermerhorn St.; Tue–Fri 10am–4pm, Sat, Sun 11am–5pm, admission $7

On the East River
Old Fulton, which runs almost parallel to Brooklyn Bridge, and then Front St. lead to the former harbour known as **DUMBO**, standing for »down under the Manhattan Bridge overpass«. The »new village« is an up-and-coming area. Artists first moved into the huge warehouses; currently many are being converted to flats, studios and shops. The DUMBO Art Under the Bridge Festival in mid-October gives a good impression of the scene.

OTHER SIGHTS IN BROOKLYN

Carroll Gardens, Boerum Hill
The residential area between Brooklyn Heights and Park Slope with its quaint streets has transformed into one of the most popular neighbourhoods in New York. Along Smith Street and Court Street, you'll find one charming restaurant or café after the other, with significantly lower prices than in Manhattan.

Prospect Park
Prospect Park with its mature trees, broad lawns, playgrounds and a small zoo lies in the heart of Brooklyn. Its main entrance is on Flatbush Ave. opposite the oval **Grand Army Plaza** with the 24m/78ft-high Soldiers' & Sailors' Arch (1870), modern sculptures and a John F. Kennedy monument (subway: Grand Army Plaza or Prospect Park). Immediately west of the Grand Army Plaza is the most beautiful building of the pretty neighbourhood Park Slope: the **Montauk Club** was built in 1891 and modelled on the Ca' d'Oro in Venice. The frieze is decorated with scenes from the history of the Montauk people, who once lived in eastern Long Island. Prospect Park was donated in 1858 by the Litchfield family and designed by the landscape architects Olmsted and Vaux, who considered it to be their masterpiece (they also designed the

Sports course in Prospect Park

more famous ▶Central Park). There is rowing on Prospect Lake in the south of the park in the summer, and ice skating on the Kate Wollman Rink. Other attractions are Litchfield Mansion, the former home of the donor, and **Leffert's Homestead**, a farmhouse from the year 1776, which was brought here in 1918 and is now a museum with furnishings of that time.

Greenwood Cemetery (25th St./Fifth Ave., subway: 25th St.), about 1.5km/0.9mi south-west of Prospect Park, is a completely different world. There are hundreds of Victorian-style mausoleums, monuments and statues in this cemetery, which was opened in 1840 and designed in the style of a romantic park. Enter through the Gothic Revival brownstone gatehouse with a 30m/100ft gate tower, which is decorated with reliefs. Along with graves from earlier times, which were moved here from Manhattan, numerous prominent people from the 19th century found their final resting place here, among them Peter Cooper (1791–1883, rail-

Greenwood Cemetery

MARCO ⏚ POLO TIP

Dining with a view · Insider Tip

The skyline of south Manhattan and classical American cuisine can be enjoyed in the luxury restaurant River Café (daily Sun noon–3pm, 5.30pm–11pm, ▶p.xxx). Chamber music concerts take place regularly from Thursday to Sunday on a barge on the East River: Barge Music, Fulton Ferry Landing (tel. 1 718-624-2083; www.bargemusic.org).

way magnate and inventor); Samuel Finley Breese Morse (1792–1872, inventor of the telegraph that was named after him; on his grave: »S. F. B. M.«); Elias P. Howe (1819–67, inventor of the first functional sewing machine); and Lola Montez (1818–61, a dancer known for her influence on the Bavarian King Ludwig I; on her grave: »Mrs Eliza Gilbert«). Among the largest grave monuments are the Niblo Tomb (at Crescent Water) of the theatre and restaurant owner William Niblo, and the Whitney Tomb (on Ocean Hill) of the cotton magnate Stephen Whitney. A visit at the end of May or early June, when the cherry trees and rhododendrons are blooming, is especially pleasant.

The Botanic Garden borders on Prospect Park to the north-east. Designed by the Olmsted brothers in 1910, it has not lost any of its charm in 90 years of existence. More than 12,000 different kinds of plants grow on the 20ha/50ac of land. The main attractions include a garden of decorative herbs, the Cranford Rose Garden with a large collection of roses, a Japanese hill and pond garden with a teahouse and Shinto shrines as well as a new greenhouse with an impressive collection of bonsais. A visit to the garden at the end of April or beginning of May, when the Japanese cherry trees are in blossom, is especially enjoyable. For visually impaired visitors there is a garden

*Brooklyn Botanic Garden

! **Insider Tip**

Nathan Handwerker is said to have invented the hot dog in 1900, and indeed the hot dogs at Nathan's snack shop are especially good. An eating contest is held here on 4 July every year. The current record: 55.5 hot dogs in 12 minutes (1310 Surf Ave./Stillwell Ave.; subway: Coney Island/ Stillwell Ave.).

Theater Café & Grill: 1031 Brighton Beach Ave, tel. 1 718-6 48-31 00

Amusement park: summer daily 6am–1am

The **New York Aquarium**, in about the middle of the Boardwalk, recreates the natural habitat of marine animals, for example in its Berrmuda Triangle, a section about native marina fauna and one on the Red Sea. In the warmer months (June– Sept) the Aquatheater has shows with dolphins and sea lions, in the colder months with Beluga whales. Visitors can also watch the daily feeding of the sharks, penguins, seals, walruses, whales and electric eels.

❶ Surf Ave., West 8th St., subway: Stillwell Ave.; daily 10am – 5pm, Sept–May until 4pm, admission $11.95; tel. 1 718 2 65 47 40, www.nyaquarium.com

** **Brooklyn Bridge**

✳ **C 19**

Location: Between south Manhattan and Brooklyn across the East River

Subway: Manhattan: Brooklyn Bridge-City Hall; Brooklyn: High St.

South-east of ►City Hall the lengthy ramp of the Brooklyn Bridge ascends to the oldest bridge over the East River.

Mighty construction of stone and steel

The plans for the first steel suspension bridge in the world, which rests 40m/130ft over the water on two mighty piers about, were drawn up by the engineer Johann August Röbling, originally from Germany. He died two years later from injuries incurred during a work accident. His son Washington Roebling continued the work. In 1872 he suffered from the bends after he left a caisson too soon, before the pressure had been equalized. His wife Emily took over the construction project; the partially lamed Roebling directed the work from home and watched through his telescope from the window of his house in Brooklyn. The bridge was inaugurated in May 1883 after 16 years of construction. It is 1,052m/1,150yd long without the ramps (the entire span is 2–3km/1.2–1.8mi). The **walkway**, reserved for pedestrians, runs 5.5m/18ft above the six-lane road; walkers, joggers and cyclists have an impressive view of Manhattan with its skyscrapers and of the South Street Seaport as well as the Upper Bay with the Statue of Liberty in the distance, especially in the evening. At night the bridge is seen as an impressive string of lights between Brooklyn and Manhattan.

★★ Brooklyn Museum

⚓ Outside the city centre

Location: 200 Eastern Parkway
Subway: Eastern Parkway/ Brooklyn Museum
Admission: $12

🕐 Wed–Fri 10am–6pm, Thu until 10pm, Sat, Sun 11am–6pm
www.brooklynmuseum.org

Were the Brooklyn Museum in Manhattan and not in the north-east of Prospect Park in Brooklyn, it would most likely be one of the most popular museums in New York. Its Egyptian department and collection of American art up to the present day are famous.

The foundation stone for the five-storey building, designed by McKim, Mead & White, was laid in 1895. The museum was intended to surpass the Louvre, at least in area. But after Brooklyn was incorporated into New York a large part of the construction plans remained unrealized. Since then the museum has been redesigned several times, such as in 1934 when the original exterior stairs leading up to the portico were removed and replaced with three spartan entrances on the ground floor. In 2004 the museum received a glass entry pavilion (architect: Polshek). The semicircular front entrance with its stepped roof is reminiscent of the original stairs, but keeps the entrance on ground level and makes the dark building more inviting. The museum is a comfortable half-hour subway ride from Manhattan.

Collection

In the **sculpture garden** in the museum courtyard, parts of demolished New York buildings are displayed. On the **ground floor** art from Africa, Oceania, North and South America is shown, including an important collection of artefacts from indigenous American cultures. The **second floor** is dedicated to art from China, Japan, Korea, Southeast Asia, India and Persia. The third floor is dedicated to the wrld famous collection of **Egyptian art** is and the exhibition 700 Years of European Painting. French art of the 19th century is represented impressively by Monet's *The Doge's Palace* from 1908, among other works. The focus of the **fourth floor** is the »Period Rooms«, furnished in various styles. Furniture as well as silver, pewter, ceramic and glass utensils can also be viewed. The collection American Identities on the **fifth floor** has masterpieces like Albert Bierstadt's *Storm in the Rocky Mountains*

A Striking Construction

Whether from Fulton Park at the foot of the eastern pier in Brooklyn or from the promenade more than 40m/130ft above the water: Brooklyn Bridge offers grandiose views of the Manhattan skyline. With its 532m/582yd freely suspended deck and its two piers the bridge is itself quite striking.

❶ It began with an idea e

Röbling is said to have had the idea of building a bridge over the East River when he was stuck yet again on the ferry in the middle of the partially frozen river. After long, drawn out negotiations he was given the commission to build in 1866.

❷ Constuction of the piers

The foundations for the piers were built using a new method: two 55x35m/60x38yd caissons of wood, 15m/16.4yd high, were weighted on top and slowly sunk into the East River. Pressurized air forced the water out. Inside this air bubble, the so-called »Sandhogs« shovelled and blasted their way 20m/21.8yd down through the mud and gravel river bed. The caissons were then anchored and filled with cement. The 92m/299ft-high stone piers with two 40m/13ft-high, 11m/12yd-wide Gothic pointed arches each stand on these foundations.

❸ Wire cables

278 single wires were combined to form one strand, and 19 strands to form one cable. Each of the four 38.5cm/15.1in-thick main cables con-

sists of a total of 5,659km/3,537mi of twisted wire. The cable ends are held by anchor plates within 3-storey granite vaults, which also served as storerooms.

❹ Angle cable technique

The idea of the angled cable technique, where diagonal cables connect the bridge girders directly with the pylons and give additional stability, came from Röbling

❺ Opening

After 16 years the bridge was inaugurated on 24 May 1883. At a cost of $15 million the bridge was twice as expensive as originally planned. The construction cost the lives of 20 people, most of them dying of the bends when working under water. 150,000 pedestrians walked across the bridge on opening day. But only after 21 elephants from the Barnum Circus had »proven« the structural strength of the bridge was it opened for traffic. Today more than 130,000 cars travel here in six lanes, while 5.5m/18ft above the street a promenade for pedestrians and bikers offers an opportunity to observe the construction close-up and a grandiose view.

(1866), Thomas Cole's *Picnic* (1846) and Georgia O'Keeffe's *Brooklyn Bridge* (1948). The almost 60 Rodin sculptures are also very beautiful. After a visit to the museum the neighbouring **Botanic Garden** is an inviting place to take a stroll (▶Brooklyn, Botanic Garden).

* Cathedral of St John the Divine

✦ G 5

Location: 1047 Amsterdam Ave./ 112th St.
Subway: Cathedral Parkway
❶ Daily 7am–6pm
Tours: Mon 11am, 2pm, Tue–Sat

11am, 1pm, Sun 1pm,
Admission: $6
Tel. 1 212-316-7540
www.stjohn divine.org

If this church (begun in 1891) were ever completed it would be the largest in the world. It was begun by the architects Heins & LaFarge in Byzantine-Romanesque style (apse, choir and crossing) and after their death continued by Ralph Adams Cram over the following 30 years with a new design in the Gothic style.

This Episcopalian cathedral has five aisles, is 183m/200yd long, currently 44m/48yd wide and in the main aisle 38m/123.5ft high. The church is impressive primarily because of its dimensions. It has a mass of decorative furnishings, including Italian paintings (16th century), Barberini tapestries after Raphael (17th century), icons, a Bohemian candelabrum and numerous sculptures. The Romanesque choir apse is divided into seven chapels (glass windows by J. Powell, London; beautiful dome in St Martin's Chapel). Behind the main altar is the grave of the Bishop Horatio Potter (1887), who initiated the building of the church. In the eight-sided baptistery are eight figures of historic New York personalities. The chancel is made of Tennessee marble. The crossing, over which a

| ! | *All creatures great and small* | Insider Tip |

MARCO ⊕ POLO TIP

»All things wise and wonderful, the Lord God made them all...«, and suddenly, along with the human choir, whales are singing (albeit from a recording), wolves howling, and birds twittering. Every year on the first Sunday in October, the day of St Francis of Assisi, our four-legged and feathered friends receive a blessing in St John the Divine. The service begins at 11am – tickets are available from 9am – and ends with a small public celebration in the park around the church.

137m/445ft-high steeple is supposed to stand someday, only has a provisional cupola; from here there is a good view of the rose window, which was completed in 1933. In the exhibition room on the south-west side (later transept) there is a model of the cathedral, whose two towers were supposed to be 76m/247ft high. A memorial in the Missionary Chapel commemorates the Holocaust and war crimes in Bosnia-Herzegovina, while another monument honours the 343 firemen who died when the World Trade Center collapsed. The Peace Fountain, sculpted by Greg Wyatt, has stood south of the church since 1985. The grounds of Columbia University extend a little further north (▶Harlem).

** Central Park

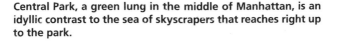

✳ E 10–6

Location: In the centre of Manhattan, between 59th and 110th St.
Subway: Visitor Center (The Dairy): 68th St.; Belvedere Castle: 81st St.;

North Meadow: 96th St.
Visitor Center: Tue–Sun 10am–5pm
Tel. 1 212 7 94 65 64
www.centralparknyc.org

Central Park, a green lung in the middle of Manhattan, is an idyllic contrast to the sea of skyscrapers that reaches right up to the park.

Its size is 340ha/840 acres (= 5% of the entire surface area of Manhattan; Monaco is 195ha/482 acres in size) and stretches from 59th to 110th St. (length 4km/2.5mi) and from Fifth Avenue to Central Park West, the extension of Eighth Avenue (500m/550yd wide). The park is bordered on the east and west by premium residential areas. Thus some of the richest people in New York live on the **Upper East Side**, on Fifth and Park Avenue; and the so-called Museum Mile, Fifth Avenue along Central Park, is the location of some of the most important museums of the city. The **Upper West Side** by contrast has a much broader appeal.

Romantic carriage rides start at Central Park South. On Central Park Drive, which runs around the park, a path is reserved for bikers, joggers and inliners. But disciples of other forms of physical exercise, like practising yogis, rock climbers or anglers can also be found in the park. Altogether the park has over 90km/55mi of paths, 8,968 benches and reputedly 26,000 trees. Bird experts have their pleasure, too: 258 of the over 800 bird varieties of North America live in Central Park, at least when passing through.

Getting around in Central Park

The idea of a park for the quickly expanding city was born in the 1840s. It was laid out from 1859 to 1870 on what was then the northern periphery of the city to plans by Frederick Law Olmsted and Calvert Vaux and modelled on the Bois de Boulogne in Paris. Ten million wagon-loads of earth had to be brought in and the ground cleared of rocks and boulders. The many bridges and the four somewhat lower east-west roads were present from the beginning. Central Park is closed to traffic during rush hour (8–10am and 5–7pm) so that bikers, roller skaters, inliners and horse-drawn carriages can use the broad streets exclusively. Apart from that the park is populated

200 gardeners and 1400 assistants look after New York's green oasis

by strollers, picnicking families and dog walkers, who expertly walk several dogs at a time. The much more frequented southern part of the park is gentler, while the northern part (above 86th St.) is left in its natural state, with a more interesting landscape and fewer visitors. The park is in general very safe but, as in any of the world's large cities, you should stay on the well-lit main paths and avoid the dark corners after nightfall.

A WALK IN THE PARK

It's best to enter the park from Grand Army Plaza. Directly at the south-east entrance (60th St.) is **The Pond**, with a bird sanctuary on its west side, and to the north is the **Wollman Rink**, for roller-skating, inline skating and hockey in the summer, and in the winter ice skating (it is possible to hire skates at the rink).

In the zoo large animals such as polar bears roam rather small living quarters. Take a look at the small monkeys and snakes in the so-called Tropic Zone and the penguins in the Polar Circle, an exemplary polar landscape.

Central Park Zoo

❶ Daily 10am–5pm, Sat, Sun until 5.30pm, in winter until 4.30pm; subway: Lexington Ave. /63rd St.; admission $18; www.centralpark zoo.com

The Dairy, a park building by Olmsted and Vaux west of the zoo, is the seat of the park administration. Park maps and information on all park activities are available here.

The Dairy

❶ **Visitor Center**; Tue–Sun 10am–5pm; tel. 1 212-794-6564, www. centralparknyc org

The Mall, an avenue of elm trees with sculptures of poets and composers, begins at the **Sheep Meadow**, a huge lawn where sheep still grazed until 1934. Self-promotion New York style can be witnessed here: amateur preachers, athletes and freaks, ball-playing youths, picnicking families and frustrated variety artists make this a colourful venue. Cross the Mall to get to **Bethesda Terrace** featuring a fountain decorated with figures by Emma Stebbin in the middle. Beyond lies **The Lake**, a branching romantic expanse of water on which Venetian gondolas float. Boats, bikes and inline skates as well as food are available in **Loeb's Boathouse** (behind Bethesda Terrace).

The Mall

On its north side, at the highest point, stands **Belvedere Castle** (weather station), which was modelled after a European castle; inside there is a small exhibition on the park's fauna. To the west is the **Delacorte Theater**, where in the summer Shakespeare and other plays are performed free (entrance: West 81st St.).

Strawberry Fields Opposite West 72nd St., Strawberry Fields is a memorial to John Lennon, who was killed in front of the Dakota Building on Central Park West in 1980. Fans still lay flowers on the mosaic set in the pathway bearing the single word »imagine«, the title of Lennon's famous song.

Conservatory Pond East of the Lake is the small Conservatory Pond; on the west side a statue commemorates the fairy-tale writer Hans Christian Andersen (Georg Lober, 1956), and the bronze group to the north Alice in Wonderland (Jose de Creeft) delights children. On the adjoining **Great Lawn** ball games often take place; in the summer concerts are held by the New York Philharmonic Orchestra. Behind the ▶Metropolitan Museum of Art stands the Egyptian obelisk **Cleopatra's Needle**, which comes from Heliopolis, where it was erected in around 1500 BC by Thutmosis III. The obelisk once stood in Alexandria and was given to New York at the end of the 19th century by the Khedive Ismail Pasha. Today, however, Cleopatra's Needle is completely weathered. Its partner stands in London on the Thames. The final stop is the so-called **Reservoir**, a large fenced-in lake. The water reflects the bordering skyscrapers and the 2.5km/1.5mi-long path around the Reservoir is popular with runners. North of the Reservoir there are fewer facilities – one is the **Conservatory Gardens** in the French style – but more untamed natural beauty (entrance 105th St. and Fifth Ave.).

> **MARCO POLO TIP**
>
> ❗ *Open air* **Insider Tip**
>
> In summer, the Summer Stage programme organizes free concerts in the open air. The annual theatre festival is called »Shakespeare in the Park«, though that doesn't mean it consists exclusively of Shakespeare plays. Tickets are available from 1pm daily at the Delacorte Theater (tel. 1 212-539-8750) – expect long queues! Tel. 1 212-539-8500, www.centralpark.com, ▶MARCO POLO Insight p.92). Live jazz, salsa and funk are the focus of the Harlem Meer Festival, every Sunday in summer outside the Charles A. Dana Discovery Center (tel. 1 212-860-1370, www.centralparknyc.org).

Harlem Meer At the extreme north-east is the Harlem Meer, where rowing boats can also be hired; in the winter the western part is transformed into an ice skating track. Beyond 110th St. (now Central Park North) ▶Harlem begins.

Refreshment stops In Central Park there are several places to get refreshments: **Loeb's Boathouse**, a small restaurant on The Lake; and the **Tavern on the Green**, near the park entrance.
Loeb's Boathouse: Sunday 9.30am–4pm for brunch, tel. 1 212-517-2233
Tavern on the Green: Central Park West/67th St.; daily 10am–5pm, chamber music 11am–3pm; table reservoations tel. 1 212-874-7874

Chelsea

✴ A–D 12–14

Location: West Manhattan
Subway: 14th St., 23rd St.

Chelsea is an area in south-west Manhattan, extending roughly between 14th and 34th St. and between Fifth Ave. and the Hudson River.

Historic Chelsea, known as the Historic District, between 9th and 10th Ave. and 19th and 23rd St. is a quiet residential area which still has many buildings from the 19th century. Taxi firms and car repair shops mark the scene in West Chelsea, the area west of 10th Ave. between 21st and 24th Street, which has developed into a magnet for young art. The piers on the Hudson are a Mecca for sports fans and Eighth Avenue the centre of the gay scene.

SIGHTSEEING IN CHELSEA

A good starting point is the General Theological Seminary (9th Ave./20th, 21st St.), the oldest seminary of the Episcopal Church in America. The inner courtyard is worth a look; the westernmost building was built in 1836 and is the oldest example of the Gothic Revival style in New York. The seminar owns the world's largest collection of Latin Bibles. Opposite is Cushman Row (406–418 W 20th St.), which has won several prizes as New York's most beautiful street block. The seven buildings in the Greek Revival style were built between 1839 and 1840. Following 22nd Street past St Paul's church leads to the legendary **Chelsea Hotel**, which was originally built in 1884 as an apartment building (23rd St., between Seventh and Eighth Ave.; ▶MARCO POLO Insight p.68). Rock musicians and other colourful characters like Salvador Dali and Thomas Wolfe used to stop here. At the western end of 22nd St. is the **Chelsea Art Museum**, which is notable for its collection of post-war abstract Expressionism, including works by Corpora, Lakner and Kirkeby.

Historical Chelsea

❶ 556 W 22nd St., Tue–Sat noon–6pm, Thu until 8pm, admission $8; www.chelseartmuseum.org

The Recreation Area, where once ocean liners and freighters docked, is like an oasis in the city of millions with its golf courses, skating rinks, swimming pools, promenades and jogging paths on the bank of the Hudson (▶MARCO POLO Insight p.220). In nearby West Street are the Chelsea Studios, in which well-known TV series such as *Law & Order* are filmed.

*Chelsea Piers

Meatpacking District	Even more than West Chelsea, the so-called Meatpacking District is on the way to replacing SoHo and TriBeCa as New York's trendy neighbourhood. In the late 1940s, big refrigeration plants made this the logistical centre of the meat business. In the 1970s and 1980s, cutting-edge nightclubs moved in. Citizens' initiatives thwarted plans for demolition and redevelopment, and the district around Gasevoort/14th St. with its giant warehouses, restaurants and trendy shops is now protected heritage. Two new attractiona, the ▶High Line Park and the new ▶Whitney Museum of American Art, are located here, too.

West Chelsea The area west of Ninth Avenue is especially trendy. Artists wanting to win a place in the progressive art scene have their galleries or studios between West 22nd and West 29th St., if possible on West 26th, the new **Gallery Row**. Numerous galleries have moved here because ▶SoHo has become too commercial for them or the rents near the ▶Museum of Modern Art have become too expensive. The Dia Center for the Art was the vanguard (which has since opened a museum in Beacon on the Hudson River (▶p.175), and a row of galleries have followed such as Matthew Marks, Metro Pictures, Paula Cooper, Barbara Gladstone and many more (▶Enjoy New York, Museums and Galleries). Recently exclusive shops have been opening here too, like Comme des Garçons, which was built by Takao Kawasaki based on an idea by Rei Kawakubo (520 W 22nd St.). Modern dance is practiced in the **Joyce Theater**.

Joyce Theater: 175 Eighth Ave./19th St.; tel. 1 212-242-0800

> **!** *Chelsea Market* **Insider Tip**
>
> **MARCO ⊕ POLO TIP**
>
> An old biscuit factory (where the famous Oreo Cookies were invented!) has become Chelsea Market with its shops and restaurants. After 5pm the world's best brownies are sold at half price at the Fat Witch (75 9th Ave, between 15th and 16th St., www.chelseamarket.com).

Madison Square Garden	Madison Square Garden, located between Seventh and Eighth Ave. and 31st and 33rd Street, is a concrete cylinder, a stadium with 20,000 seats. Alongside games of the Knicks basketball team and the Rangers hockey team, other major sporting and musical events take place here. Beyond that the complex includes a theatre with 5,600 seats, cinema, bowling alleys, exhibition areas, offices, shops and restaurants. Pennsylvania Station was originally located here. Today's **Penn Station** (1968) for Amtrak long-distance and commuter trains to Long Island and New Jersey is below ground.

General Post Office	The »Roman temple« with its Corinthian columns, a classic example of the Beaux Arts style, originally stood opposite the old Pennsylvania Station. The latter was built in 1910, the General Post Office in

Chelsea Piers Recreation Area – ocean liners and freighters once moored here

1913 according to plans by the architects McKim, Mead & White. In 1963 the old Penn Station was torn down despite massive public protest and in its place an unimaginative new building was built; thus the General Post Office seems somewhat out of proportion without its counterpart. In the course of the westward expansion of Midtown there are plans to replace the underground Penn Station with an entry building above ground. The General Post Office is seemingly ideal for this purpose. The plans of SOM architects provide for preserving the façade with the imposing outdoor steps, which is a protected monument, and the old post office counter hall for use by US Mail, while converting most of the building behind it into the new Penn Station. The main element of the construction is a 40m/130ft-high fan-shaped glass hall, which will bisect the block north-south and through which daylight is to fall onto the underground train platforms. The question of whether and how to implement these plans has been a subject of heated debate for a number of years.

Fitness Counts

New York's concrete jungle has much to offer those addicted to fitness, and not only in Central Park, where athletes can be found at any time of the year and where ice skating is obligatory in the Christmas season, as it is in Rockefeller Center. Just think of the skyscrapers that invite sports fanatics to »take the stairs«: once a year in the Empire State Building a popular race to the 102nd floor is held – and at least the runners who reach the finish line at almost 400m/1300ft high can breathe better than in the smog at ground level.

Of all the countless health clubs in New York the **Chelsea Piers** are the most popular among athletes. New York's largest fitness club was created on four former piers between 17th and 23rd Street, pointing like fingers into the Hudson River. Once, large transatlantic steam ships docked at the piers, which were opened in 1910, and in 1912 the relatives waited for the survivors of the Titanic catastrophe here. The era of the big transatlantic steamers ended in the 1960s, and the quays declined until even the police didn't dare go there. At the beginning of the 1990s a New York businessman showed interest in the area. His daughter, a passionate ice skater, had not been able to find an ice rink in all of New York. He discovered a gap in the market: the city needed an ice rink and he wanted to build it on the only available free space in the Big Apple, the Chelsea Piers. But the city said that the investor could only have the pier he had chosen if he took them all – **for a rent of $200,000** per month. Thus the 120,000 sq m/143,500 sq yd complex, after an investment of more than **$100 million**, was a bit bigger than planned – »really only a hock-

ey rink gone wild«, as he himself admitted.

Golfing on the Piers

Apart from skiing, riding and playing tennis, almost every other imaginable type of sport can be done here. One whole quay is available to inliners, on one pier there are two ice rinks, a third pier has the fitness area, and a fourth is exclusively for golf. There is also a five-block-long building, the Field House, with numerous fitness areas, spa zones, restaurants and all sorts of shops. The inline tracks, the ice rinks and the golf course can be used by anyone who pays the fee of $60. Only the Sports Center and the Field House, the actual fitness area, are members only ($100 per month).

Ex-soldier as a Trainer

Here an ex-trainer in the **»leathernecks«** (that's what the soldiers of the United States Marine Corps are called) can really get you to build up a sweat, and you can tone up your muscles on the newest fitness equipment, as well as ascend the 15 x 33m/16.4 x 36yd **artificial climbing wall**, the largest on the American east coast. Of course all sorts of sports disciplines such as football, basketball, swimming (indoor pool), Asian martial arts and even beach volleyball are available. In addition there is special training for business management and children's gymnastics. Since the ice rinks were built on Chelsea Piers, the city has also had an ice theatre company, which trains here daily for the season's gala performance; and the golf course, with its artificial green, the 600,000 cubic metre/760,000 cubic yard netted area and the split-second ball return, refutes the criticism that golf ruins the landscape. Anyone looking for real adventure can take a kayak course – with the goal of paddling around Manhattan and, as the trainer remarks with a grin, braving dangers like »shipping, city garbage and corpses«.

Open around the clock

The fitness area closes at midnight, the golfing range is open until 3am and the ice rink never closes. Chelsea Piers can only show profits if the facilities are used regularly. But New York won't close down the investors: the number of visitors has surpassed all estimates. So it is no wonder that next to the 28 available sports, 20 films have been made here and in the almost ten years of its existence over 230,000 birthday parties have been celebrated here. Detailed information: Chelsea Piers, 23rd St./Hudson River; tel. 1 212-336-6666, www.chelseapiers.com

A golf driving range with an impressive backdrop. And no balls get lost.

Jacob K. Javits Convention Center

Further west on Eleventh Ave. between 34th and 38th St. (subway: 34th or 42nd St.) stands the Jacob K. Javits Convention Center, a massive convention centre by the architects I. M. Pei and James Ingo Freed. In its giant glass walls the New York skyline is reflected by day.

Garment District

The Garment District stretches between Eighth Ave. and Broadway to 40th Street. Here, countless fashion and textile producers have their offices. In the so-called Accessories District between 23rd St. and Herald Square there are numerous sewing and tailoring businesses. The backbone of the Garment District is Seventh Avenue, also known as »Fashion Avenue« in this section south of ▶Times Square. **Macy's** is located here as well, the largest department store in the world (Seventh Ave. and 34th St.). Not far to the east looms the ▶Empire State Building.

✸✸   Chinatown

━━━━━━━━━━━━━━━━━━━━━━ ✦ C 17/18 ●

Location: South Manhattan
Subway: Canal St., Grand St.

Masses of people, exotic smells, vegetable and fish shops, rundown houses, colourful pagodas, countless small shops with cheap watches, scarves and other odds and ends, ubiquitous Chinese script – that's Chinatown, Asia in America.

www.explore
chinatown.
com

Currently about 150,000 people live in the 120-year-old area. With up to 400 restaurants, over 300 flourishing textile businesses (thanks to cheap labour) and five Chinese daily newspapers, Chinatown is a city of its own in the middle of Manhattan. And it's growing: Little Italy has been more or less bought up and large parts of the Lower East Side are already in Chinese hands. Other Chinese neighbourhoods are Sunset Park (Brooklyn; predominantly Hong Kong Chinese live here), Elmhurst (Queens; mostly Taiwanese and today probably the largest Chinese city outside China) and Willowbrook (Staten Island). The first Chinese settlers were sailors who came to New York in 1847 on board the junk Kee Ying and stayed; they were followed about 20 to 25 years later by Chinese who came to work as labourers on the building of the transcontinental railroad to California and who lived on land that belonged to John Mott and Joshua Pell. The large inflow of up to 2,000 a month began in 1965 when immigration from the Far East was made easier. Even the immigration reform of 1986 could not stop it. »The snake« is what the journalist Gwen Kinkead calls the pipelines of human smuggling from China, Taiwan or Malaysia into the USA. The

China in New York: Pell Street

smugglers, so-called snakeheads, demand up to $50,000 per person, which is either paid by relatives in the USA or by the immigrants in the form of years of labour. Chinatown has always been self-contained. About 40 family clans form the social network. They provide old-age care, job referral, child care and unofficial legal judgments. Since the clans are quarrelling today they have lost influence. Police statistics state that the Chinese neighbourhoods are the safest in New York – because no one reports anything. But crime is a problem. Power is in the hands of organized gangs that make up a Chinese mafia.

IN CHINATOWN

Did you know

MARCO POLO INSIGHT

Because Chinese immigrants refused to adopt the »American way of life« and worked for cheap wages, they met with the opposition of white workers. This attitude led to the »Chinese Exclusion Act« of 1882, which prohibited the further immigration of Chinese. A serious side effect was that in around 1900 there were only 150 women among the 7,000 Chinese in Manhattan. Only since 1943 have Chinese been allowed to pour into New York unhindered.

The core of the Chinese area stretches between Canal St., Broadway and the Bowery, the two main streets are Mott Street and Pell Street. One of the oldest houses in Manhattan stands on the corner of Pell St. and the Bowery: the **Edward Mooney House** of 1785. The plaza opposite was named after the monument to the Chinese philosopher Confucius (551–479 BC). The large arch on the east of the plaza is the entrance to Manhattan Bridge.

South-west on Chatham Square, the Kim Lau Memorial commemorates Chinese-American soldiers killed in action. In 1997, the year in which the British crown colony Hong Kong was given back to China, the statue of the anti-British »opium warrior« Lin Zexu was erected as a demonstration of Chinese pride. In the **Eastern States Buddhist Temple**, between restaurants and souvenir shops, over 100 Buddha figures sit in the smoke of countless incense sticks (64 Mott St.).

A small **Museum of Chinese in America** tells about the origins of the Chinese and their working conditions.

Museum of Chinese in America: 215 Centre St.; subway: Canal St.; open: Tue, Wed, Fri–Sun 11am–6pm, Thu until 9pm, admission $10, www.mocanyc.org

Columbus Park The area Columbus Park, the only open land in Chinatown and a popular meeting place for New York Chinese, was part of the Five Points slum in the 19th century. Martin Scorsese's film *Gangs of New York* (2002) tells the history of this notorious slum.

★ City Hall & Civic Center

✦ B 17/18

Location: City Hall Park, Broadway
Subway: Chambers St., Brooklyn Bridge/City Hall

In Lower Manhattan, between Broadway, Park Row and White Street, in the so-called Civic Center District stand a series of city, state and federal offices for about 300,000 people. All possible styles of architecture are represented.

In the small, triangular **City Hall Park**, laid out in 1811, a statue by F. McMonnies commemorates Nathan Hale, who was hanged in 1776 by the British as a spy. In the same year one of the first public readings of the Declaration of Independence took place here. City Hall lies in the park along with the offices of the mayor and the city council (51 members). The city hall's south face was originally covered with marble and is today clad in limestone. It was designed in 1803–12 by J. F. Mangin and J. McComb in the Federal style with echoes of French

The Municipal Building rises above City Hall Park

Renaissance with a columned portico, extending wings and a domed bell tower (the figure of Justice on top). Their design earned them a prize of $350. The back of the building was built in sandstone, supposedly because at the time of construction the building was so far out of town that it wasn't considered necessary to build it in marble. Inside, a double circular stairway leads to the second floor. In the Governor's Room (originally for the state governor) the historic furniture used by the first US congress, the chair used by George Washington during his inauguration as president and the lectern at which he composed his first speech to Congress can still be seen. On the walls of this and other rooms are portraits of war heroes and honoured guests of the city: in the Council Chambers there is one of Lafayette (painted by the inventor S. F. B. Morse in 1824) as well as of Washington and Hamilton (both by J. Trumbull).

On the other side of Broadway (no. 233) is the Woolworth Building. It was built in 1913 to plans by Cass Gilbert and was, at a height of 241m/792ft and with 60 floors, the tallest building in the world until the completion of the ▶Chrysler Building 17 years later. The architecture critic Paul Goldberger called it the »Mozart among skyscrapers«. The Gothic details are well adapted to the vertical form of the building, and the tower rises naturally above the building. The richly decorated three-storey lobby is worth a look.

**Woolworth Building

North of City Hall is the Old New York County Courthouse, also called Tweed Courthouse (52 Chambers St.), a neo-Renaissance building from 1870 (architects: John Kellum and Leopold Eidlitz), in which one of the courts is housed. The building got its nickname from William M. »Boss« Tweed, one of the most notorious political leaders of New York.

Old New York County Courthouse

Diagonally opposite (31 Chambers St.) is the Hall of Records, built in 1907 in Beaux Arts style; the former courthouse is today the city archive (architect: John R. Thomas). The façade is decorated with allegorical scenes and historic portraits; the statues along the main façade commemorate New York mayors and governors.

Hall of Records

The Municipal Building (city administration) at the end of Chambers St. (1 Centre St.) stands 177m/576ft immediately above the Brooklyn Bridge subway station. It was built in 1914 by the architects McKim, Mead & White. The superstructure, an ensemble of towers, is the most striking feature, crowned by the golden sculpture *Civic Virtue* by Adolph Weinman. The building was, incidentally, the model for the main building of the University of Moscow.

Municipal Building

Woolworth Building

Police Headquarters   Police Headquarters, one of the newest buildings of the Civic Center, was built in 1973 by Gruzen & Partners and is connected to the Municipal Building opposite by a plaza. The sculpture *Five in One* (Bernard Rosenthal, 1974) in front of the police headquarters symbolizes the five New York boroughs.

U. S. Courthouse   The federal court on Foley Square lies in the centre of the Civic Center. It was built in 1936 according to plans by Cass Gilbert, the architect of the Woolworth skyscraper, and his son, and is believed to have been inspired by the campanile of St Mark's in Venice.

New York County Courthouse   Across from the U. S. Courthouse is the district court, built in 1912 by Guy Lowell in the shape of a hexagon with a Roman temple façade. Here Sidney Lumet made the famous film *Twelve Angry Men* in 1957 with Henry Fonda in the leading role.

U. S. Federal Building   The U. S. Federal Building on the other side of the plaza was built in 1967 by Alfred Easton Poor, Kahn Eggers (26 Federal Plaza). The small windows make the façade look like a chessboard. Occupants include the New York branch of the U.S. Department of Immigration.

Criminal Courts Building and Prison   The Criminal Courts Building (100 Centre St.) was built in 1939 by Harley Whiley Corbett. The so-called Night Courts are held in this building on weekdays between 5pm and 1am, and are usually open to the public. A new prison was built to replace the notorious city prison »The Tombs«, which meanwhile has been demolished. The »Bridge of Sighs« connects the courthouse to the prison.

* The Cloisters

✳ Outside the city centre

Location: Fort Tryon Park at the northern tip of Manhattan
Subway: 190th St., continue with bus 4
❶ March–Oct daily 10.00am–5.15pm
Nov–Feb until 4.45pm

Tours: Tue–Fri, Sun 3pm
Tel. 1 212-9 23-37 00
Admission: $25
(includes same week admission to the MET)
www.metmuseum.org

The Cloisters, a museum for medieval art, is located in Fort Tryon Park high above the Hudson River at the forested northern tip of Manhattan. Although it dates from the 1930s, the building seems astonishingly authentic.

History   The architect Charles Collens combined parts of four cloisters from the Middle Ages and added to them. The striking main tower is a

The Cloisters

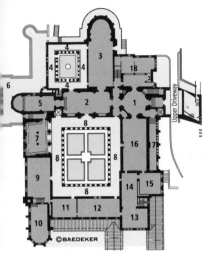

Museum for sacred medieval art and architecture

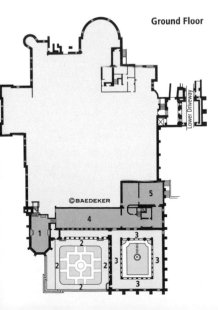

Ground Floor

Main Floor

1 *Entrance Hall*
2 *Romanesque Hall* (portals from France)
3 *Fuentidueña Chapel* Apsis of the church San Martin de Fuentidueña at Segovia (central Spain)
4 *Saint Guilhem Cloister* Cloister of the Benedictine abbey St-Guilhem-le-Désert (southern France)
5 *Langon Chapel* Part of the church Notre-Dame du Bourg in Langon (southwest France)
6 *West Terrace*
7 *Pontaut Chapter House* Chapter house of the monastery Notre-Dame de Pontaut (southwest France)
8 *Saint Michel de Cuxa Cloister* Cloister (in part supplemented) of the monastery St-Michel-de-Cuxa (southern France)
9 *Early Gothic Hall* (sacred statuary)

10 *Gothic Chapel* (▸ Lower floor)
11 *Nine Heroes Tapestries Room* Tapestries of the nine heroes of world history
12 *Unicorn Tapestries Hall* Tapestries with scenes of a unicorn hunt
13 *Boppard Room* Stained glass windows from the Carmelite monastery St. Severin in Boppard on the River Rhine
14 *Burgos Tapestry Room* Flemish tapestry from the Cathedral of Burgur (northern Spain)
15 *Spanish Room* (Campin Room) Mérode wing altar from Flanders; Gothic painted ceiling from Castile
16 *Late Gothic Hall* Hall in Late Gothic style of a medieval refectory
17 *Froville Arcade* Gothic arcade from the monastery Froville (Lotharingia)
18 *Books & Reproductions*

Ground Floor

1 *Gothic Chapel* patterned after the church interior of the Gothic cathedral St-Nazaire in Carcassonne
2 *Bonnefont Cloister* Monastery cloister

Bonnefont-en Comminges (southern France)
3 *Trie Cloister* Cloister of the monastery Trie near Toulouse (southern France)
4 *Glass Gallery*
5 *Treasury*

Medieval art in the north of Manhattan: The Cloisters

replica of the tower of the French monastery St-Michel-de-Cuxa (12th century). The Romanesque cloister of The Cloisters comes from there as well. The basis of the collection was provided by the sculptor George Grey Barnard (1863–1938), who brought back many works of art from his trips to Europe. In the 1925 the Metropolitan Museum of Art bought the collection. The money came from John D. Rockefeller Jr., who also donated the land (including the bank of the Hudson opposite) and the means to build the museum. In clear weather there is a unique view of the Hudson, the Washington Bridge and the (undeveloped) western river bank. The admission ticket is also valid for the ▶Metropolitan Museum on the same day.

Collection   The exhibition of Romanesque and Gothic architectural fragments, illustrated manuscripts, stained glass, artefacts of enamel, glass, ivory and silver as well as paintings and sculptures is chronologically organized. It begins with the Romanesque period (around AD 1000) and ends with the Gothic period (around 1550). The core of the museum is the cloister on the main floor and entrance level, from the monastery Saint Michel de Cuxa in the north-eastern Pyrenees (12th century), which was dissolved during the French Revolution but is inhabited by monks again today. The small cloister from the St Guilhem monastery founded in 806 by Montpellier dates from the 13th century. Among the main attractions are the seven tapestries that depict a unicorn hunt (**Unicorn Tapestries** Room; made around 1500 near Brussels as replicas of Parisian designs). The tapestries show a hunt for the innocent unicorn, with its infamous murder and ensuing resurrection; both the execution and the multi-layered meaning make the tapestries an outstanding achievement of European textile art and courtly elegance of the late Middle Ages. The six glass windows in the **Boppard Room**, from the Carmelite monastery of St Severin in Boppard on the Rhine (1447), came into the possession of the Cloisters by a circuitous route in 1937. Along with Gothic ceiling paintings from Castile and furniture from the 15th century in the **Campin Room**, the altar triptych, whose centrepiece shows the *Annunciation* (around 1425) by Robert Campin from Tournai, is particularly worth seeing. The **Gothic chapel** on the ground floor, an imitation

? *Did you know*

The larger of the two cloisters on the lower floor comes from the Cistercian monastery Bonnefont-en-Comminges south-west of Toulouse (13th–14th century). The medicinal herbs and spices in the garden were also cultivated in the Middle Ages. The adjacent cloister is from the monastery Trie (from Tarbe, southern France); it was built in the 15th century and destroyed 100 years later by Huguenots.

of the Cathedral of St Nazaire in Carcassonne, contains funeral monuments from the 13th and 14th centuries. Along with sculptures and painted glass from the 15th century in the **Glass Gallery**, look out for the altarpieces *Birth of Christ* and *Dream of the Three Kings from the Orient* from the school of Rogier van der Weyden, and the courtyard of a house in Abbéville. A special attraction of the **Treasury** is the book of hours of the Duc Jean de Berry (Belles Heures), a prayer book illustrated by the Limbourg brothers before 1410.

Columbus Circle

✳ **D/E 10**

Location: Central Park West, 59th St.
Subway: Columbus Circle

Busy Columbus Circle on the south-west corner of Central Park is one of the squares created by ▶Broadway in its course through Manhattan.

The outstanding feature is that the streets here form a circle, which happens nowhere else in New York. In the centre of the circle, on a pedestal, stands Columbus (Gaetano Russo, 1894). The west side is occupied by the **Time Warner Center**, completed in 2004 (architect: David Childs, SOM). With its two 229m/750ft-high, diagonally cut glass towers, it takes up the course of Broadway and continues the tradition of double towers on the western edge of Central Park. On 55 floors, along with the media corporation of the building's owner Time Warner, there are various exclusive shops, first-class restaurants, the Mandarin Oriental luxury hotel, concert halls (»**Jazz at Lincoln Center**«; information: www.jalc.org) and high-priced condominiums. On the northern edge of Columbus Circle stands the 207m/678ft-high, 44-floor former Gulf & Western Building, from the year 1969, today the Trump International Hotel Tower, occupied by luxury apartments and a hotel. Since its renovation by Philip Johnson and Costas Kondylis it has been covered by a skin of tinted glass. Two Columbus Circle has been home to the Museum of Arts and Design (▶ p.131) since 2008. The Hearst Tower, a little to the south on 8th Ave. between 56th and 57th St., a shiny rhombus-patterned tower set on the originally six-storey 1920s building of the media magnate Hearst, is the celebrated New York debut of Norman Foster's architectural practice (2000–06).

East Village

─────────────────────────── ✷ **C 15/16**

Location: South of 14th St. and east of the Bowery
Subway: Astor Place

East Village, once the northern part of the Lower East Side, is the area east of Broadway between 14th and Houston Street. In the 19th century the wealthier New Yorkers lived here. Later immigrants from Germany, Poland, Russia and Puerto Rico displaced the rich, who moved northwards. In the 1950s, when ▶Greenwich Village was favoured by the chic set, the artists, writers, musicians and students who had been driven out of the Village discovered this neighbourhood.

St Mark's Place, actually the extension of Eighth St., became the centre of the **hippy scene** and along with the surrounding side streets was renamed the East Village. In the 1980s art galleries and trendy restaurants moved here and the area became the centre of New York sub-culture. Within a short time the neighbourhood changed into a popular residential and entertainment area. Even though the East Village cannot be called middle class, the times when no-one dared go out at night around Tompkins Square are over. Particularly at weekends, the countless hotspots and restaurants around St Mark's Place are teeming with life, and during the daytime numerous small antique shops and boutiques are waiting to be discovered.

! *A relic* **Insider Tip**

The Yaffa Café (St Mark's Place/97th St.) is a relic of wild times past with its garish decorations and secluded garden. In late August and early September it is a venue for the unconventional Howl! Festival with its 260 events (www.howlfestival.com).

The cast-iron sculpture *Alamo* (Bernard Rosenthal, 1967) on Astor   **Astor Place**
Place marks the entrance to the subway station (Lafayette St./Fourth
Ave.). On the south side of Astor Place stands the **Cooper Union
Building**, a massive brownstone house, which was founded in 1859
by the railway magnate, inventor and philanthropist Peter Cooper in
order to help gifted children from poor families get a free education.
In 1860, in the Great Hall, President Abraham Lincoln delivered an
impassioned speech against slavery.

Across from the main building is the Cooper Union's **41 Cooper
Square**, designed by Pritzker-winning architect Thom Mayne of
Morphosis and completed in 2009. The wholly contemporary architecture of the new academic building with its at once bold, aggres-
sive and curvy exterior, described by the New York Times as »tough
and sexy«, makes a bold architectural statement, reflecting character,
culture and vibrancy of both the university and of New York itself. 41
Cooper Square is considered one of the most interesting examples of
great contemporary architecture in the city. As becomes apparent
when walking through the streets, the entire neighbourhood has
metamorphosed into a modern architectural laboratory of sorts.
Along with the New Museum of Contemporary Art designed by architects Kazuyo Sejima and Ryue Nishizawa of SANAA, there are a
number of very modern residential buildings along Bond Street,
among them one designed by Herzog & de Meuron Basel, a Swiss
architectural firm.

**More than 2 million books at Strand Book Store,
828 Broadway/12th Street**

The so-called **Colonnade Row**, four of originally nine once magnificent villas (429–434 Lafayette St.), was built in 1836 in the Greek Revival style. The white marble, however, lies hidden under a dark patina. Opposite is the **Public Theater** (425 Lafayette St.), which was opened in 1854 as the Astor Library and now hosts the New York Shakespeare Festival and Joe's Pub. Not far from here is another house in the Greek Revival style. The **Old Merchant's House** was built in 1831, and shortly afterwards it was bought by the wealthy businessman Seabury Tredwell. It contains the original furnishings.

Old Merchant's House: 29 E Fourth St.; Sun–Thu noon–5pm, admission $10

> **MARCO POLO TIP**
>
> ! *Angelica Kitchen* **Insider Tip**
>
> This is a classic address for vegetarian and vegan cuisine. The New York restaurant scene would be much poorer without Angelica's, where delicacies such as walnut and lentil paté, couscous vegetable salad and seasonal roast vegetables are on the menu. A colourful mix of customers knows that all of this is every bit as healthy as it sounds (daily 11.30am–10.30pm; 300 E 12th St., between 1st and 2nd Ave., tel. 1 212 2 28 29 09; subway: 14th St./Union Square and 1st Ave.; main courses from $10).

Stuyvesant St. leads to the church **St Mark's in-the-Bowery** (Second Ave. /10th St.). The second-oldest church in New York, dating from 1799, stands on ground rich in history: this site was the estate of the Dutch governor Peter Stuyvesant (1610–72; he is buried in the neighbouring cemetery). The church, built in the colonial style with a classical tower and Roman portico with cast-iron screens, played an important role in the main period of the hippie movement, whose centre was St Mark's Place only two blocks away. Today cultural events are still held here. **Grace Church**, a little way to the west, is a masterpiece of Gothic Revival by James Renwick (1846; Broadway/Tenth St.).

Little Ukraine   Since the 1970s about 30,000 Ukrainians have lived in the neighbourhood, as shown by shops and restaurants such as the Kiev (117 Second Ave.), a church and a small **Ukrainian Museum**. On display in the new building is Ukrainian folk art, including examples of the famous Pysanky (painted Easter eggs) as well as woven and needleworked textiles, ceramics, wood and metal work.

Ukrainian Museum; 222 E Sixth St., between Second Ave. and Cooper Square; Wed–Sun 11.30am–5pm; admission $8

German community   Towards the end of the last century a large German community lived in the East Village. Several buildings still testify to this, including the house once used by the German-American shooting club at St Mark's Place 12 (1885), the Ottendorfer branch of the Public Library (135 Second Ave.; 1884) and the Stuyvesant Polyclinic, until 1918 known as the Deutsche Poliklinik (137 Second Ave.; 1884). The English poet W. H. Auden lived at number 60 St Mark's Place until his death.

The descendants of immigrants from Poland and the Ukraine share the little Tompkins Square Park with busy office workers, chess players and a few homeless people. East of the East Village is **Alphabet City**, which gets its name from the Avenues A, B and C and which was once a notorious area. Where heroin was sold until the end of the 1990s, there are now chic restaurants.

★ Ellis Island

Outside the city centre

Location: west of the southern tip of Manhattan
Subway: South Ferry; the ferry to the island runs from/to Battery Park

🕐 Daily 9.30–5pm
Admission (with Statue of Liberty): $17
www.nps.gov/elis

Ellis Island, located off the shore of Jersey City to the west of the southern point of Manhattan, is one of the 40 islands in New York's waters. Originally a fortified site and ammunition depot, the island achieved fame as the immigration station for new arrivals between 1892 and 1917, when the federal government took over control of the flood of immigrants into New York (▶MARCO POLO Insight p.336).

People who wanted to emigrate had to endure physical checkups and questioning before getting permission to continue to Manhattan or New Jersey. The sick, single women or the politically suspect (about 2%) were sent back or interned on the island until their appeal had been heard and decided upon. The largest numbers arrived in the period from the 1890s until the beginning of the First World War, when about 17 million people were shunted through. The crowds were sometimes so huge that every official had to question 400 to 500 people a day, meaning that the fate of entire families was sometimes decided in a few minutes – which earned Ellis Island the name »Island of Tears«. After 1917 Ellis Island served primarily as a camp and clearance area for the deported and politically persecuted; during the

Second World War it was an internment camp for foreigners. An impressive description comes from **Egon Erwin Kisch**, author and journalist from Prague: »Am again a prisoner on the ship. I see New York through the closed porthole, which I have been approaching for fourteen days, war days on the Pennland (Holland-America Line)... The Immigration Officer said that my passport was not in order, for a Chilean visa from Paris was not enough for a transit visa to America ... While he spoke with me another official showed him a piece of paper, doubtless about me. – »I know,« he said. So I have to go to the »island« – a euphemism for Ellis Island, the Island of Tears ... Off the Pennland, on which we were for more than fourteen days, down with the baggage (mine stayed in Belgium) onto the ice-cold docks, where customs inspection takes place, then on a tender to the prison island guarded by the Statue of Liberty...« (»Notes 23–28.12.1939«; Landing in New York).

Great Registry: where the immigrants' details were recorded

Photos, artefacts and films document the circumstances under which **Museum**
immigrants came to the USA. A computer tells visitors when their
ancestors came to Ellis Island. In the **museum** they follow the route
that the immigrants had to take: from the baggage room, where possessions were inspected, to the Great Hall or Registry Room on the
second floor where the immigrants first had to answer officials' questions and then pass a medical examination. If everything went well
the procedure took three to five hours, after which the immigrants
received their papers. At the northern end of the island is the Wall of
Honor, in which about 500,000 names of immigrants are engraved.

** Empire State Building

✦ **D 13**

Location: 350 Fifth Ave./34th St.
Subway: 34th St.
❶ Daily 8am–2am

Admission: $29
Tickets online:
www.esbnyc.com

**Until completion of ▶World Trade Center the Empire State
Building was the tallest building in New York for a few years,
and it remains one of the most famous buildings in the world
– 3.5 million people visit it every year. From the observatory
on the 102nd floor there is an incomparable view of Manhattan; in clear weather the visibility is said to be 130km/80mi.**

In 1929, construction began on the site where once the first Waldorf-
Astoria Hotel stood. After only 19 months the 381m/1,250ft (with
antenna 443m/1,454ft) colossus was complete; it was named after the
nickname of the State of New York. The Art Deco building is a kind
of city in itself – over 30,000 people live and work here. The building
used 365,000 tons of steel, cement and granite; 100km/60mi of water
pipes and 5,630km/3,498mi of telephone line were laid. 73 lifts travel through 11km/7mi of shafts, in only 45 seconds they transport
people and freight up to the top. There are also stairs: runners at the
peak of fitness require eleven minutes for the 1,860 steps in the annual Empire State Run. The mast on the roof was originally intended
to be an anchoring place for airships but is now used as an antenna
for radio and television programmes. In cinema, the building was the
final place of refuge for the giant gorilla King Kong, before he
plunged to his death – though the famous final scene of the film was
made in a studio. Thanks to window frames made of stainless steel
the Empire State Building radiates a special glow, both day and night.
The top 30 floors are illuminated after dark until midnight by large
searchlights, on special occasions even in colour: on Independence
Day in red, white and blue, on Valentine's Day in red, and on St Pat-

MARCO POLO INSIGHT

Conquering the Heights

New York is a city of contrasts: rich and poor, loud and quiet, high and low. A few streets away from extremely expensive shops there are poor neighbourhoods, and in the middle of the loud, colourful bustle there are peaceful corners where almost nothing of the constant noise of the city can be heard (▶MARCO POLO Insight p.350).

One of the many contrasts of the city can be seen when approaching New York in an aeroplane: if you look down on Manhattan, you notice that the skyline does not form a continuous line, but instead the skyscrapers congregate in Midtown and at the southern tip, while in the middle most buildings are of medium height. The reason is **geological**: Midtown and the south of Manhattan are on a bedrock of massive granite, which allows tall buildings to be built; this is not possible on the ground in between. Manhattan's skyline is probably the most famous in the world. But the skyscraper era actually began in the mid-19th century in **Chicago**. At first conventional

One of the best views on Downtown Manhattan offers Staten Island Ferry – for free

stone and brick buildings were built: the more storeys added, the thicker the lower walls had to be. Then the cast-iron beam was invented, and shortly afterwards the steel skeleton. The electric lift had already been developed. In 1884 the first building with a steel frame was built in Chicago, which gave the Second City the highest building in the world – the word **skyscraper** was born.

Motivation for New York

Now the New Yorkers were spurred to act, since they already recognized the advantages of high-rise buildings. The steel skeleton allowed not only thinner walls and larger windows, which were in great demand then – they theoretically allowed buildings to be of unlimited height (ideal above all when land is very scarce). In 1902 Manhattan saw its first skyscraper: the 21-storey Flatiron Building on the corner of Fifth Ave./23rd St. The building attracted onlookers long after its completion, above all men, for the narrow edge of the building with the open plaza in front was so windy that women's skirts were blown about. The Flatiron is only one example for the first of four phases of New York high-rise history. »Utility« was in the foreground at that time: the new structural possibilities were used mainly to put one storey on top of another, without regard for the surrounding streets and the amount of sunlight they got. Some of the early high-rises nevertheless display **aesthetic architecture**, such as the Woolworth Building, the so-

called »Mozart of the skyscrapers«, with its neo-Gothic stone ornaments. In 1916, a year after the completion of the Equitable Building, which shamelessly took up the area of one whole block in the vertical and caused a storm of protest, the city passed the Zoning Law, **building regulations** that were intended to prevent the streets from being turned into canyons without light. The building of high-rises consequently changed. The wedding cake style was developed, the second phase: the higher a skyscraper was built, the narrower it became on top.

Chrysler and Empire State

The best-known examples are the Chrysler Building of 1930, with its Art Deco point which glitters like a diamond at sunset: it consists of cobalt-wolfram steel which has **diamond splinters** mixed into the alloy. Another example of the second phase is the Empire State Building on Fifth Avenue, which at 381m/1250ft was the tallest building in the world for over four decades after its completion in 1931. With its spire, which was originally supposed to be an **anchor for airships** and now has a television antenna attached, it even measures 443m/1454ft. An airship never anchored at the Empire State Building – the era of airships was almost over – but on 28 July 1945 a B-25 US Air Force bomber did fly into the building at the level of the 79th floor at about 300m/975ft in dense fog. The observation deck of the Empire State is closed about 40 days every year – for fear that strong winds might blow the visitors away. When filming *Sleepless in Seattle* the main actors Meg Ryan and Tom Hanks were tied to the railing as a precaution. The Empire State Building is not only the most impressive building in Midtown by day: at night the point is illuminated – red-green in the Christmas season, blue-white at the opening of the Yankee's baseball season and red, white and blue on the birthday of a US president. Incidentally, it is constantly stated that mostly Native Americans work as **ironworkers** on the steel skeleton because they have such a good head for heights. In fact, most of the ironworkers in Manhattan were and are »Newfies«, people whose families originally came from Canadian Newfoundland.

Modern Phase

After the second phase, in which the architects increasingly let historical echoes of contemporary art, above all the Beaux Arts, influence the building of high-rises and which created some of the most beautiful New York skyscrapers, the »modern« phase followed – but with hardly any noticeable and few style-making buildings, apart from the **Seagram Building**, a modern classic, built in 1958 by Mies van der Rohe, and the Lever House by his student Gordon Bunshaft. These two skyscrapers on Park Avenue have been imitated in the world thousands of times. In the 1970s the postmodern style developed, whose most definitive example is the AT&T Building (1984) described as »Chippendale« because of its idiosyncratic roof construction, and the **Trump Tower**, completed in the same year, with its spectacular atrium. A characteristic of this fourth phase is the plaza style of building.

Stricter Building Regulations

In 1961 the Zoning Laws were revised; the building authorities had recognized that the regulations were not enough to allow space,

Woolworth Building

Constructing World Trade Center, 1970

air and light between the buildings. Now the builders had to make sure that part of the surface area was used for a public plaza; in exchange the houses could be built flat and did not have to recede as they got higher. Not everyone liked the box-shaped building style: Bunshaft built two office high-rises for Manhattan in 1972 which remind critics of sailors' pants or knocked-out teeth. The twin towers of the World Trade Center, opened in April 1973 and 417m/1,368ft and 415m/1,362ft high respectively, took the title of **tallest building in the world** away from the Empire State Building after 40 years.

But they only kept their first place for a short time: in 1973 Chicago beat the Big Apple with the 443m/1,454ft-high Sears Tower. In the meantime there are higher skyscrapers outside America. The 452m/1,484ft-high Petronas Towers stand in Kuala Lumpur (Malaysia) and the »king of skyscrapers« is the 509m/1,670ft Taipeh 101 in Taipeh, the capital city of **Taiwan**. But the **Burj Khalifa** in the United Arab Emirates, 828m/ 2,717ft high, topped them all in 2010. The 541m/1,776ft-high Freedom Tower, now known as *1 WTC*, on the site of the World Trade Center, will only be occupied up to 335m/1,100ft (70 storeys), above which will be a lattice skeleton and a point. But the skyline of Midtown and Downtown Manhattan remains the most famous in the world and the symbol for New York. (Supplementary literature: Andreas Lepik, Skyscrapers, Prestel Publishing 2004)

rick's Day in green (lighting schedule: www.esbnyc.com). The building is worth a visit both in the daytime and the evening – there are two observatories, one on the 86th and the other on the 102nd floor – but the security checks for visitors are very strict since 9/11.

Insider Tip
You pay an additional $17 to visit the observation deck on the 102nd floor , but the view isn't really better than from the 86th floor. Expect long lines when buying tickets and waiting to get on the lift. On hazy days, it's best to go early in the morning..

** Fifth Avenue

✦ C–J 15–4

Location: From Washington Square Park along Central Park northwards

Fifth Avenue has always been New York's most magnificent thoroughfare and, because there is no main square, it is also the centre of the city. The big parades start here (Steuben Parade, St Patrick's Day Parade), and it is also closed to traffic for other festivities.

Fifth Avenue starts downtown at Washington Square in ►Greenwich Village, and runs straight to the Harlem River, dividing Manhattan's streets into West (W) and East (E). At the end of the 19th century, the Rockefellers, Fricks, Forbes, Astors, Vanderbilts, Goulds and others who wanted to flee the congestion of southern Manhattan had townhouses built on its first mile or so, which earned it the nickname »**Millionaires' Row**«. Its more recent nickname, »Boulevard of Golden Credit Cards«, comes from luxury shops like Tiffany and Cartier between 49th and 59th St. The rich of the 20th century settled further along, next to Central Park. Today the sights concentrated along Fifth Avenue (►Empire State Building, ►Rockefeller Center, ►Museum of Modern Art, Trump Tower, ►Central Park as well as the Museum Mile, to name but a few) exert an unparalleled attraction, not only on tourists but also on New Yorkers.

ON FIFTH AVENUE

Between 34th and 59th Street
The **Flatiron Building** at the intersection of Fifth Avenue, Broadway and 23rd Street made architectural history as the first skyscraper in Manhattan (►Flatiron District). For those taking a stroll, the most interesting part of Fifth Ave. is between 34th and 59th Street. A special magnet for tourists is the ►Empire State Building (Fifth Ave./34th St.), whose observation platforms also give a good view of the course

The atrium of Trump Tower is not only reserved for millionaires

of the street. Art lovers should visit the nearby ►Morgan Library and Museum (E 36th St.), and a very special pleasure is the little **Bryant Park** behind the ►New York Public Library (476 Fifth Ave., between 40th and 42nd St.). Those interested in architecture should make a detour to E 42nd St., where there are several buildings worth seeing, including the ►Grand Central Terminal and the ►Chrysler Building.

Back on Fifth Avenue, the **Chase Manhattan Bank** (Fifth Ave./43rd St.) was built in 1954 to plans by Skidmore, Owings & Merrill and was one of the first glass buildings. In the block between Fifth and Sixth Ave., near 47th St., the diamond trade has become established. For the most part it is in the hands of Chassidic Jews, who control 80% of American trade in these gems. According to estimates the **Diamond District** employs 26,000 people. While the total sales turnover here is not known, the city collects almost $60 million in tax revenue from this area. Continuing along Fifth Avenue, the 19 buildings of the ►Rockefeller Center are next, and on the other side of the street stands ►St Patrick's Cathedral with the Villard Houses behind it. The neighbouring 189m/621ft-high, 50-storey **Olympic Tower** (645 Fifth Ave.) was built in 1976 to plans by Skidmore, Owings & Merrill. This aluminium-covered building, once the New York headquarters of Aristotle Onassis's empire, united shops, offices and con-

Back on Fifth Avenue

dominiums under one roof for the first time. The public arcades inside, with palm trees and a waterfall, do not however create a real-life atmosphere. In the **Tishman Building**, also called 666 Fifth Avenue, a 39-storey, aluminium-clad high-rise from 1957, there is also a waterfall designed by the artist Isamu Noguchi.

11 E 52 St., between Madison and Fifth Ave., is the address of the Austrian Cultural Forum. Regular events take place in the narrow, 24-storey, new glass-and-cement building by architect Raimund Abraham (information: tel. 1 212-319-5300, www.acfny.org). On the corner of Fifth Ave./W 53rd St. stands **St Thomas's Church**, built in 1913 by Cram, Goodhue and Ferguson in the neo-Gothic style. In the side street there are three worthwhile museums, among them the ►Museum of Modern Art. The University Club, built in 1899 in Renaissance style (Fifth Ave./W 54th St.), was designed by McKim, Mead & White.

*Carnegie Hall A detour takes you to one of the most famous concert halls in the world, Carnegie Hall (154 West 57th St./Seventh Ave.). The steel magnate Andrew Carnegie donated the house with almost 2,800 seats; Tchaikovsky conducted the opening concert in 1891. Until the building of the ►Lincoln Center, Carnegie Hall was the home of the New York Philharmonic orchestra. This brick and glazed-tile temple of music in Italian Renaissance style was to have been demolished in the 1960s, but instead was given protected status and carefully restored. Events still take place here (►p.91). The **Rose Museum** shows

FAO Schwarz on Fifth Ave. is a legend

gifts from the artists who have performed here. Cesar Pelli was the architect of the neighbouring **Carnegie Hall Tower**. The skyscraper with offices and extensions of Carnegie Hall was erected over a concrete tube that was poured on site, then covered with bricks and glazed tiles like the Hall itself. In its shadow just a few metres away is the 66-storey black **Metropolitan Tower** (Harry Macklowe, 1987). A block to the south is the third giant, Helmut Jahn's 70-storey **Cityspire** (1987) with its cupola reminiscent of the cathedral in Florence. Together, Carnegie Hall Tower, Metropolitan Tower and Cityspire make an impressive ensemble.

Rose Museum: 154 West 57th St./7th Ave.; daily 11am–4.30pm; tours, when no concert is taking place: Mon–Fri. 11.30am, 2pm, 3pm, Sat 11.30am, 12.30pm, Sun 12.30pm; admission $10; tel. 1 212 9 03 96 29, www.carnegie-hall.org

Moving towards Central Park, exquisite shops are lined up one next to the other. The department stores **Saks Fifth Avenue** (611 Fifth Ave., between 49th and 50th St.) and **Takashimaya** (693 Fifth Ave., between 54th and 55th St.), are popular, as are »theme shops« such as the **Disney Store** (711 Fifth Ave./55th St.), **Niketown** – a multi-storey shop offering everything from the world of sports (6 E 57th St., between Fifth and Madison Ave.) – or **Tiffany**, the jewellery shop which opened in 1837 and was made famous by Truman Capote's tale and the film *Breakfast at Tiffany's* (727 Fifth Ave., www.tiffany.com).

> **?** MARCO POLO INSIGHT
>
> *For rich and beautiful people ...*
>
> 13,000 millionaires live in Manhattan, it is said – enough to populate a small town! The boom in real-estate prices is matched by that in superstar restaurants such as Le Parker Meridien, where the caviar omelette costs $1000. If that's too much, consider eating Japanese at Masa, where the cheapest lunch is a steal at only $300. And why should luxury be monopolized by humans? The dog beauty parlour at the Ritz Carlton offers full treatment including a name-tag in 22-carat gold for $1095.

The Corning Glass Building (717 Fifth Ave./56th St.) was built in 1959 to plans by Harrison & Abramowitz, the architects of the ▶Rockefeller Center and the Metropolitan Opera in the ▶Lincoln Center. The Steuben Shop in the ground floor offers a broad selection of glass, historical and modern.

Corning Glass Building

In 1984 the real-estate magnate Donald Trump built a monument to himself on the corner of Fifth Ave./E 56th St. The 202m/663ft-high, 68-storey glass palace is based on a design by Der Scutt. The six-storey atrium is certainly an eye-catcher (▶photo p.243). Breccia marble from Italy was used for the walls and floors here, its colour mixture of pink, peach and orange making everything appear gilded. A wa-

Trump Tower

Millionaire's Mile – Central Park East

Central Park East was once the preferred address of the super-rich, and is still one of the most coveted areas in the city. Follow this walk to see »who lived where?«. In addition to splendid mansions, you pass many museums.

The **Vanderbilt House**, a huge residence built from white limestone and red brick (Fifth Ave./86th St.), dates from 1914. In 1944 the wife of the railroad millionaire Cornelius Vanderbilt IV bought it with part of the fortune that he had acquired by dubious means. One block further south is **1040 Fifth Avenue**, made famous by Jacqueline Onassis, the widow of President Kennedy, who bought the penthouse on the 15th floor a few months after his assassination and lived there until her death in 1994. The less famous but extremely wealthy Benjamin Duke lived in the house built in 1901 at the **corner of Fifth Ave. and 82nd St.** He and his brother founded the American Tobacco Company.

A house modelled on a palace in Bordeaux, sometimes described as the most beautiful residence in New York, also belonged to the Dukes. Today it houses the **NYU Graduate School of Art History** (Fifth Ave./78th St.). The decorative columns between Fifth Ave. and Madison Ave. belong to the magnificent **home of Joseph Pulitzer**, a publisher from Austro-Hungary (1847–1911) after whom the Pulitzer Prize was named.

The mansion of the steel magnate Henry Clay Frick in **70th St.**, which occupies a whole city block, was planned from the beginning as an art gallery. Today it is the home of the ▶**Frick Collection**, covering several centuries of European painting. 47–49 East 65th St., further south-east, is the address of the **Roosevelt Twin Town House**, which was owned by President Franklin D. Roosevelt. Opposite Central Park, Ulysses S. Grant, a former US president, lived with his mother from 1881 to 1885 at 3 East 66th St.; here he wrote his memoirs.

A view inside the mansion of the art collector Henry Clay Frick

terfall tumbles 60m/200ft down to the ground. Restaurants, cafés and countless shops are housed here, above them are offices and condominiums, of which the largest on the top floor can be had for a mere $10 million. Trump Tower is connected with the attractive glass garden of the former IBM Building (590 Madison Ave., ▶Sony Building). Trump Tower would be only half as beautiful without the reflection in its façade of the **Crown Building** (730 Fifth Ave.), formerly called the Heckscher Building, which was built in 1921 (architects: Warren & Wetmore) in the French Renaissance style.

Grand Army Plaza forms a dignified provisional finale to Fifth Avenue with the Pulitzer Fountain (1915) in its centre. Here are the former **Plaza Hotel** (59th St.), which was built in 1907 in the style of a French Château by Henry J. Hardenbergh, the south-east entrance to ▶Central Park – the horse-drawn carriages start their trips through the park here – and the giant toy shop **FAO Schwarz** (767 Fifth Ave./58th St.) in the **General Motors Building**, which was built in 1968 by Emery Roth & Sons with Edward Durell Stone. Unfortunately the 215m/705ft-high, 50-storey building has destroyed the much praised harmony of Grand Army Plaza. Furthermore, take a look at the building of the **Metropolitan Club** (corner of 60th St.), from 1893 by Stanford White in the style of a Florentine palazzo. Northwards, between the ▶Frick Collection (70th St.) and the Museum of the City of New York (103rd St.), stretches the **Museum Mile** with the ▶Whitney Museum, the ▶Metropolitan Museum of Art, the ▶Neue Galerie, the ▶Guggenheim Museum and the Cooper Hewitt Museum.

*Grand Army Plaza

* Financial District

────────────────── ✧ A/B 19

Location: Lower Manhattan
Subway: Wall St., Rector St.

The financial district in southern Manhattan is so named for the New York stock exchange and the many banks and credit institutions in the area, primarily on Wall St., the city canyon which rarely sees sunshine.

A WALK THROUGH THE DISTRICT

Wall Street is generally believed to have derived its name from the fortified wall that ran through this area to protect the New Amsterdam settlement against British colonial incursions and attacks from

*Wall Street

Trinity Church surrounded by skyscrapers

»Indians« (Native Americans). The events of 11 September 2001, including the crippled telecommunications network caused by the attacks, have greatly changed business in the financial district. Trading on the stock market crashed, and many financial firms have left this area and moved to midtown or to the suburbs. Another reason for the flight is the traffic congestion brought on by the small one-lane roads with numerous stoplights and stop signs and lack of staggered lights as exist elsewhere in the city. Many of the former bank buildings were converted into luxury residential buildings, such as the former headquarters of J. P. Morgan & Company (►p.252) on 23 Wall Street.

*Trinity Church

For 300 years Trinity Church has stood at the start of Wall Street, where it is now wedged between the high-rises of the financial district. The present church was erected in 1846 in the Gothic Revival style from brown sandstone (architect: Richard Upjohn). The 92m/300ft tower was the tallest building in New York in the 19th century. There were two previous buildings of the same name: the first church, from the year 1698, was a simple building without a steeple which burned down in 1776. The following building was dedicated in 1790 and torn down in 1839 because it was structurally unsound. The bronze doors by Richard Morris Hunt (1828–95) on the three entrances from Broadway show biblical scenes (main entrance and north portal) as well as events from the history of America and Trinity congregation (south portal). In the interior, the stained -glass windows and the back wall of the altar with Christian scenes engraved in stone from Caen (France) are worth taking a look at (guided tours: daily 2pm). The **museum** explains the beginnings of New York and the church, which in 1705 got most of its property from Queen Anne and is one of the richest Episcopalian congregations in the city. In New York's oldest **cemetery** numerous historical personalities are buried, including Alexander Hamilton, buried in a pyramid-shaped tomb, the first US Secretary of the Treasury (1755–1804), who was shot in a duel by his opponent Aaron Burr (▶Harlem, Morris-Jumel Mansion Museum), and Robert Fulton, who constructed the first functional steamship (1765–1815). Opposite the church (Broadway/Wall St.) stands the high-rise of the **Irving Trust Company**, a massive limestone block (1 Wall St.; architect: Ralph Walker, 1931). The exquisitely decorated Art Deco lobby is worth a look.

Trinity Church Museum: Trinity Place; Mon–Fri 9am–530pm, Sat, Sun 9am–3.45pm, www.trinitywallstreet.org

From here it is only a few steps to Federal Hall. This building was completed after eight years in 1842 and inaugurated as the customs house at the intersection of Wall/Nassau St.; it represents the pinnacle of neo-classical architecture in New York. Its Wall Street façade, in the shape of a Doric temple, is a simplified Parthenon without a frieze. The interior consists of a rotunda, which actually seems to be more Roman than Greek. From 1862 to 1920 Federal Hall was a department of the U. S. Treasury; it has been a museum since 1955. President George Washington, who took his oath of office in 1789 where his statue now stands, is remembered here in particular. At that time the old city hall (1701) stood here. It was modernized by Pierre L'Enfant, famous as the urban planner of the nation's capital Washington, which was the seat of the U.S. Congress in 1789–90.

Federal Hall National Memorial

❶ 26 Wall St , Mon–Fri 9am–5pm

The New York Stock Exchange (20 Broad St.), NYSE for short, is the largest stock exchange in the United States and, in spite of many crises, the most important in the world. On an average trading day about 1.5 billion stocks worth more than $46 billion change hands (record: October 10, 2008 at $ 7.3 billion; in 2008 the total was $ 802,027 billion. In London the volume is about $30 billion). During the finance crisis the Dow Jones fell by 53.8 per cent between October 2007 and March 2009. The biggest fall was on 6 May 2010, when it lost 9,869.62 points or 9.19 per cent. The value of all 3,507 companies listed on the NYSE in late 2008 sank more than 60% during the financial crisis as. The New York stock exchange was founded in 1792: at that time a few stock dealers used to meet regularly under the sycamore trees along Wall Street in order to deal in government loans from the American Revolutionary War. The building with a façade in

New York Stock Exchange

A Centre of World Finance

The New York Stock Exchange (NYSE) opened in 1792, with trading in just five stocks. By the time of the great Wall Street Crash in 1929 at the latest, it had become a worldwide symbol of stock trading. Apart from the NYSE, the biggest electronic exchange in the United States, NASDAQ, the world's biggest commodity exchange, NYMEX, and several other important trading institutions are based in New York. More than half a million people are employed in finance in the metropolitan area.

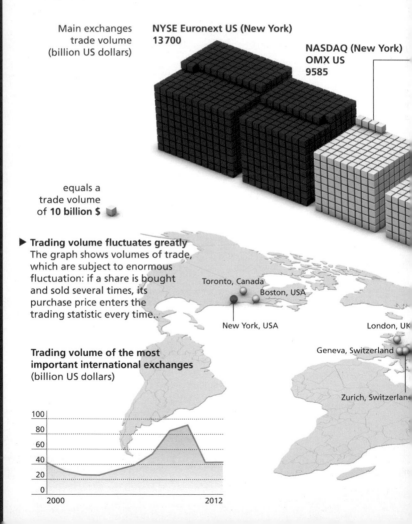

Main exchanges
trade volume
(billion US dollars)

NYSE Euronext US (New York)
13 700

NASDAQ (New York)
OMX US
9585

equals a
trade volume
of **10 billion $**

▶ **Trading volume fluctuates greatly**
The graph shows volumes of trade, which are subject to enormous fluctuation: if a share is bought and sold several times, its purchase price enters the trading statistic every time.

Toronto, Canada
Boston, USA
New York, USA
London, UK
Geneva, Switzerland
Zurich, Switzerland

Trading volume of the most important international exchanges
(billion US dollars)

100
80
60
40
20
0
2000   2012

GFCI Ranking

The Global Financial Centres Index is an important instrument for stockbrokers. It compares the competitiveness of the world's leading trading places. Apart from economic data, the assessment is based on educational standards, availability of workplaces and political criteria. This ranking differs from the list based on trade volumes.

▶ **Important finance centres**
  GFCI rank (points)

1 New York	786
2 London	784
3 Hong Kong	761
4 Singapore	751
5 Zurich	730
6 Tokyo	722
7 Seoul	718
8 Boston	715
9 Geneva	713
11 Frankfurt am Main	709
14 Toronto	651

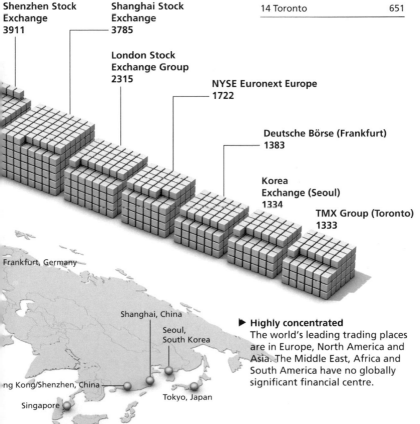

Japan Exchange Group (Tokyo)
6516

Shenzhen Stock Exchange
3911

Shanghai Stock Exchange
3785

London Stock Exchange Group
2315

NYSE Euronext Europe
1722

Deutsche Börse (Frankfurt)
1383

Korea Exchange (Seoul)
1334

TMX Group (Toronto)
1333

Frankfurt, Germany

Shanghai, China

Seoul, South Korea

ng Kong/Shenzhen, China

Singapore

Tokyo, Japan

▶ **Highly concentrated**
The world's leading trading places are in Europe, North America and Asia. The Middle East, Africa and South America have no globally significant financial centre.

In front of the NYSE

the style of a Roman temple, designed by George B. Post, was built in the year 1903. In the legendary trading room there is seemingly chaotic activity. Since 9/11, visitors are no longer permitted entry. Those interested in the history of Wall Street should instead go to the **Museum of American Finance**.

New York Stock Exchange: latest information tel. 1 212-656-3000, www.nyse.com

Museum of American Finance: 48 Wall St.; subway: Wall St.; Tue–Sat 10am–4pm, admission $5, www.moaf.org

At 23 Wall St., on the corner of Broad Street, stands the fortress-like **Morgan Guaranty Trust Company** (architects: Trowbridge & Livingston). Close by is the Bank of Manhattan (40 Wall St.), now the **Trump Building** (H. Craig Severance, Yasuo Matsui, 1929). The tower, with its pyramid-like crown, is 282.5m/927ft high. The banking house with two rows of giant Greek columns (55 Wall St.) was built in 1841 for the New York stock exchange and designed by Isaiah Rogers; in 1907 it was renovated and expanded by the architects McKim, Mead & White. Opposite is the 40-storey office high-rise of the **Morgan Bank**, a tower of granite and reflecting glass built in 1988 to plans by Roche, Dinkeloo & Assocs. At a height of 289.6m/951ft it is the tallest building in the financial district. At this point, Wall St. meets Water Street. A short detour to the left leads to Wall Street Plaza (Water/Pine St.), built in 1973 to a design by the Chinese American I. M. Pei. There is a nice **view** across the East River from the somewhat higher plaza between the buildings at 55 Water St.

Fraunces' Tavern Museum
Follow Water St. south-west to reach a block with 18th-century houses. Fraunces' Tavern was built in 1719 and taken over in 1763 by Samuel Fraunces, who opened an inn here; it is the oldest house in Manhattan (54 Pearl St./Water St.). George Washington spent his last days as general here in the winter of 1783: on 4 December he said farewell to his officers and withdrew to his estate in Mount Vernon

near the city that would later become the capital named after him. In 1837 and 1852 the building burned down but was rebuilt in 1907 in neo-colonial style. Today's building is a new construction by William Mersereau from the year 1928 in 18th-century style. On the ground floor there is a restaurant (tel. 1 212-968-1776), and on the two upper floors a museum about the history of America.

❶ 54 Pearl St./Water St.; Tue–Sun noon–5pm; admission $7

Return along Pearl to Pine Street, where the beautiful Art Deco American International Building stands at 70 Pine St.; its lobby is worth a look. A couple of steps north-east between Nassau and William, Pine and Liberty St. is the headquarters of the **Chase Manhattan Bank** with a huge plaza (1 Chase Manhattan Plaza). The design of the 248m/813ft-high, 60-storey high-rise of steel and glass – an example of International Style – was by Gordon Bunshaft from the office of Skidmore, Owings & Merrill. Its completion in 1960 marked the beginning of the modernization of the financial district. On the plaza stands the large sculpture *Four Trees* by **Jean Dubuffet** (1972). The 14m/46ft-high, 25-ton sculpture made of aluminium, steel and plastic was called »a monument of the spirit, a landscape of esprit« by the artist. The Sunken Garden, a lowered plaza with a fountain and seven basalt blocks, is at the same time the light source for the bank under the plaza. It is the work of the Japanese artist Isamu Noguchi (1961–64).

American International Building

The intersection of Liberty and William St. and Maiden Lane is named after the artist Louise Nevelson (1900–88, ▶Famous People). The sculpture *Shadows and Flags* (1977) in the middle of the street, which consists of seven iron figures of varying heights, is her work.

Louise Nevelson Plaza

The Federal Reserve Bank in William St. was built in 1924 in classical style and is known as the Fed (entrance: 33 Liberty St.). It is one of twelve Federal Reserve banks, which circulate US dollars. Here – and not in the US gold depot Fort Knox in Kentucky – about half of the world's gold is stored, amounting to 700,000 gold bars. Only about 2% belong to the United States, the rest to 60 other countries and organizations such as the International Monetary Fund. A giant security system guards them. The safe is about 30m/100ft underground, is half as big as a football field and has 122 numbered cells in which the bars are stacked like bricks. Each one is 99.5% pure and weighs 12.5kg/28lbs. Most of the gold came to the USA during the Second World War. If a national bank sells its gold today, it is simply carried from one cell to another. The bank refuses to divulge who has sold how much gold.

Federal Reserve Bank

❶ Mon–Fri 10am–4pm, tours 9.30am–3.30pm, tel. 1 212-720-6130; www.newyorkfed.org

Marine Midland Bank The 223m/725ft dark glass tower of the Marine Midland Bank (Gordon Bunshaft from the office of Skidmore, Owings & Merrill, 1967) stands at 140 Broadway on a receded base; the 7m/23ft-high *Red Cube* by Isamu Noguchi (1973) is a real eye-catcher.

Equitable Building Opposite the Marine Midland Bank towers the Equitable Building, built in 1915, a giant 160m/525ft-high massive stone block (120 Broadway). It casts a shadow over the whole area. Protests about this caused the Zoning Law to be passed in 1916. This law stated that high-rises had to be built with set-backs, so that they became narrower with increasing height.

33 Maiden Lane The office high-rise reminiscent of a knight's castle, 33 Maiden Lane, is the work of Philip Johnson, a master of the International Style, who obviously helped himself here from the smorgasbord of architectural history.

One Liberty Plaza Building The small plaza on Liberty St. (between Broadway and Church St.) is a place for lunch for crowds from the surrounding offices and banks especially at midday – the bronze sculpture depicting a financier searching through his briefcase by J. Seward Johnson Jr. hints at this. The east side of the plaza is occupied by the 245m/804ft-high former U. S. Steel Building, today One Liberty Plaza (Skidmore, Owings & Merrill, 1972).

Flatiron District & Union Square

✦ D 14

Location: Between Fifth and Park Ave., and 14th and 29th St.
Subway: 23rd St., 14th St.

The Flatiron Building at the intersection of Fifth Ave. and 23rd St., one of the first and most unusual skyscrapers in New York, is the centre of a new trendy area with select shops and restaurants ranging from the cosy to the off-beat.

∗Flatiron Building The striking triangular shape of the »Flatiron« gave the building its name. It was New York's first skyscraper in the – then new – steel skeleton construction. The architect D. H. Burnham could not build in any other way on the acutely angled land at the intersection of Fifth Ave. and 23rd St. The building was erected in 1902, is 76m/250ft high and with its 20 floors looks more like an oversized apartment building.

The »flatiron« heralded the skyscraper era

Among the pictures in the corridors are Vermeer's *The Officer and the Laughing Girl* (around 1656) and *The Music Lesson* (1660) in the **South Hall**. Goya painted *Don Pedro, Duke of Osuna* (around 1790), Renoir the *Mother and Two Children* (1870). The dresser and bureau were created by Jean-Henri Riesener around 1780 for Marie-Antoinette. The **Library** mainly displays portraits, including one of the art collector *Henry Clay Frick* by Johansen (1943) and *George Washington* by Gilbert Stuart. In the **North Hall** the portrait of *Comtesse d'Haussonville* by Ingres (1845), *Portal of Valenciennes* (1709–10) by Watteau and Monet's *Winter in Vetheuil* are especially worth seeing. A glass roof lightens the **West Gallery**, which contains Rembrandt's self-portrait of 1654 and his *Polish Rider* (1658), Veronese's *Wisdom and Strength* and *The Choice of Hercules*, *The Smithy* by Goya (1818), portraits by El Greco, van Dyck, Hals, Bronzino and Velázquez's *Philip IV of Spain* (1664). The adjoining **Enamel Room** contains, among other works, Jan van Eyck's *Virgin and Child with Saints and Donor*, *St Simon* by Piero della Francesca and a four-part altar by the same artist from the church S. Agostino in Borgo San Sepolcro (Italy). In the **Oval Room**, Frick's former study, two portraits by van Dyck and Gainsborough are displayed facing each other. In the **East Gallery** are *The Sermon on the Mount* by Claude Lorrain, portraits by Jacques Louis David, Goya and Whistler. This leads to the **Garden**

Frick Collection

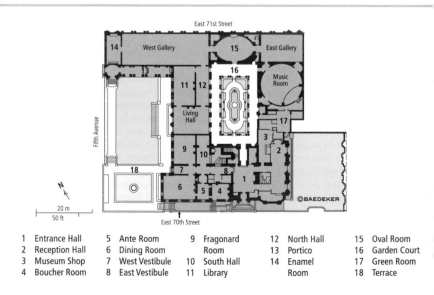

1 Entrance Hall	5 Ante Room	9 Fragonard	12 North Hall	15 Oval Room
2 Reception Hall	6 Dining Room	Room	13 Portico	16 Garden Court
3 Museum Shop	7 West Vestibule	10 South Hall	14 Enamel	17 Green Room
4 Boucher Room	8 East Vestibule	11 Library	Room	18 Terrace

Court, a glass-covered inner courtyard with a small table, benches and a bronze angel by Jean Barbet. In the **Lecture Hall**, lectures and introductions to the collection are occasionally held.

★ Gracie Mansion

J 9

Location: East End Ave./E 88th St. (in Carl Schurz Park)
Subway: 86th St.
Visits: Wed on appointment

gracietours@cityhall.nyc.gov
Admission: $7
www.nyc.gov/gracie

This house, which was built in 1799 by Ezra Weeks for the Scottish importer Archibald Gracie in the Federal Style, has been the residence of the mayor of New York since 1942.

Although the current mayor Bill de Blasio lives here, Gracie Mansion, which has been renovated and expanded several times, is open to the public on Wednesday. It lies in the north of **Carl Schurz Park**, which is especially popular in the summer, and is located along the bank of the East River between 84th and 90th Street. It was named after the German-American journalist and politician Carl Schurz (1829–1906; ▶Famous People). A pretty promenade runs along the bank of the East River. The first stretch is named after John Finlay, the publisher of the *New York Times*. From here there is a fine view of the Queensboro Bridge, Roosevelt and Ward's Island and Hell Gate, the connection between the East River and Long Island Sound.

Yorkville, the area between East 79th and 96th St. as well as East River and Lexington Ave., was once the **German quarter** of Manhattan, and 86th Street was known as the »German Broadway«. Today only the names of a few cafés, restaurants and shops remind of this. The German population has shrunk to a small core since real-estate speculation and the removal of older houses pushed the rents up. German settlement in this area began at the end of the 19th century and reached its peak before the beginning of the Second World War. The rapid decline of Yorkville as a German quarter began about 1960. The so-called **Henderson District** (on the East River) consists of 24 pretty terraced brick houses from the late 19th century and is a sought-after address today.

Yorkville

? *Excursion to death*

MARCO ⊕ POLO INSIGHT

15 June 1904 marked the end of Little Germany in New York. Edward T. O'Donnell's book *Ship Ablaze* relates the background of how 2,000 residents of Little Germany died in a boating catastrophe.

** **Grand Central Terminal**

E 12

Location: E 42nd St./Park Ave.
Subway: Grand Central
Tours: Wed 12.30pm with the
Municipal Arts Society, meet under
the clock at the information desk;
Fri 12.30pm with the Grand Central

Partnership, meet at 120
Park Ave. Atrium opposite
the station
www.grandcentralterminal.com

Cathedral of progress
In 1871 the railway magnate Cornelius Vanderbilt opened the first railway station here, from which the trains of the private railway line New York Central left for Chicago and Canada.

Today's building by the architects Reed & Stern, a masterpiece of Beaux Arts style, in which Baroque and Renaissance elements have been merged, was opened in 1913. It is one of the biggest passenger stations in the world. All tracks were put below ground – 41 on the upper and 26 on the lower underground level – so that the land above could be profitably developed. Four subway lines and a shuttle to Times Square also run from here.

At its heart is a giant **station concourse**, and above the elaborate marble floor domes an artificial sky with over 2,500 stars (Paul Helleu). The double staircase is also impressive, based on the Paris opera house and reminiscent of the glory days of train travel. From above the information booth shines a giant brass clock, and the candelabra are plated with gold and nickel. Renovation in the 1990s installed numerous restaurants and shops in the, among them the famous **Oyster Bar**, which has excellent seafood cuisine (▶p.121). On the lower floor the Grand Central Market, with a broad selection of shops and fast-food for every taste, is an inviting place to have a look around. The station long ago reached full capacity. To extend it, a tunnel 12km/7.5mi long from Queens is planned, which will divide at the terminus into two upper, two lower and one middle level, making Grand Central the world's biggest subterranean station.

MetLife Building
In 1963 the 59-storey Pan Am Building (today MetLife Building) was built. The architects were Emery Roth & Sons, and Walter Gropius and Petro Belluschi also worked on the plans.

Back on 42nd Street
Back on 42nd Street, there are several interesting buildings: diagonally across from Central Station is the 26-storey Altria Building (former Philip Morris Building, 120 Park Ave.; Ulrich Franzen, 1983). Other notable buildings on 42nd St. are the Home Savings of America Building (former Bowery Savings Bank; 110 E 42nd St.), whose richly appointed teller hall is an absolute must (York and Sawyers, 1923). The neighbouring 56-storey Chanin Building (122 E

Grand Central Terminal is a pivotal point for commuters

42nd St.) is a successful example of Art Deco style (Sloan & Robertson, 1929); here, take a look at the beautiful lobby.

The architectural highlight of the street is indisputably the Chrysler Building, built in 1930, with which the car manufacturer Walter P. Chrysler wanted to immortalize himself. At almost 319m/1,037ft it was the tallest skyscraper in New York for a year, but lost this honour when the Empire State Building was completed in 1931. The crown, with its stainless steel arches and triangle windows which give the building its characteristic appearance, can be seen from almost everywhere. Architect William Van Alen was inspired by the Art Deco style when creating the Chrysler Building, which was at first denounced as bizarre. Art Deco is also represented in the lobby and the 18 lifts (with different wood inlay work) which have been restored in the original style. Visitors may only enter the lobby (during office hours).

**Chrysler Building
►MARCO POLO Insight
p.264

❶ 405 Lexington Ave./42nd St. Subway: Grand Central. Visitors are only allowed into the lobby, Mon – Fri 8am – 6pm

Mobil Building Opposite is the 45-storey Mobil Building (150 E 42nd St.). It was built in 1955 of stainless steel to plans by Harrison & Abramovitz and was intended to prove that glass and aluminium are not the only building materials of the future.

Daily News Building The former Daily News Building (220 E 42nd St.) was built in 1930 in Art Deco style for the newspaper that had the largest circulation of the time – film buffs will recognize it as the building of the *Daily Planet*, which Clark Kent (alias Superman) entered and exited, either on foot or by air. The façade is impressive: the rising, prominent vertical bands of light brick make the 37-storey building seem taller than it really is. The flat roof designed by the architects Howells and Hood is also unusual. The extension along Third Ave. followed in 1958 to plans by Harrison & Abramovitz. Take a look at the Art Deco lobby with its large rotating globe.

Ford Foundation Building Architectural history was also made in 1967 by the Ford Foundation Building, which was designed by Kevin Roche and Dinkeloo (320 E 43rd St.; entrance on 42nd St.). The L-shaped ground plan of the 12-storey building includes an almost 1,400 sq m/1,700 sq yd winter garden. The intention of the builder and architects was to create an environmentally sound building.

Tudor City Opposite the Ford Foundation the so-called Tudor City, completed in 1928, extends between E 40th and E 43rd Street. The complex, in the neo-Gothic Tudor style, consists of about twelve buildings with about 3,000 apartments, a hotel and two parks, and is an oasis in the middle of Manhattan. When the colony was built, the UN headquarters (►United Nations Headquarters) did not yet exist, and there were industrial sites and slaughterhouses on the East River; for this reason there are hardly any windows facing the river.

✷ Greenwich Village

——————————————————— ✷ **B/C 14–16**
Location: Between 14th and Houston St. and west of Broadway
Subway: Fourth St./Washington Sq., Sheridan Sq., Eighth St.

New Yorkers just call it »The Village«. Greenwich Village is situated between 14th and Houston Street and between the Hudson River and ►Broadway; the small part west of Sixth Avenue is also called West Village.

When the village of Greenwich was founded in 1696, it lay far outside the city. By 1811, when the chequerboard street grid of Manhattan was adopted, Greenwich was already a small town, whose small, winding streets had names that remain to this day. In the course of the 18th and 19th centuries the district developed into a refined residential area, to which old brick buildings bear witness. It became important when from about 1900 for about 30 years it was the haunt of New York's Bohemia, who patronized the small theatres and many bars. During prohibition, **bars known as speakeasies** met the demand for illegal alcohol. The number of poets, authors and painters who lived in the Village is legion, and included James Fenimore Cooper, Edgar Allan Poe, Richard Wright, Henry James, John Dos Passos, Marianne Moore, Mark Twain, Sinclair Lewis and Dorothy Thompson, Thomas Wolfe, Hart Crane, Mary McCarthy, E. E. Cummings, William Styron and Edward Albee as well as Edward Hopper, William Glackens and Rockwell Kent. Today Greenwich Village is a respectable residential area; there are a few modern high-rises, but the impression of a small town with many homes with pretty inner courtyards and the winding narrow streets remains. The rents are among the highest in New York. A stroll through the historic area, whose centre lies immediately west of Washington Square, is most worthwhile. In the evening in particular it is a popular attraction with its legendary jazz clubs (among them the Blue Note and the Village Vanguard), theatres, cafés and restaurants.

The extravagant marble arch commemorates George Washington's inauguration

An Iconic Skyscraper

By building a company headquarters, the automobile manufacturer Walter P. Chrysler aimed to erect a monument to himself. This he did successfully: the Art Deco skyscraper by architect William van Alen is one of New York's most beautiful buildings.

Although Chrysler never occupied the building, it kept the name. The commission brought the architect no luck, however. Chrysler accused Van Alen of taking bribes, he received no fee and his career as an architect was at an end.

❶ Conquering the peak

With the construction of the Chrysler Building suffering delays, the Bank of Manhattan on Wall Street was already being acclaimed as the tallest building in the city at 283m/920ft. It had 71 storeys, the Chrysler only 65. Then Van Alen pulled his trump out of the heating shaft: the 56m/182ft high, 27 ton stainless steel crown, which rose up at his command. But the triumph, 77 storeys and 319m/1037ft high, only lasted for a short time. The architects of the Empire State Building raised their building by ten storeys to a total of 102 storeys, and in 1931 it took the record with 381m/1238ft. Even though Chrysler never moved in to the building, it kept his name. But it brought the architect no luck. After

Chrysler accused him of taking bribes, Van Alen did not receive his commission and his career was finished..

❷ Zoning Law

So that sunshine and air reach street level the first zoning law was passed in 1916: after a certain height a skyscraper has to taper off toward its peak. This high rise model, which narrows towards the top, made architectural history.

❸ A hymn to the automobile

The shining stainless steel tower resembles the flanges of a radiator grill, the eight gigantic waterspouts shaped like the head of an eagle pattern on the Chrysler Plymouth hood ornament. The stepped wall offsets are decorated with winged hoods, wheels and stylized cars. The idiosyncratic Art Deco, successor to Art Nouveau, originated in Europe. The Chrysler Building is one of the most accomplished examples of its American counterpart.

❹ Lobby

The lobby was meant to be an exhibition area for Chrysler cars. It is decorated with Moroccan marble, white onyx and fine wood intarsia work; Tutankhamun's burial chambers were the model for the lift doors. The ceiling painting by Edward Trumbull shows a worker during the construction of the building and scenes from the history of technology and transport.

Only the lobby is open to the public

*Washington Square   The main square of the area is Washington Square. Once execution ground, paupers' graveyard and parade ground, it is now a place where New York romps; at weekends a microcosm of the city with people of all races, nations and ages, who play, make music, roller skate or just enjoy the sun. The square is dominated by the mighty **Washington Centennial Memorial Arch**. The 26m/85ft-high triumphal arch (by Stanford White) was erected in 1892 to commemorate the inauguration of George Washington. In the north of the square stands a statue of the first president (by Alexander Calder, 1918), and south of the arch is a monument to Garibaldi (by Giovanni Turini; 1888), the hero of Italian independence who lived on Staten Island from 1848 until 1854.

! *Did you know* **Insider Tip**

MARCO ⊕ POLO TIP

Greenwich Village has its own newspaper: *The Village Voice* reports weekly on American politics and culture, as well as the nightlife in the popular area of the Big Apple – and at no charge.

The square is bordered by the buildings of **New York University**, the largest private university in America, founded in 1831 by Albert Gallatin. New York University's Grey Art Gallery mainly displays American art from about 1940 until the present day.

❶ 100 Washington Square East between Washington and Waverly Place; Tue, Thu, Fri 11am–6pm, Wed until 8pm, Sat until 5pm; www.nyu.edu/greyart

The Row   North-west of Washington Square lies **The Row**, a group of elegant townhouses in the classical Federal Style. They inspired Henry James to write the novel *Washington Square* (1881). From here it is not far to the **Washington Mews**, former stables on a pretty cobbled street which today belong to New York University. The **Northern Dispensary** (165 Waverly Place), a three-sided building on the corner of Waverly Place, was built in 1831 during a cholera epidemic. In **McDougal Alley**, a small street north-west of Washington Square, Gertrude Vanderbilt Whitney (1875 until 1942) opened a gallery in the early 20th century that later developed into the ▶Whitney Museum of Art. The brick-built **Judson Memorial Church** south of Washington Square commemorates the Baptist Adoniram Judson, who went to Burma as a missionary in the early 19th century. The church has magnificent stained glass windows by the New York artist John La Farge. Bleecker Street, of which Simon & Garfunkel sang on one of their first albums, is the commercial centre of the Village with its many theatres, restaurants, bars and antique shops. The **Bayard Building** (65 Bleecker St.) is the only New York building by the Chicago archi-

tect Louis Sullivan (1898). At 100 Bleecker St. stands the sculpture *Bust of Sylvette* by Pablo Picasso. The 11m/36ft, 60-ton concrete sculpture rises four storeys high in front of the three towers of the faculty residences of New York University (I. M. Pei, 1966). Despite its size, the sphinx-like figure radiates an unusual grace.

Christopher Street Until the 1960s the gay and lesbian scene in New York was repressed. A full-blown rebellion took place on 27 June 1969, after the police stormed Stone Wall Inn (51 Christopher St.) and arrested some of the homosexual clientele. Three nights of resistance followed. This and many other actions led to a change in the law, which gave gays and lesbians the same rights as the rest of the population. Today people in the Village don't hide their sexual inclination anymore. »Christopher Street Day« is celebrated all over the world to commemorate the »Stonewall Rebellion«. **Sheridan Square**, where Christopher St. and Seventh Ave. intersect, is the second centre of the Village after Washington Square.

Jefferson Market Library The Jefferson Market Courthouse Library (425 Sixth Ave./10th St.) is an especially interesting building. Built in 1876 in wonderfully overloaded Venetian Gothic, it was a courthouse until 1945 and reopened in 1967 as a branch of the ▶New York Public Library.

Other streets Other streets worth checking out in the Village are Minetta Lane, Bedford Street – no. 75 is the oldest remaining Village house (1799) – the winding Commerce Street, and Grove Street, as well as St Luke's Place (between Leroy and Hudson St.) with a group of completely preserved houses from 1855, and Hudson Street with the **St Luke-in-the-Fields** church (no. 485) dating from 1822 which was badly damaged by fire in 1981. In spite of later changes to the building it still looks like a village church. In this part of Hudson St. there are countless antique shops.

** Guggenheim Museum

G 8

Location: 1071 Fifth Ave./88th St.
Subway: 86th St.
❶ Sat–Wed 10am–5.45pm,
Fri until 7.45pm

Admission $22,
Sat 5.45pm–7.45pm:
Pay What You Wish
www.guggenheim.org

The Guggenheim has one of the world's best collections of modern art – from 20th-century works to contemporary offerings. The museum is the creation of the mining industrialist Solomon R. Guggenheim (1861–1949).

Frank Lloyd Wright's sculpture-like Guggenheim building

Guggenheim originally collected old masters until the German artist and later museum director Baroness Hilla Rebay introduced him to abstract art. In 1943 the Swiss collector commissioned Frank Lloyd Wright (1869–1959) to plan a museum to display the works of art in the »Solomon R. Guggenheim Collection of Non-Objective Paintings« which had been housed temporarily since 1939. 14 years passed until all of the city's requirements were met, and building finally began in 1957. Wright never saw the opening: he died six months before the museum was completed in 1959. **History**

Wright's only museum and his only building in New York is a great work of architecture, even though a number of critics doubt its suitability as a museum. For Wright himself his aesthetic form meets the function halfway. »A museum«, so he postulated, »is an organic structure with one large room on one continuous storey.« He detached himself from the usual division of museums into halls and created one single cylindrical 28m/90ft interior in which the light source is daylight through a glass dome. A conically widening, 432m/472yd-long spiralling ramp with a 3% incline winds around **Frank Lloyd Wright's museum building** the room and exhibits the works of art in over 70 niches and small galleries. The natural lighting is supplemented by some indirect lighting along the ramp. This arrangement of space results in an easy-to-survey and systematic exhibition that leads the visitor clearly in the logical order of the exhibits: downwards, after taking a lift to the top. The foundation had to fight more than 20 court cases until they were allowed to build a highly necessary extension – which Wright had already planned in 1951 (10m/33ft higher than the present extension) – next to the rotunda which is under a preservation order. In 1992 the 14-storey gallery house with several double storeys was finished (architect: Charles Gwathmey). The spiral is now used only for temporary exhibitions; the main collection is in the extension. But even now there is still not enough room for the New York foundation – actually a »collection of collections« – since the Thannhauser, Niedendorf, Dreier, Peggy Guggenheim and Panza collections, among others, were added to the Guggenheim complex. The Guggenheim had to expand: there are now branches in Venice, Bilbao, Berlin and Las Vegas.

Collection The collection consists of more than 8,000 paintings and sculptures – from the famous pictures of the Thannhauser collection including those by Camille Pissarro, the oldest Guggenheim artist, all the way to Pop Art. This excellent overview of modern to contemporary art is displayed in a rotating selection of about 350 masterpieces. The Munich art dealer Justin K. Thannhauser, who died in 1976, willed the museum his collection of 75 Impressionist and post-Impressionist masterpieces. In another gallery, art from the time between the World Wars is exhibited, chronologically a continuation of the Thannhauser Collection with works by Kandinsky, Mondrian, Mirò, Chagall and Léger. The collection donated by the Italian Count Panza consists of 200 works of Minimal and Concept Art, monochrome painting and environments.

✳ **Harlem**

✦ **F–K 1–6**

Location: North of Central Park
Subway: 125th St.

Express subway trains, once immortalized by Duke Ellington in *Take the A-Train*, take less than ten minutes from Times Square to 125th St., Harlem's shopping street. Since the turn of the millennium Harlem, the predominantly African American neighbourhood in north Manhattan between 110th and 162nd Street, has been experiencing its second renaissance.

Peter Stuyvesant founded the settlement Nieuw Haarlem (named after the Dutch city) in a hilly area in 1658, and it kept its rural character for a long time. In 1832 the first train connection to the urban south of Manhattan was built, and Harlem developed into a refined summer resort. One by one, settlements of solid brownstone houses like Morningside, Hamilton and Washington Heights (named after the later president, whose troops camped here in the War of Independence against the British) were built. After the start of the 20th century the subway connection from Harlem to south Manhattan started a building boom, but the apartments turned out to be unrentable. So Philip A. Payton Jr., an African American real estate agent, persuaded the owners who were concerned about their income to rent the empty apartments to the steadily growing African American population. Thus the »Black capital of America« was founded. As early as 1910 almost all of Harlem's residents were African American. With them came writers, painters and musicians. In the 1920s the neighbourhood flourished in the first **Harlem Renaissance**.

!   *The Harlem Flophouse*   **Insider Tip**

MARCO ⊕ POLO TIP

This bed & breakfast in a renovated brownstone building is like an art gallery. Antique furnishings like bathtubs with lion's feet recall the first Harlem renaissance. The owner Rene Calvo serves the homemade breakfast personally and is ready to advise and help with sightseeing (242 W 123rd St., near Frederick Douglass Blvd., tel. 1 212-662-0678, www.harlemflophouse.com).

Lenox Lounge, one of Harlem's famous jazz clubs

Brownstones in 120th Street

The renaissance of African American self-confidence was promoted by African American writers, painters and musicians and celebrated in legendary clubs like the Cotton Club or the Apollo Theater – though in times of segregation only in front of a white audience. The collapse began after the stock market crash in 1929, when the area sank into the bitterest poverty and misery. In the 1970s and 1980s Harlem was a synonym for decline, oppression, drugs and violence. The demography shifted as well. Today **125th Street, also known as Martin Luther King Jr. Boulevard**, is the centre of African American Harlem; in East Harlem, east of Fifth Ave., immigrants from Puerto Rico (El Barrio) are concentrated; in the far north those from the Dominican Republic and Honduras. It is still apparent – apart from a few skyscrapers – that Harlem was built around the turn of the century as a residential area for the upper middle class. The buildings are of a better quality than in other Manhattan neighbour-hoods and the streets are broader than any others in New York (e.g. Lenox Ave., next to 125th St. the real centre of Harlem). Although very little is left of the middle-class polish of that time, the signs of recovery cannot be missed. The population is growing, and the crime rate has dropped here even more than in the rest of New York. A new business opens almost every day. Tourism has discovered the reawakened cultural life of the city and the tourist attractions. About 40,000 tourists visit this neighbourhood every year, and the number is growing.

Is it dangerous to walk around in Harlem? It would be negligent to deny that there are dangers. But anyone who follows the usual rules that apply in any large city will be as safe here as Downtown. In the evenings it is better to go directly to your destination in Harlem, like a jazz or dance club or a theatre. Harlem Heritage Tours or Harlem Spirituals, among others, offer guided bus and walking tours through Harlem (▶p.158).

Security

SIGHTSEEING IN HARLEM

Columbia University, located between 114th and 120th St. and Amsterdam and West End Ave. (subway: 116th St./Columbia University), was founded in 1754 as King's College and as such is the oldest university in New York. Alongside Harvard, Yale and Princeton it is one of the most respected universities in the country. With about 19,000 students Columbia is not the largest university in New York (New York University on Washington Square has 40,000 students). Among its graduates are more than 50 Nobel Prize winners as well as Isaac Asimov, J. D. Salinger, James Cagney and Joan Rivers. In 1897 building work started on today's campus under the architect Charles McKim, who also designed the **Low Library**. The classical columned building with its impressive outdoor stairway today houses the university administration. The statue of the Alma Mater is by Daniel Chester French (1903). The university library is the Butler Library at the southern end of the campus. Immediately east of the Low Library is **St Paul's**

*Columbia University

Chapel, which was built in 1904 to plans by John Howell. Its style is a mixture of Italian Renaissance, Gothic and Byzantine architecture; occasionally free concerts are held here. There are various sculptures on the campus including ones by Rodin, George Grey Barnard, Jacques Lipchitz, Kees Verkade and Henry Moore. On the other side of Broadway is Barnard College for women, which was opened in 1889.

►Cathedral of St John the Divine

It is worth visiting Riverside Church to see its 120m/394ft-high tower (first a lift, then about 150 steps), from which there is a great view. The church was inspired by the cathedral in Chartres and was built in 1930. It has a glockenspiel with 74 bells (Sunday noon and 3pm) as well as an organ with 22,000 pipes; in the interior take a look at the 16th-century stained glass windows from Bruges and a Madonna by J. Epstein.

St John the Divine

Riverside Church

❶ 490 Riverside Drive/122nd St.; subway: 116th St./Columbia University; tours Mon–Fri 9am–4pm, free admission

Grant's Tomb, the imposing grave in honour of Ulysses S. Grant diagonally opposite, commemorates the 18th president of the USA and commander-in-chief of the Union troops in the American Civil War

> **!** *Gospel in the churches* **Insider Tip**
>
> **MARCO ⊕ POLO TIP**
>
> The lively style of worship and the infectious music of the gospel choirs are the biggest attraction in Harlem. There are bus tours (for example Harlem Spirituals Gospel Jazz Tours, tel. 1 212-391-0900), but you can go to Harlem under your own steam, too. The most famous choirs are at the Abyssinian Baptist Church (►p.276), Metropolitan Baptist Church (151 West 128th St./Powell Boulevard) and Mount Moriah Church (2050 Fifth Ave.). Tickets are available at tourist information offices.

(1822–85; John H. Duncan, 1890). It is in the northern part of **Riverside Park**, which is on the eastern bank of the Hudson River between 72nd and 155th Street and divided by Henry Hudson Parkway. The park was laid out in 1875 by Frederick Law Olmsted, who also designed ►Central Park. Numerous monuments stand here: the Jewish Martyrs Memorial (near 83rd Street) commemorates the Holocaust, the Soldiers' & Sailors' Monument (89th St.) those who fell in the Civil War, the Fireman's Memorial (100th St.) the New York firemen, and a statue of a figure on horseback, the Civil War general Franz Sigel (1824–1902; 106th Street).

The legendary **Apollo Theater** was opened in 1913, but until 1934 its doors were closed to African Americans. In the next 40 years Bes-

Apollo Theater

125th Street, Harlem's main street

sie Smith, Billie Holliday, Huddie Ledbetter, Duke Ellington, Count Basie, Dizzie Gillespie, Thelonius Monk, Ella Fitzgerald and Aretha Franklin were among its stars. At the beginning of the 1970s it was converted to a cinema and finally closed in 1976. Since its renovation in the 1980s amateur and comedy shows have taken place here.

❶ 253 W 125th St.; subway: Lenox Ave./125th St.; tel. 1 212-531-5300, www. apollotheater.com

*Studio Museum

The Studio Museum, just a few blocks away, is the only official institution in the USA for African American art. In rotating exhibitions art from the 20th and 21st centuries is shown

❶ Studio Museum: 144 W 125th St.; subway: 125th St.; Sun, Wed–Fri noon–6pm, Sat 10am–6pm; www.studiomuseuminharlem.org, admission $7; tel. 1 212-864-4500

*Schomburg Center for Research in Black Culture

Those interested in African American culture should visit the Schomburg Center for Research in Black Culture. The basis of the collection is the private collection of Arthur Schomburg (1874–1938). This bank employee, who was originally from Puerto Rico, protesting against the dominant opinion of his time that African Americans had no history, collected 5,000 books, 300 manuscripts, 2,000 prints and portraits as well as other material. The building (1991) designed by Bond Ryder Associates has an octagon at one end and a tower at the corner of 135th St.

❶ 515 Lenox Ave., between 135th and 136th St.; subway: 135th St.; Mon–Wed noon–8pm, Thu, Fri 11am–6pm

Abyssinian Baptist Church

Of the older buildings in the area, the many churches and religious establishments are especially interesting. The most famous of the approximately 400 churches in Harlem is the Abyssinian Baptist Church, built in 1924 in the neo-Gothic style, where the father and son both named Adam Clayton Powell – the son sat in Congress in 1944 – preached their fiery sermons.

❶ 132 W 138th St.; subway: Lenox Ave./135th St.; Sunday: sermon with gospel worship at 11am; www.abyssinian.org

Strivers' Row

The roomy brownstone houses in Strivers' Row (138th and 139th St. between Adam C. Powell Blvd. and Seventh Ave.) are among the most beautiful in all of New York. They were built in 1891 to prove that affordable apartments could also be tasteful and spacious. Nowadays the pretty houses are traded by white speculators for high prices.

Audubon Terrace

Donated by Archer M. Huntington (▶Famous People), the complex built in 1908 in the neo-classical style is named after the scientist John James Audubon, who once owned the land and is buried nearby in Trinity Cemetery. The sculptures on the main square were created by the sculptor and wife of the donor, Anna Hyatt Huntington. Several special institutes are housed in the building: the **American Numismatic Society** with an important coin collection, the **American Academy of Arts and Letters**, a group of respected American poets, painters, architects and composers, and the ***Hispanic Society of America** , founded in 1904 by Huntington, a museum with exhibitions on the culture of Spanish-speaking ethnic groups from prehistoric times until the present. The collection of paintings includes works by Joaquín Sorolla y Bastida, El Greco, Velázquez and Goya, and the museum also displays archaeological finds, goldsmith work, Islamic art from the Middle Ages, carpets and porcelain from the times of the expulsion of the Moors, as well as craft items.

❶ Broadway, between 155th and 156th St.; subway: 157th St. Tue–Sat 10am–4.30pm, Sun 1pm–4pm

The well-restored country estate a little to the north is one of the oldest buildings in Manhattan. It was built in 1765 in the Georgian style by Roger Morris and served in 1776 as George Washington's headquarters, when American troops fighting the British had withdrawn to New York. In 1810 the trader Stephen Jumel bought it as his country estate. He and his wife Eliza furnished it in the French Empire style. Today it is a nine-room museum with many pieces of original furniture from the 18th and 19th centuries as well as paintings, drawings, silver, porcelain and crystal from the early USA.

*Morris-Jumel Mansion Museum

❶ 65 Jumel Terrace, between 160th and 162nd St.; subway: 163rd St.; Wed–Sun 10am–4pm, admission $5

▶The Cloisters

The Cloisters

* High Line Park

➡ B 12 – 14

Location: between Gansevoort and 34th St.
Subway: 14th St., 23rd St., 8th Ave.
❶ Daily 7am–11pm; accessible

without steps: 14th St. West 16th St., 23rd St. and West 30th St.;
www.thehighline.org

The High Line was originally an elevated track for freight trains that operated in New York from 1934 to 1980. After decommissioning it was forgotten and neglected.

Plans to demolish it were opposed by a citizens' initiative founded in 1999. It later became one of the many projects in the so-called Plan

A green fairy tale

NYC 2030. The result is a raised promenade, a hybrid of steel and vegetation, at a height of 9m/30ft, with lawns, wild flowers and dense shrubbery, furnished with benches and deck chairs, which passes through the gallery district of Chelsea. It is the work of the architects Diller, Scofidio and Renfro, and the landscape architects Field Operations.

Sights along the High Line

The High Line connects the Meatpacking District in West Chelsea (►Chelsea) with Clinton/Hell's Kitchen. While the first two sections, already completed, run between existing rows of buildings, the third section, now under construction, includes Hudson Yard, a major development area in Manhattan. When this part too has been opened, the park will run 2.33km/1.5mi parallel to the Hudson River.

The conversion of the High Line made industrial wasteland into a hip place and a **focus for new architecture**. Art and design galleries have sprung up along its length, and new hotels, restaurants, cafés, apartments and office buildings have followed. Some of the notable buildings (from south to north) are the new ►Whitney Museum, The Standard Hotel (848 Washington St.; Todd Schliemann from Polshek Partnership Architects), with foundations consisting of concrete pil-

From industrial wasteland to a hip location: the High Line

lars that straddle the High Line; two works by Della Valle Bernheimer: 459 West 18th Ave. and 245 10th Ave.; between them and a little to the west an eye-catching tower by Jean Nouvel (100 11th Avenue) with a multi-layered arrangement of windows that looks like a kaleidoscope. Neil Denari's steel-and-glass HL 23 (515–517 W 23rd St.) has a striking aerodynamic façade; to save space, the 14-storey building leans into the air space above the High Line.

Recommended places to take a break are a German-style beer garden with wooden benches and bratwurst beneath The Standard Hotel (entrance on Washington St.), the Rooftop Bar of the same hotel for a fantastic panoramic view, the cosy wine bar in The Upholstery Store (713 Washington St.) and Pastis, which serves international bistro food opposite the Hotel Gansevoort (9 Ninth Ave.). Chelsea Market (9th–10th Ave., 15th–16th St., ▶p.218) is also worth a visit. There is access to the Hudson River from Chelsea Waterside Park at 22nd and 24th St.

Insider Tip

Jewish Museum

G 8

Location: 1109 Fifth Ave./92nd St. **Admission:** $15
Subway: 86th St. Tel. 1 212 4 23 33 07
❶ Sat–Tue, Fri 11am–5.45pm, **www.thejewishmuseum.org**
Thu until 8pm

Founded in 1904 by the Jewish Theological Seminary of America, the Jewish Museum is located on the Museum Mile, a little north of the ▶Guggenheim Museum. After the ▶Museum of Jewish Heritage it is the second-largest Jewish museum in New York. Since the 1940s it has resided in the former town home of the banker Felix M. Warburg, which was built in 1908 in the neo-Gothic style (expanded in 1993). The museum owns a large collection of Jewish art as well as historic Judaica. 4,000 years of Jewish history are on display in numerous galleries. Cult objects from synagogues and private households of many countries, including Torah scrolls, Shabbat lamps, Kiddush goblets, jewellery and implements from the extensive Harry G. Friedman collection are on display. The main collection includes the Benguiat Collection, which in turn contains objects dating from the Middle Ages to modern times. Café Weisman serves kosher food.

❶ Sat–Tue, Thu 11am–5.45pm, Fri until 4pm

At Park Ave./92nd St., near the Jewish Museum, stands *Night Presence IV*, a sculpture almost 7m/23ft high by Louise Nevelson (1972); nickel and copper have been added to the steel, which accounts for the black-brown colour.

Sculpture by Louise Nevelson

* Lincoln Center for the Performing Arts

—————————————————————— ✳ D 9/10

Location: 65th St./Columbus Ave.
Subway: 66th St.

New York's large centre for the performing arts was built under the directorship of W. K. Harrison, mainly in the 1960s. Events include theatre, opera, ballet and concerts. The building not only gave a neglected area of New York a new face, it also pointed the way for many other cities in the USA, in which similar cultural centres have been built since then.

The building costs of $165 million were raised privately; public funds were used only to buy the land. Different architects designed the individual buildings, which nevertheless appear unified by their stark classical appearance. The stone used for all of the buildings was Italian travertine. The artistic arrangement of the cultural centre was important to the builders and architects, so that a visitor would not only be attracted by the culture on offer and the architecture but also because of the works of art by famous artists. After 50 years of service, the world's first, and still its largest, arts centre urgently needed modernization. A thorough remodelling was carried out up to 2011 by the architects Diller, Scofidio and Renfro, opening up the formerly closed ensemble and adding a restaurant.

❶ Information on the activities in the Lincoln Center: www.lincolncenter.org. Information and registration for guided tours in the »Atrium at Lincoln Center«, tel. 1-212-875-5350.

Lincoln Center Plaza The site is centred on the plaza open to Columbus Ave., around which the three main buildings and side buildings are grouped. The fountain in the middle by Philip Johnson is made of dark marble. In August street theatre and other performances are held here, mostly free of charge.

Avery Fisher Hall The first building to be erected was the one on the north side of the plaza, designed by M. Abramovitz in the form of an ancient Greek temple, and opened in 1962 as the Philharmonic Hall; it was later renamed Avery Fisher Hall and is the home of the New York Philharmonic Orchestra. The concert hall with 2,800 seats and an organ with 5,500 pipes has been renovated several times in order to improve the acoustics. In the foyer, the 5-ton metal sculpture *Orpheus and Apollo* by Richard Lippold is worth seeing. Along with the New York Philharmonic, which gives four concerts a week from mid-September to

Metropolitan Opera House. main building of Lincoln Center

mid-May, famous US and foreign orchestras and soloists are guests in the concert hall. The Philharmonic also gives concerts in the parks in the summer.

Opposite Avery Fisher Hall is the David H. Koch Theater (formerly the **New York State Theater;** Philip Johnson, Richard Foster, 1964), home of the New York City Opera Company and the New York City Ballet. The three-storey foyer of the theatre with 2,700 seats is decorated with a bust of Mahler by Rodin, a mask of Beethoven by Bourdelle and two large statues of women by Elie Nadelmann.

David H. Koch Theater

The main building of the Lincoln Center is on the west side of the plaza: the Met, one of the leading opera houses in the world and home of the Metropolitan Opera Company and the American Ballet Theater. Designed by W. K. Harrison and opened in 1966, the building impresses with its five tall, arched windows, which give a clear view of the richly furnished foyer. The two large murals in the foyer by Marc Chagall, *Les Sources de la Musique* and *Le Triomphe de la Musique*, are protected from the sun in the mornings and unfortunately cannot be seen then. The auditorium seats 3,800 guests; the large crystal chandeliers come from Austria. In the corridors are portraits of famous singers who have performed in the Met. Behind the Met, in Damrosch Park, outdoor concerts are held in summer in the Guggenheim Bandshell.

Metropolitan Opera House (Met)

❶ Tours: Oct–June, 1.5 hrs, reservations tel. 1-212-769-7020 (10am–3pm), www.metoperafamily.org

Reclining Figure West of Avery Fisher Hall there is another courtyard with a large, square decorative basin, in the middle of which stands **Henry Moore's** 6-ton bronze group *Reclining Figure* (1968). The Vivian Beaumont Theater, designed by Eero Saarinen (1965), houses the Lincoln Center Theater (1,140 seats). The little Mitzi E. Newhouse Theater nearby (300 seats), a kind of workshop theatre, is also very successful.

Library & Museum of the Performing Arts This narrow building by Skidmore, Owings & Merrill from 1965 stands between the Metropolitan Opera House and the Vivian Beaumont Theater. The museum archives materials on the history of theatre, film, dance and music, including a collection of sound carriers. The Bruno Walter Auditorium, named after the German conductor, is part of the library and media centre, a branch of the ►New York Public Library in which concerts, exhibitions, lectures, poetry readings and film showings take place. Outside the museum stands **Alexander Calder's** black steel sculpture *Le Guichet* (1972).

❶ Mon, Thu noon–8pm, Tue, Wed, Fri 11am–6pm, Sat 10am–6pm; free admission

Juilliard School of Music Across West 65th St. to the north, New York's most important conservatory is housed in a building conceived by Pietro Belluschi in 1968, which along with a modern stage for opera, lecture halls and practicing rooms includes **Alice Tully Hall** for chamber music and solo concerts. The Walter Reade Film Theater here is the venue for the **New York Film Festival** every year in the early autumn.

American Folk Art Museum In the American Folk Art Museum, the most important museum for naive art in the US, rotating exhibitions show folk art and applied art from America as well as from other countries, including textiles, quilts and also paintings and sculptures from the colonial period until the present day. Visit the main building of the museum on 53rd St., next to the MoMA (►Museum of Modern Art).

❶ 2 Lincoln Square/Columbus Ave., between 65th and 66th St.; Tue–Thu, Sat 10.30am–5.30pm, Fri until 7.30pm, www.folkartmuseum.org

Little Italy

✴ C 16/17

Location: North-west of Chinatown
Subway: Spring St., Prince St.

North-west of ►Chinatown lies Little Italy, one of the smallest ethnic neighbourhoods in Manhattan. Because of the expanding Chinese community the area has almost lost its identity.

Once more than 40,000 people lived in the area between Canal, Houston, Elizabeth and Lafayette St., but today there are only about 5,000, mostly older Italian Americans, the younger generation having long since moved northwards to Nolita (= North of Little Italy). The most important north-south streets are Mulberry and Mott St.; east-west are Grand and Broome Street. There are countless Italian restaurants and cafés on Mulberry St., and Italian shops and men's clubs complete the picture. The centre of the neighbourhood is the **former police station** (240 Center St.), which takes up the whole block between Grand, Center and Broome St. The building was completed in 1909 in the style of a French hôtel de ville and was later converted into a multi-storey luxury apartment building. Little Italy is most worth a visit during the second week in September, during the Festa di San Gennaro (▶p.104); St Januarius is the patron saint of the neighbourhood. At that time there are sales and food stalls along Mulberry St. and other streets in Little Italy.

Lower East Side

✳ **C/D 17/18**

Location: Between First Ave. and East River (downtown)
Subway: Delancey St.

No ethnic neighbourhood in Manhattan is as difficult to pin down as the Lower East Side, where even today there are still some tenements, giant housing blocks where immigrant families were housed from 1880 until 1914. Unlike ▶Harlem, which was originally a residential area for the upper middle class, the Lower East Side was built for the poor and until 1900 was one of the most densely populated areas in New York.

At the beginning of the 20th century the Lower East Side was a purely Jewish area, to which about 500 synagogues and school buildings testify. But only a few still serve their original purpose, among them the elaborately restored **Eldridge Street Synagogue**, built in 1887 by orthodox Ashkenazi Jews from eastern Europe (12–14 Eldridge St., between Division and Canal St.). The Chinese entered the area from Chatham Square across East Broadway (just as in ▶Little Italy), and after the Second World War a new wave of Spanish-speaking immigrants from Puerto Rico, Central and South America washed across the Lower East Side. Since the 1980s young artists and musicians have moved here, so that the neighbourhood today has a very mixed population and a lively infrastructure. In particular the Bargain District, the **area around Orchard St.** with its many fashion, shoe, fur and other shops, attracts shoppers. This area is very busy on

Former Jewish quarter

The life of immigrants in Lower East Side Tenement Museum

Sundays (the Jewish shops are closed on Saturdays) with a bazaar-like atmosphere reminiscent of North Africa or the Middle East. Since the prices are low and the quality often unusually high, many people from Uptown make major purchases here.

Eldridge St. Synagogue Museum: 12–14 Eldridge St., between Division and Canal St., Sun–Thu 10am–4pm

*Lower East Side Tenement Museum The Lower East Side Tenement Museum, at 103 Orchard St. in an apartment building from the turn of the 19th to 20th century, is definitely worth a visit. It shows the life of the immigrants, marked by deprivation in the late 19th century.

❶ Guided tours: daily 10.15am–5pm on request in the visitor center (daily from 10am on), admission $22; tel. 1-212-431-0233, www.tenement.org

✴✴ Manhattan

✦ A–J 1–19

Location: between Hudson River, East River
and Harlem River

At 58 sq km/22 sq mi Manhattan may be New York's smallest borough, but it is the best known and the centre of the city. Along with a few smaller islands, it consists of the 21km/13mi-long and only 3km/2mi-wide island of the same name between the Hudson River, East River and Harlem River, and is home to about 1.5 million people. On this, the most famous island in the world, the main attractions and greatest numbers of hotels, restaurants, musical theatres and jazz clubs are found – this is the reason that, for most visitors, Manhattan is New York.

Native Americans still lived on Manhattan Island at the beginning of the 16th century. Then the explosive development which would create a world metropolis began. Nowhere are the results of such development so clearly seen as here. The city's character is defined by its residents, immigrants or their descendants, who in part still live in certain neighbourhoods like Chinatown or Little Italy; but it is also defined by the stunning skyline of Manhattan, the most beautiful conglomeration of skyscrapers on the smallest area, a unique collection of building styles both historical – classical, Gothic, Art Deco – and modern.

**Skyline

Manhattan is arranged like a chequerboard; twelve consecutively numbered avenues run north to south, more than 200 streets from east to west. The term **downtown** has become a worldwide synonym for »city centre«. Here it refers to the settlement area south of 14th Street where the streets mostly have names and not numbers. Many of the oldest, as well as the most modern and tallest buildings, are at the southern tip. The ▶Financial District is the business heart of the city. Immediately next to it along the Hudson is one of the city's most beautiful green oases. In addition, some neighbourhoods bear witness to the fact that immigrants used to settle in their own ethnic groups. **Midtown**, the busy centre of Manhattan and the heart of New York, stretches between 14th Street and ▶Central Park. Here stand the most imposing skyscrapers, which have shaped the city's appearance since the 1920s, among them the ▶Empire State Building, the ▶Chrysler Building, the MetLife Building and the ▶Rockefeller Center. Midtown is also the Mecca of entertainment with the Theater District on Broadway and ▶Times Square, Carnegie Hall, Radio City Music Hall and Madison Square Garden. **Uptown** is the area east

City planning

Beneath Manhattan

The greatest number of high rises is amassed on the southern edge of Central Park (Midtown) and at the southern tip of Manhattan (Downtown). The main reason for this is the character of the ground.

❶ Secure foundation
IIn Midtown and Downtown bedrock lies just below the surface and provides a secure foundation, allowing the construction of very tall buildings.

❷ Levels 1 & 2
The shafts for electrical and telephone cables, water and steam as well as gas

lie up to 9m/29ft deep (since the blizzard of 1888, 51 million kilometres/31.7 million miles of telephone cable have been buried underground). The subway tunnels run between 9m/29ft and 60m/197ft below ground; the subway station at 63rd St., for example, lies 60m/197ft underground..

❸ Level 3
New York needs 5.3 trillion litres/1.4 trillion gallons of water daily. As of the 1970s a new water tunnel is being blasted through the bedrock about 240m/786ft below ground to supplement the current water pipes.

❹ East River
The river is about 25m/82ft deep.

❺ Road and train tunnels
The road and train tunnels run 50m/164ft below ground, for example the Queens Midtown Tunnel.

and west of Central Park (▶below). North of Central Park lies Upper Manhattan, ▶Harlem where mainly African Americans and Hispanics live and where Columbia University is located.

UPTOWN: UPPER WEST AND UPPER EAST SIDE

The Upper West Side extends from Columbus Circle (near 59th Street; ▶Lincoln Center) to 110th St. and from the Hudson River to Central Park West (subway: 86th St.). Unlike the Upper East Side (▶below) this area is more down-to-earth, and the streets have names. Thus Eighth Ave. becomes Central Park West, Ninth becomes Columbus Ave. and Tenth becomes Amsterdam Avenue. The first building on the Upper West Side was the ▶American Museum of Natural History. From 1880 the building of numerous luxury apartment buildings followed (▶below). Today writers, actors and other artists as well as young families with children live here. In the last years a lively **restaurant scene** has developed here, which is easy to explore on foot. Along Amsterdam and Columbus Ave. between 66th and 86th Street there are countless restaurants and cafés, in which almost every cuisine in the world is represented. At the weekends New Yorkers meet here for their favourite pastime: brunch. Unfortunately there is often a wait for a table. But people don't mind, because they know the rule: where there's a queue, the food is good!

Upper West Side

Here is a list of some striking apartment buildings: **San Remo**, the double-towered apartment building on Central Park West (no. 145 and 146/74th St.), was built in 1929–31 to plans by Emery Roth. Dustin Hoffman, Paul Simon and Diane Keaton are among its famous residents. The architect of the Art Deco **Century Apartments** (25 Central Park West) was Irwin Chanin, 1931. The two-storey apartments of the **Hotel des Artistes** (1 West at 67th St.; George Mort Pollard, 1907) have been home to Isadora Duncan, Rudolph Valentino and Noël Coward. On the ground floor is the equally famous Café des Artistes. The **Beresford Building,** a monumental palazzo at 211 Central Park West (north of ▶American Museum of Natural History), is one of the most posh addresses in Manhattan. The tennis star John McEnroe and the actor Rock Hudson are among the celebrities who used to live here. The trademark of the building, which was designed by Emery Roth, are the three towers on the roof. Varying façades and numerous decorative elements take away some of the building's weightiness. The castle-like **Dakota** was built in 1880–84 as the first private building on the Upper West Side (1 W 72nd St.). The contractor of this luxurious building was Edward S. Clark, Singer sewing-machine heir. He commissioned Henry J. Hardenberg, later the architect of the Plaza Hotel, to produce the plans. The luxu-

Striking apartment buildings

ry suites have accommodated Judy Garland, Lauren Bacall, Leonard Bernstein and John Lennon, who in 1980 was shot outside the house by a mentally disturbed fan. The house has also been immortalized in film: in 1968 Roman Polanski filmed *Rosemary's Baby* here. A detour towards the Hudson River leads to more houses from the late 19th century. The ornate Beaux Arts **Ansonia Hotel** was built in 1899 to plans by Paul E. M. Duboy (2101–2119 Broadway, near 73rd St.). Its two swimming pools, a fountain in which seals played, as well as an internal mail chute system were legendary. Since the rooms in the hotel were especially sound-proof, it was popular among musicians. Among its guests were Arturo Toscanini, Enrico Caruso, Igor Stravinsky and the baseball legend Babe Ruth. A little way north stand the **Apthorp Apartments**, another impressive complex, built in 1906–08 for William Waldorf Astor (2207 Broadway, between 78th and 79th Street). Nearby is Zabar's, the famous New York delicatessen and household goods shop (2245 Broadway).

Insider Tip

Upper East Side

The Upper East Side, between Grand Army Plaza (near 59th Street) and 96th St., between Fifth Ave. and East River, is one of the most

South Manhattan is especially impressive when seen from the water

exclusive neighbourhoods in Manhattan. Here some of the richest residents live in ornate villas, the »Gold Coast Properties« on Fifth and Park Ave.; east of Lexington Ave. the middle classes are also represented. The Upper East Side is known for its exclusive shops and restaurants, and for some of the most important museums on the **Museum Mile**, on Fifth Ave. at Central Park.

** Metropolitan Museum of Art · Met

✳ F/G 8/9

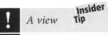

Location: 1000 Fifth Ave./82nd St.
Subway: 86th St.
❶ Sun–Thu 10.30am–5.30pm, Fri, Sat 10.30am–8.45pm
Admission: $25 (incl. The Cloisters)

www.metmuseum.org
Museum Highlight Tour: daily 10.15am–4.30pm

The museum known as the Met for short is among the most important art museums in the world, on a par with the British Museum in London, the Louvre in Paris and the Hermitage in St Petersburg. Its opening exhibition in 1872 with Cypriot antiquities and a small art gallery was modest, but today the museum owns around 3.5 million works of art representing almost all epochs of art history.

The geographically and chronologically arranged exhibits range from the Egyptian Temple of Dendur to the façade of a Wall Street bank. Experts value the collections of Egyptian and medieval art. The European Paintings department shows all famous painters, while the American Wing exhibits the most important American artists as well as authentic period rooms. The sheer quantity of works is overwhelming: it is best to get to know how the museum is organized and then concentrate on what you want to see.

Collection

The museum was opened in 1870 on the initiative of a few private citizens who thought that the time had come for the residents of New York (then almost one million) to have an art museum. The Metropolitan Museum of Art, called the Met for short, was

> **! A view** Insider Tip
>
> **MARCO ⦿ POLO TIP**
>
> Whatever else you leave out in the Met, don't miss the sculpture garden on the roof, which is open from spring until autumn. It has a small selection of contemporary sculpture, refreshments, and above all a stunning view of Central Park and the skyline of Manhattan.

The Met is the greatest museum in the New World

first located on West 14th St., at that time the city centre. A short time later the city gave the museum a piece of land on the eastern edge of the newly created ►Central Park, on which Calvert Vaux, who was also in charge of the design of the park, built a red-brick building in 1880 – which today can only be seen from Central Park itself. The current main building on Fifth Ave. followed in 1879–98. Its middle section is by the architects Richard Morris Hunt and Richard Howland Hunt (father and son), while the two wings are by McKim, Mead & White. The newer additions were built under the guidance of architects Roche, Dinkeloo and partners: the Robert Lehman

Wing (1975), the house of the Temple of Dendur in the Sackler Wing (1978), the American Wing for the American collection (1980), the Michael C. Rockefeller Wing for the ethnological department (1982), the Lila Acheson Wallace Wing for 20th-century art (1987), the Henry R. Kravis Wing (1991) and the Milton Petrie European Sculpture Court, the garden courtyard for European sculpture. Even though the museum has over 300 exhibition rooms it can only display about one quarter of its collection, which grows faster (mainly through gifts) than the space can be expanded. In addition there are regular special exhibitions of high calibre.

Enter the museum at Fifth Ave. via the steps, a popular place to sit outdoors when it is warm. In the so-called Great Hall, the foyer, is the **information area**, where museum maps and brochures are available. On this floor there are also **museum shops** and two cafés (on the lower level a cafeteria and on the upper level a restaurant for museum members only). It is also possible to rent **audio guides** on the highlights of the museums here. To the right of the Great Hall lies the Grace Rainey Rogers Auditorium, where concerts and lectures take place regularly. There is a **Museum Highlight Tour** around the best-known works of art. ▶The Cloisters, which is dedicated to the art of the Middle Ages, is also part of the Met.

Museum service

FIRST FLOOR

The **Egyptian collection** on the first floor is among the most important in the world and spans more than three and a half millennia. The **Temple of Dendur** (1st century BC), built for the Roman Emperor Augustus, had to be removed when the Aswan Dam was built so that it would not be submerged. It came to America as a present from Egypt and was re-erected true to the original in an extension constructed especially for the temple. From the time of the Old Kingdom (3rd–6th dynasty, 2600 until 2160 BC) the **mastaba of the palace administrator Perneb** and the tomb chapel of Prince Raemkai (5th dynasty) are on display. The Middle Kingdom (11th and 12th dynasties, 2040–1785 BC) is represented by grave offerings and painted stele from excavations in Thebes. Showpieces from the New Kingdom (18th–20th dynasty, 1552–1070 BC) are the helmeted head of Ramses II and 14 statues of **Queen Hatshepsut** from the temple Deir el-Bahri near Thebes.

> **!** Don't miss — Insider Tip
>
> MARCO ⊕ POLO TIP
>
> - Temple of Dendur
> - Frank Lloyd Wright's study
> - Astor Court
> - Rembrandt self-portrait in the European painting collection
> - Sculpture garden on the roof

Lloyd Wright and more than 1,000 paintings and sculptures can be seen.

Arts of Africa, Oceania and the Americas   Nelson Rockefeller had this wing built in memory of his son Michael, who died while on an expedition in the South Seas. The **ethnological collection** with several thousand objects shows African, Pacific and American art.

Modern art   The museum annex named after Lila Acheson Wallace, who co-founded the *Reader's Digest* and died in 1984, is dedicated to 20th-century art. The basis is Alfred Stieglitz's collection, which his widow Georgia O'Keeffe gave to the museum. The work of European and American artists is represented on three floors, including Henri Matisse, Vassily Kandinsky and Picasso; also Weber, Stella, Georgia O'Keeffe, Gorky, Hopper, De Kooning and Rothko, Eric Fischl or Matta.

For a special experience, take a look at the **Cantor Roof Sculpture Garden** which displays works by Louise Bourgeois, Reuben Nakian and Louise Nevelson. From here there is a unique view of the Manhattan skyline. In the mezzanine there are photographs and the Paul Klee collection, which was left to the museum in 1984 by the Paris art dealer Heinz Berggruen. Beyond that, applied art is also shown: vases, glasses, jewellery, lamps and furniture.

SECOND FLOOR

European painting   The collection of European painting and sculpture with around 3,000 works from the 13th to the 18th century takes up most of the room on the second floor. Among the attractions are works by Raphael, Titian, Tintoretto, Veronese, Giotto and Tiepolo, as well as by the Dutch masters Hals, Rembrandt, Vermeer and Ruysdael. French painting is represented by Poussin, de La Tour, Watteau and Jacques-Louis David, Flemish and German art by Jan van Eyck, van der Weyden, Hans Memling, Rubens, Lucas Cranach, Dürer and Holbein the Younger, among others. A large proportion of the Spanish paintings come from the private collection of the New York department-store owner Benjamin Altman: El Greco, Zurbarán, Velázquez, Murillo and Goya are especially noteworthy. Hogarth, Reynolds, Gainsborough, Constable and Turner represent English painting.

19th-century European paintings and sculpture   The French art of the 19th century is spread out over 21 exhibition rooms: Classicism, Romanticism and Realism are represented by J. A. D. Ingres, Turner and Delacroix. The focus of the collection is on the **Impressionists and post-Impressionist**s with works by Ed-

Greek sculptures in the Met

ouard Manet and Claude Monet. The Met owns around 100 pictures by Edgar Degas, one of the most comprehensive collections of this master in any museum. In addition Henri Fantin-Latour, van Gogh and Paul Cézanne, as well as Renoir, Seurat, Toulouse-Lautrec, Signac, Bonnard and Gauguin are displayed. In a long sculpture gallery stand sculptures by Auguste Rodin, Bourdelle, Maillol and Jules Dalou.

In ten galleries Islamic art from the 8th to the 19th century is documented. The objects come from Iran, Iraq, Egypt, Turkey, Spain and India. A set of doors from Samarra (8th/9th century) document early Islam, as well as a bowl with ornamental Kufic writing from the 10th century and Fatimid carving from the 10th and 11th centuries. From Persia there is a tiled prayer niche from Isfahan (1354) and a richly illuminated manuscript of the Persian national epic Shah-Nameh (14th century).

Islamic Art

Entering through the new and striking entrance on Madison Avenue, visitors find a variety of rooms and exhibition spaces on Floor 1. The Morgan Stanley Galleries show loan exhibitions of original manuscripts, drawings and rare books, while medieval and Renaissance treasures are found in the Clare Eddy Thaw Gallery. Mr Morgan's Study, where Pierpont Morgan once held meetings – also known as the West Room – contains paintings and sculpture from his original collection of which the most outstanding objects are the famous wedding portraits of Martin Luther and Katharina von Bora by Lucas Cranach the Elder. A Tintoretto (Portrait of a Moor), a painting by Hans Memling (Man with a Carnation), two Bohemian panel paintings from the 15th century and Italian small statuary from the Donatello school are also on display. Another treasure is the Stavelo reliquary, a fine gold and enamel object by Godefroi de Claire (around 1150). The heart of the campus is Gilbert Court, suffused with natural light; adjacent to this the impressive Rotunda leads on to Mr Morgan's Library, packed floor to ceiling with European literature from the 16th through to the 20th century. Since its re-opening, the Morgan has double its previous exhibition space, much of which is on Floor 2, devoted to exhibiting the various collections.

Reading Room The Morgan Shop near the entrance is well-stocked with books, cards and reproductions of exhibits. In the Morgan Dining Room, the menu is inspired by New York's cuisine of the early 20th century. The museum also serves as a research library for the humanities; naturally lit, the Reading Room at the top of the building provides a working environment for scientists and researchers. In the Gilder Lehrman Hall on the lower level, lectures and readings take place.

** Museum of Modern Art · MoMA

✳ E 11

Location: 11 W 53rd St. and W 54th St.
Subway: Fifth Ave./53rd St., Rockefeller Center
🄾 daily 10.30am–5.30pm, Fri until 8pm

Tours only for registered groups, tel. 1-212-708-9685
Admission: $25, Fri from
www.moma.org

The Museum of Modern Art, also called the MoMA or Modern, was founded in 1929 by the three friends: Abby Aldrich Rockefeller, Lillie P. Bliss and Mary Quinn Sullivan, wives and daughters of rich industrial barons. Today it has the largest and most important collection of modern art in the world.

This »canon of art history« includes over 100,000 works of art. The works are exhibited on four floors (the fifth and sixth floors have temporary exhibitions) chronologically from top to bottom: paintings and sculptures from classics of post-Impressionism (on the top floor) to contemporary star artists (second floor), prints and book illustrations (second floor), drawings, an architecture and design collection, a photographic collection from the invention of photography in the early 19th century up to the present (third floor), as well as the largest film collection in the USA.

The first exhibition in November 1929 was in the Rockefellers' town house at today's location, and was opened with 100 French Impressionist paintings (all loaned). The collection grew through generous donations and soon needed its own museum. The building was ded-

History of the museum

A quiet evening at MoMA

Museum of Modern Art

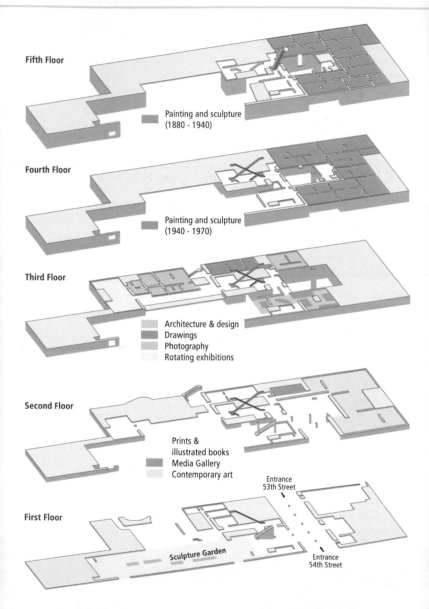

Fifth Floor

Painting and sculpture
(1880 - 1940)

Fourth Floor

Painting and sculpture
(1940 - 1970)

Third Floor

Architecture & design
Drawings
Photography
Rotating exhibitions

Second Floor

Prints &
illustrated books
Media Gallery
Contemporary art

First Floor

Entrance
53th Street

Sculpture Garden

Entrance
54th Street

icated in May 1939 in a modern style considered controversial at the time (English International Style) by the architects Philip Goodwin and Edward Durell Stone and has since then been expanded on numerous occasions. In 1964 the east wing and the sculpture garden were added according to plans by Philip Johnson, in 1984 the Argentine architect Cesar Pelli doubled the exhibition area with an annex. Under his guidance the 44-storey apartment tower was built over the main house (the sale of the luxury apartments financed the continuation of the collection). At the end of 2004 the MoMA was reopened after conversion and expansion by the Japanese architect Yoshio Taniguchi, the façade of black granite, glass and aluminium continuing seamlessly from the old building.

! *Don't miss* **Insider Tip**

MARCO⊕POLO TIP

- Van Gogh, *Starry Night* (1889)
- Monet, *Water lilies* (around 1920)
- Picasso, *Demoiselles d'Avignon* (1907)
- Matisse, *La Danse* (1909)
- Brancusi, *Bird in Space* (1928)
- Gerhard Richter, *18 October 1977*
- Sculpture garden

Museum services

Information on film screenings, special exhibitions and other events is available on tel. 1 212-708-9480. There are two cafés in the museum (on the first and fourth floors), a restaurant, The Modern, in the lobby on the first floor and a well-stocked bookshop.
Restaurant: The Modern, tel. 1 212-333-1220

MoMA Design Stores

The **museum shops** of the MoMA are almost an attraction in themselves (two other MoMA Design Stores can be found opposite the museum.
MoMA Design Stores: 44 W 53 St., and in SoHo, 81 Spring St.: Sat–Thu 9.30am–6.30pm, Fri 9.30am–9pm, www.momastore.org

IN THE MUSEUM

Foyer

The heart of the new building is the 33m/108ft-high foyer (also called ground or first floor), with its two entrances (from 53rd and 54th Street). On the east side a giant window gives a view of the famous **sculpture garden**, which has also been expanded, where Rodin's bronze Balzac stands guard separated from the street by a high aluminium wall. From here, an escalator goes up to the **main gallery** in the second floor. In the middle stands **Barnet Newman's** Broken Obelisk, on the wall Claude Monet's triptych **Water Lilies** (around 1920). From here a connecting passage with pictures by Willem de Kooning, Jasper Johns and Brice Marden leads to the **contemporary gallery**, which is reserved for art from 1970 onwards.

Fifth floor   The following short description of the museum begins on the fifth floor, where European art from 1880 until 1940 is shown. Paul Signac's portrait of the art dealer and collector Félix Fénéon (1890) starts the exhibition off, followed by works by Cézanne (Bathers, around 1885), Van Gogh (Starry Night, 1889; his only oil painting in the museum), Gauguin, Seurat, Rousseau, Matisse (the MoMA has the largest collections of his works, including *La Danse*, 1909, and *Swimming Pool*, 1932), and Picasso, whose **Les Demoiselles d'Avignon** (1907) is considered to be the first Cubist painting ever, as well as Dubuffet, Giacometti and Bacon.

> **?** *Did you know*
>
> **MARCO ◉ POLO INSIGHT**
>
> The »museum of museums« is one of the most expensive in America, with an admission price of $25. There is no admission charge on Fridays after 4pm. Avoid the long queues by reserving tickets in advance at www.moma.org.

Fourth floor   The development of art in the second half of the 20th century, including American art, follows on the floor below, beginning with Pollock's *She-Wolf* (1943), on with Giacometti's *The Palace* at 4 a.m., Jasper John's *Targets*, Warhol, Bruce Nauman, Eva Hesse and Joseph Beuys.

Second floor   Contemporary art or the art scene since 1970 is the theme on the second floor, in the **Contemporary Galleries**, with works by Sigmar Polke, On Kawara, Blinky Palermo, Georg Baselitz, Gordon Matta-Clark, Kippenberger, Jeff Koons, Mathew Barney, Tuymans, Andreas Gursky, Kentridge, Jeff Wall, Rachel Whiteread and Gerhard Richter among others.

Third floor   The third floor is dedicated to architecture and design since the late 19th century. Furniture by Gerrit Rietveld, Red and Blue Chair (1918), and many excellent objects as well as architecture in models and drawings (Mies van der Rohe, Le Corbusier, Frank Lloyd Wright) are displayed. Those interested in videos are bound to find something they like in the Film & Media Gallery. The excellent **photography collection** ranges from the beginnings in 1839, through to classical and contemporary photography.

Sculpture Garden   Among trees, flowers and benches stand numerous works in the Sculpture Garden, including those by Max Ernst, Alexander Calder, Henry Moore, Maillol, Matisse, Nadelman, Nevelson, Picasso's *She-Goat* and one of Auguste Rodin's *The Burghers of Calais*.

Nearby museums   Near the MoMA are two other interesting museums, the **American Folk Art Museum** (▶p.129) and the **Museum of Arts & Design** (▶p.131).

* Neue Galerie

$\times$ G 8

Location: 1048 Fifth Ave./86th St.
Subway: 86th St.-Central Park West
❶ Thu–Mon 11am–6pm

Admission: $20 www.
neuegalerie.org

The gallery in a stylish Beaux Art building exhibits German and Austrian art of the early 20th century.

The Neue Galerie was built in 1914 by the architects of the New York Public Library, Carrère & Hasting, in the best part of New York, and has been lovingly restored. Its name refers to a famous Viennese gallery.

Among the works collected by Roland Lauder, the heir to the famous cosmetic company, and his Austrian friend, the art dealer Serge Sabarsky, are some by Gustav Klimt (including the famous *Adele Bloch-Bauer II*, 1907), Max Beckmann, Oskar Kokoschka, Paul Klee, Vassily Kandinsky and Egon Schiele. In addition there are also very beautiful furnishings and clocks from the Wiener Werkstätten as well as some sculptures. To complement the art, Café Sabarsky (closed Tue) and Café Fledermaus (closed Mon-Wed) exude the charm of a Viennese coffeehouse. The museum shop sells replicas of applied art objects as well as select books on art and literature.

Collection

* New York Botanical Garden

$\times$ **Outside the city centre**

Location: Bronx River Parkway/
Fordham Road, Bronx
Subway: Bedford Park Blvd.,
continue with bus 26; Metro-North
from Grand Central

❶ Apr–Oct Tue–Sun
10am–6pm, Nov–Mar
until 5pm
Admission: $20 (Sun
in May and June $25)
www.nybg.org

New York Botanical Garden, one of the oldest and largest botanical gardens in America, borders on the ▶Bronx Zoo to the north.

It was founded in 1891 and modelled on the Royal Botanical Gardens in Kew Gardens in London. A large part of the 1 sq km/0.4 sq mi park on both sides of the Bronx River is taken up by the Hemlock Forest, which once covered the entire Manhattan Peninsula. Look out for the Enid A. Haupt Conservatory, built in 1901, a greenhouse styled after those in Kew Gardens. In eleven galleries plants from three climatic zones grow, including orchids, ferns, cacti and tropical plants. In the Lorillard Snuff Mill of 1840, where tobacco leaves were once ground up for snuff, there is today a café, whose terrace on the Bronx River is an inviting place to take a rest. The main attractions of the Botanical Garden are the Rose Garden with countless varieties of roses, the Rock Garden (plants from all of the rocky and mountainous regions of the world flourish in a natural ravine of the Bronx River) and the Everett Children's Adventure Garden, where you can experience the growth of plants close up.

✳ **New York Public Library**

✳ **D 12**

Location: 76 Fifth Ave./42nd St.	**Tours:** Tue–Sat 11am
Subway: Grand Central, 42nd St.	and 2pm by appoint-
❶ Mon, Thu–Sat 10am–6pm,Wed	ment
until 8pm, Sun 1pm–5pm	**www.nypl.org**

The New York Public Library, second in the United States only to the Library of Congress in Washington, is despite its name a private institution and was created from the union of three private libraries.

The impressive building in Beaux Arts style was designed by the New York architects Carrère & Hastings, who are also responsible for the home of the ▶Frick Collection, among other buildings.

Today's building was built between 1897 and 1911, on a site that was once a pauper's cemetery and then the Croton Reservoir, which provided the city's drinking water. Half of the cost of $9 million was borne by the steel industrialist Andrew Carnegie. The exterior staircase, which is flanked by two stone lions (by Edward Clark Potter) is a popular lunch spot in the summer for people who work in the surrounding offices.

The giant main hall in the third floor has room for 550 people. Within a few minutes any book listed in the catalogue is made available by an ingenious computer system (total stock of the library: more than eleven million books, including copies of all of the telephone books in the United States, 14 million manuscripts and 10,000 periodicals from 128 countries). The library's special treasures include a Gutenberg Bible, a letter from Christopher Columbus, a copy of Galileo's publications and a handwritten draft of the Declaration of Independence by Thomas Jefferson. The Public Library has 85 branches, including the Library for the Performing Arts in the ▶Lincoln Center, a reference and lending library for the subjects theatre, film, music and dance, as well as the ▶Schomburg Center for the Research in Black Culture.

Behind the library is Bryant Park, named after a publisher of the *New York Evening Post*. In 1854 the first New York World's Fair was held here, and today it is one of the prettiest places in the middle of Manhattan. Along with a café and a restaurant (both immediately behind the library) there is a box office here for all musical and dance events. Statues in the park are dedicated to the journalist and politician William Cullen Bryant (1794–1878, sculptor: Herbert Adams, architect of the pavilion: Thomas Hastings in 1911), Gertrude Stein (1874–1946; Jo Davidson, 1923) and Johann Wolfgang Goethe (1749–1832; Karl Fischer, 1832). In the spring and autumn fashion shows are held here, and in the summer the **Bryant Park Film Festival.**

 *Bryant Park

❶ Bryant Park Film Festival , 8pm or 9pm in summer, tel. 1 212-768-4242, www.bryantpark.org

A fine place to read is the Beaux Arts hall of the Public Library

Around Bryant Park

On the south side of Bryant Park is the American Standard Building (40 West 40th St.), which was built in 1924 by Raymond Hood, the architect of the ►Rockefeller Center. On the north side towers the 192m/630ft-high, 50-storey **Grace Building** (1114 Ave. of the Americas). It was built in 1974 by Skidmore, Owings & Merrill, who tried here – as they did with a second building at 9 West 57th St. – to retract the upper floors by means of a curved form and thus to achieve a slender silhouette. At the corner of West 43rd St. and ►Fifth Ave. there is a branch of the Chase Manhattan Bank (1954 by Skidmore, Owings & Merrill), one of the first glass buildings in New York.

* Park Avenue

✶ D–J 5–15

Location: From Union Square northwards

Park Avenue, together with ►Fifth Ave., is one of Manhattan's most expensive streets. It starts at Union Square and runs in a straight line northwards. In the 19th century the railway tracks of the private New York Central ran along here. From 1903 these were placed underground and a broad boulevard was constructed, which was built upon bit by bit. Some of the skyscrapers have made architectural history.

The following descriptions refer to the part of the avenue between 42nd St. and 59th Street. The **starting point** is ►Grand Central Terminal (42nd St. / Park Ave.).

MetLife Building

The 59-storey former Pan Am Building was built in 1963 above the Grand Central Terminal (200 Park Ave.). Many architecture critics are of the opinion that the collaboration between Emery Roth, Pietro Belluschi and Walter Gropius produced the ugliest skyscraper in Manhattan. The building already suffered criticism while it was being built because it blocked the view of Park Ave., which until then had been unobstructed. The building was sold in 1980 by Pan Am to the insurance company Metropolitan Life. The large foyer has works of art by Josef Albers, György Kepes and Richard Lippold.

Helmsley Building

Beyond 45th Street and in the shadow of the MetLife Building stands the Helmsley Building, built in 1929 by Warren & Whetmore (230 Park Ave.); it was originally the seat of the New York Central Railroad Company, whose main railway station was the adjacent Central Terminal.

Controversial architecture: the MetLife Building in Park Avenue

Continuing along Park Ave. towards Central Park, on the left (no. 270, between E 47th and 48th St.) is the 53-storey building for the Union Carbide Company by Skidmore, Owings & Merrill (1960). Today it houses the headquarters of the Chase Manhattan Corporation. The silver-grey 50-storey tower opposite (no. 277) was built in 1962 and designed by Emery Roth & Sons.

270 and 277 Park Avenue

The world-famous hotel stands on the block between 49th and 50th Street. It was built in 1931 to plans by Schultze and Weaver and replaced the original Waldorf Astoria Hotel, which stood on the grounds of the Empire State Building until it was demolished (►MARCO POLO Insight p.66).

Waldorf Astoria

A block further on is St Bartholomew's Church (109 East 50th St.), designed in 1919 by Bertram Goodhue in the Byzantine style. Its Romanesque entrance hall is from the church built in 1903 by McKim, Mead & White (Madison Ave./44. St.). The bronze reliefs on the portal are by A. O'Connor. The altar inside the church is by Lee Lawrie, who became famous for the sculptures in the ►Rockefeller Center.
❶ Daily until dark; subway: 51st St., Lexington Ave.

St Bartholomew's Church

Immediately adjacent is the General Electric Building (570 Lexington Ave.), whose tip is literally and metaphorically a pinnacle of Art Deco style. The 51-storey building (1931) was designed by Cross & Cross for the Radio Corporation of America (RCA Victor), which moved into the ▶Rockefeller Center in 1931. The lobby is also worth seeing.

*General Electric Building

The black metal, 160m/525ft-high, 38-storey building with bronze-coloured windows, the headquarters of the whisky company, was built in 1958 and planned by Ludwig Mies van der Rohe and Philip Johnson (375 Park Ave./53rd St.). It is the only Mies van der Rohe building in New York and documents the International Style, which was developed in the USA. The architect was able to build here what he had proposed in 1920 in his famous design for Friedrichstrasse in Berlin. The interior was designed by Philip Johnson, among others, with works by Picasso, Rodin and Chagall. In the Four Seasons, the Seagram has one of the best restaurants of the city.

Seagram Building

Four Seasons: tel. 1 212-754 9494, www.fourseasonsrestaurant.com

Opposite the Seagram Building is the Racquet and Tennis Club, built in 1918 in the neo-Renaissance style (McKim, Mead & White; 370 Park Ave., between E 52nd and E 53rd Street). Immediately behind the old tennis club is the **Park Avenue Plaza** (Skidmore, Owings & Merrill, 1981). Its 44 storeys rise over a glazed plaza with various shops.

Racquet and Tennis Club

Architectural history was made by the Lever House (390 Park Ave., between E 53rd and E 54th St.), though it appears insignificant today sandwiched between giant skyscrapers. It was built in 1952 as the administrative headquarters of the food company Lever Brothers and designed by Skidmore, Owings & Merrill. The 21-storey tower above a two-storey horizontal block was New York's first glass and steel high-rise. Temporary exhibitions are held in the lobby.

Lever House

A detour leads to the Citicorp Center (153 East 53rd St., corner of Lexington Ave.), the white high-rise giant (279m/915ft, 46 storeys) with the angled roof. The original plan was for solar panels to supply the building with heat from here, but the construction proved to be insufficient for this purpose. The aluminium tower rests on four 38m/125ft pillars, which stand in the middle of each of the four sides. The skyscraper was completed in 1978, designed by Hugh Stubbins and is considered to be a symbol of the reinvigoration of the city after the economic crisis. In order to gain permission to build that high, a public plaza had to be built in the interior of the site with connections to public transport; there are many shops and cafés here.

Citicorp Center

The Citicorp Center is recognized by its angled roof

St Peter's Church	St Peter's sold the land to the Citicorp Bank on the condition that they build a new church. Today the church on the north-west corner is practically crushed by the high-rise. The artist Louise Nevelson designed the interior; the Erol Beker Chapel is especially worth a visit.
*885th Third Lipstick	In the shadows of the Citicorp Center, on the corner of Third Ave. and 53rd St., stands an office building built in 1986 by Philip Johnson and John Burgee. Because of its oval floor plan it is called »the lipstick«, and its critics also call it »the disposable lighter«. In comparison to other high-rise giants it seems insignificant, but it compensates for any lack of height through its striking shape and the high-quality materials used.
Central Synagogue	Cross 55th Street to get back to Park Avenue and pass the Central Synagogue (architect: Henry Fernbach), which was built in 1870 and is the oldest synagogue in New York in uninterrupted use.
Mercedes Benz showroom	The Mercedes Benz Showroom was designed by Frank Lloyd Wright in 1953. ● 430 Park Ave./57th. St.

Queens

—————————— ✳ **Outside the city centre**

Location: East part of Manhattan, north-east of Brooklyn

At 283 sq km/109 sq mi Queens is the largest New York borough and lies on Long Island north-east of Brooklyn. Most visitors have at least seen it in passing, on the bus or taxi ride to Manhattan, since two of the three large New York airports are here, John F. Kennedy International and LaGuardia Airport.

Did you know

Here is the key to addresses in Queens, which often have 2 or 3 numbers: 36-01 43rd Ave. means: the Museum for African Art is on 43rd Avenue, near the intersection with 36th Street.

Queens was rather insignificant until the middle of the 19th century. That changed when it was incorporated into New York in 1898 and after the building of the Queensboro Bridge in 1909. Today, 2 million people live here, and they are said to speak 120 different languages and dialects. Astoria or »Little Athens« is the largest Greek community outside Greece, Flushing proudly calls itself »Little Seoul« (but has New York's second-largest chinatown too), and there is

Queens

NASSAU

Little Neck Bay

Rikers Island

East River

MANHATTAN

Triborough Bridge

East River Drive

Bronx Whitestone Bridge

Throgs Necks Bridge

Cross Island Parkway

495

Steinway Piano Factory

LaGuardia Airport

278

Dimars Blvd.

Astoria Blvd.

Grand Central Parkway

678

Willets Pt.

Bayside Ave.

Clearview Expressway

Belt Blvd.

Northern Boulevard

Socrates Sculpture Park

★Isamu Noguchi Garden Museum

Queensboro Bridge

Vernon Blvd.

21st Street

Broadway

Museum of the Moving Image

Northern Blvd.

Flushing Town Hall

Shea Stadium

Bowne House

Queens Historical Society

Northern Boulevard

Queens County Farm Museum

Alley Park

Queens-Midtown Tunnel

Museum of African Art

Louis Armstrong House

Flushing Meadows

Corona Park

Roosevelt Ave.

Hall of Science

Queens Museum

Queens Botanical Garden

Kissena Park

Long Island Expressway

73rd Ave.

Cunningham Park

Union Tnpk.

P.S.1 Contemporary Art Center

Greenpoint

278

Queens Expwy.

Long Island Expressway

495

Queens Boulevard

Colden Center

Van Wyck Expressway

Jewel Ave.

Main St.

Grand Central Parkway

295

East River

Harborhoft Avenue

Elliott Avenue

678

Grand Central Parkway

Pilhsite Avenue

Belmont Park Race Track

Brooklyn Avenue

Williamsburg Bridge

Grand Avenue

Metropolitan Avenue

Westside Tennis Club

Hillside Ave.

Jamaica Avenue

Francis Lewis Blvd.

Laurelton Parkway

Flushing Avenue

Myrtle Avenue

Central Avenue

Myrtle Avenue

Jamaica Center for Arts & Learning

Van Wyck

Guy Brewer Boulevard

Springfield Boulevard

Montefiore Cemetery

Bedford Avenue

Bushwick Avenue

Cooper Street

Forest Park

Jackie Robinson Parkway

Jamaica Avenue

Lefferts Blvd.

Sutphin Blvd.

Merrick Boulevard

Lafayette Avenue

Broadway

Fulton Street

Atlantic Avenue

Liberty

Linden Boulevard

Rockaway Boulevard

BROOKLYN

Eastern Parkway

Liberty Avenue

Conduit Boulevard

Rockaway Boulevard

Aqueduct Race Track

Shure Parkway (Belt Parkway)

Empire Blvd.

Linden Boulevard

Nassau Expressway

Linden Blvd.

Utica Avenue

Kings Highway

Remsen Avenue

Rockaway Parkway

Avenue

Shore Parkway (Belt Parkway)

Cross Bay Boulevard

678

Brookville Park

Rockaway Boulevard

Coney Island Avenue

Ocean Avenue

Nostrand Avenue

Flatbush Avenue

Flatlands

John F. Kennedy International Airport

Avenue P

Highway

Avenue U

Marine Park

Flatbush Avenue

Floyd Bennett Field

★Jamaica Bay Wildlife Refuge Center

Shore Parkway (Belt Parkway)

Marine Parkway Bridge

Beach Channel Drive

Rockaway Fwy.

Rockaway Inlet

Beach

Rockaway Beach Boulevard

Rockaway Beach

Rockaway Point Blvd.

Atlantic Ocean

1 mi
2 km

©BAEDEKER

also a Hindu temple here, as well as a large Puerto Rican quarter and a significant Dominican community. In the 1920s and 1930s Queens was an important film metropolis, to which the American Museum of the Moving Image bears witness. Beyond that there is little worth seeing, unless you are interested in modern art, the location of the 1864 World's Fair or the tennis stadium in Flushing Meadows.

SIGHTSEEING IN QUEENS

*Isamu Noguchi Garden Museum The building is as unusual as the work of the artist Isamu Noguchi (1904–88), who is rooted in American and Japanese culture. In a former studio of the artist are sculptures, stage decorations (for Martha Graham and George Balanchine among others), furniture and other designs; adjoining are a museum shop and a cafeteria. A shuttle bus runs from Manhattan (from the Asia Society, Park Ave. and 70th St.) to the museum at weekends. One block north is the **Socrates Sculpture Park**. The former industrial area along the East River, where works by freelance artists can be seen, offers a fine view of Roosevelt Island and the Manhattan skyline

MARCO POLO TIP

Insider Tip
Summer parties at P. S. 1

In the summer, young architects and designers transform the forecourt of P. S. 1 into an abstract playground – an ideal atmosphere for weekend dance parties. In the past years a young crowd has been attracted by a grove of hammocks, water sprayers and a huge sandpit which served as a dance floor.

Isamu Noguchi Garden Museum: 9-01 33rd Road, between Vernon Blvd. and 10th St.; Wed–Fri 10am–5pm, Sat, Sun 11am–6pm; admission $10; tel. 718-204-7088, www. noguchi.org

Socrates Sculpture Park: daily from 10am; Broadway/near Vernon Blvd.; www.socratessculpturepark .org

MoMA P. S. 1 After renovation and expansion, the latest from the art scene is presented at the P. S. 1 Contemporary Art Center, now part of ▶MoMA. The former elementary school (P. S. 1 is short for Public School 1) from 1890, together with the New Museum of Contemporary Art, have filled a gap in the city art scene.

❶ 22-25 Jackson Ave./46th Ave.; subway: 23rd St./Ely Ave., Long Island City/ Court House Square, 45th Rd./Court House Square; Thu–Mon noon–6pm; admission §10; www.ps1.org, tel. 1 718-784-2084

American Museum of the Moving Image In 1920 Paramount Pictures opened in Queens what was then the biggest film studio in the city, Astoria Studios, where famous actors like the Marx Brothers, W. C. Fields, Gary Cooper and Gloria Swanson worked. The depression of the 1930s led to the film industry's move to Hollywood. Astoria Studios then filmed newsreels and training films for the army, eventually standing empty. In the 1980s Astoria Motion Picture and Television Foundation took over the complex. Since then it has been used by some independent producers. Francis Ford Coppola's *Cotton Club* and Woody Allen's *Radio Days* were produced here. In 1988 the film museum was opened in one of the studio buildings (architects: Gwathmey & Siegel). The film props there include the chariot that Charlton Heston rode in *Ben Hur* and costumes from *Star Wars*. In addition, films are shown regularly.

❶ 35th Ave. / 36th St., subway: Steinway St.; Tue, Thu 10.30am–5pm, Fri until 8pm, Sat, Sun 11.30am–7pm; admission $12; www.movingimage.us

Astoria

After a visit to the film museum it is pleasant to stroll through Astoria or »Little Athens«, as the former Greek neighbourhood is called. Though today the area is more multi-cultural, Greek restaurants, shops and cafés can still be found on Steinway Street and 30th Avenue.

Steinway pianos

The subway station Steinway St. is named after Henry Steinweg, originally from Germany, who opened his first piano factory in 1870 in Long Island City. The famous Steinway pianos are still produced here today.

❶ 1 Steinway Place, between 38th St. and 19th Ave.www.steinway.com

P. S. 1 presents the latest from the art scene

A Melting Pot of Nations

Mass immigration has led to a remarkable diversity of ethnic groups. Many of them live in their own neighbourhood, for example the Chinese in Chinatown, Poles and Ukrainians in the East Village and Arabs in Brooklyn.

▶ **Who lives where?**

Born in the USA:

- Whites
- Afro-Americans
- Hispanics / Latinos
- Asians

Born abroad:

- Central and South America
- Caribbean
- Asia
- Eastern Europe

BRONX

MANHATTAN

QUEENS

BROOKLYN

STATEN ISLAND

©BAEDEKER

▶ **Use of languages in per cent**

	New York	USA
1. English:	54.3	79.9
2. Spanish:	24.2	12.5
3. Indo-Europ.:	11.9	3.7
4. Asiatisc:	7.3	3.1
5. Other:	2.4	0.8

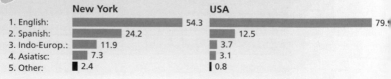

▶ **Continued attractiveness to immigrants**
People who received residence rights (million)

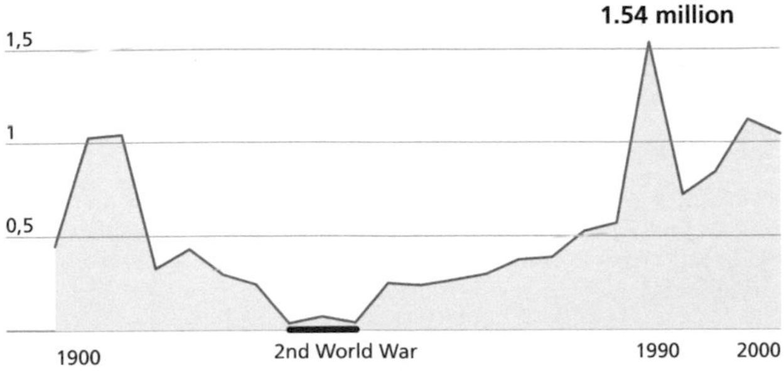

1.54 million

1,5	
1	
0,5	

1900   2nd World War   1990   2000

▶ **How many languages are spoken in NY?**
It is said that approx. 200 languages are spoken in New York. They include:

Almost 4.2 million New Yorkers speak English badly or not at all.

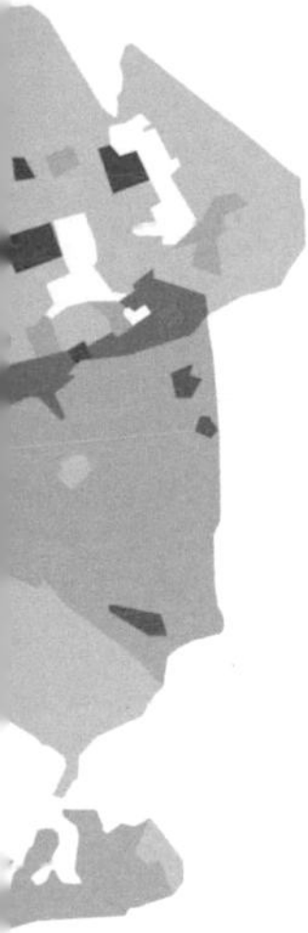

English Spanish Portuguese French Rhaeto-Romance German Hebrew Polish Italian Chamorro Yiddish Aramaic

▶ **Ethnic breakdown**

Whites 33.3%	Hispanics / Latinos 28.6%	Afro-Americans 25.5%	Asian 12.7%

Other 0.8%

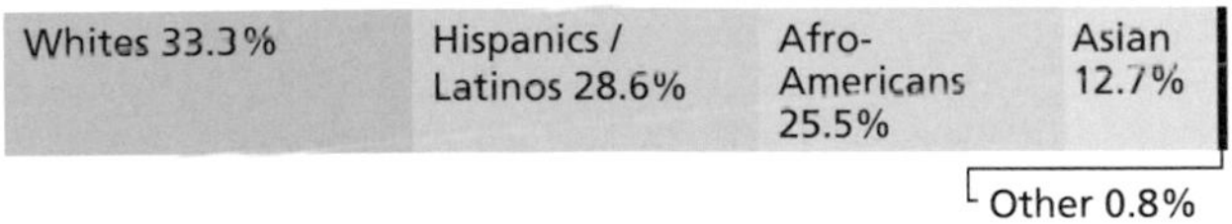

▶ **Religious diversity ...**
... is a feature of New York society

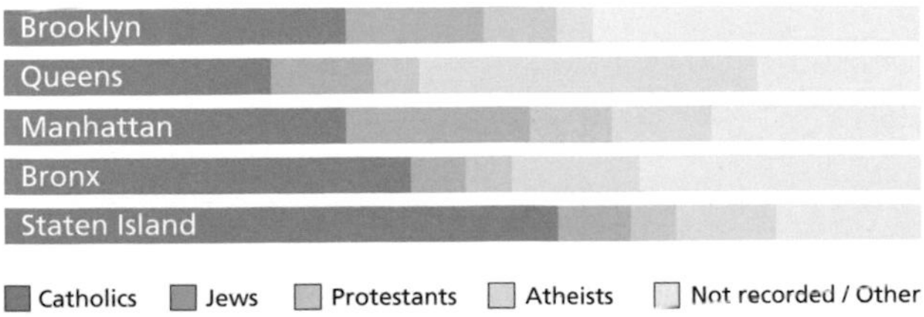

Brooklyn
Queens
Manhattan
Bronx
Staten Island

■ Catholics ■ Jews ■ Protestants ■ Atheists ☐ Not recorded / Other

»Unisphere« in Flushing Meadows

Flushing Meadows Corona Park Two World's Fairs were held on the grounds of Flushing Meadows Park in 1939–40 and 1964. The Unisphere, a 42m/138ft-high massive steel globe, remains from this time. Flushing Meadows is home to various institutions, including the National Tennis Center, where the famous U.S. Open is held every year, the 45,000 seat Citi Stadium, home of the famous baseball team the **New York Mets**, the Louis Armstrong Stadium (18,000 seats), golf courses, an ice skating rink and much more.

❶ In the north of Queens, between Roosevelt Ave., Long Island Expressway, Grand Central Parkway and Van Eyck Expressway; subway: Mets Willets Point; information on National Tennis Center: www.usopen.org

Queens Museum of Art The Queens Museum of Art gives an overview of the famous New York skyline with its model of all five boroughs at a scale of 1:1200. The model was made for the last World's Fair. The museum is in the New York City Building.

❶ Flushing Meadows Corona Park, 49th Ave., near 111th St.; subway: 111th St.; Wed–Sun noon–6pm, admission $8; www.queensmuseum.org

The New York Hall of Science, a hands-on museum of science and technology is also in the park.

New York Hall of Science

❶ Mon–Fri 9.30am– 5pm, Sun 10am–6pm; admission $11; www.nysci.org

Jazz legend Louis Armstrong (1901–71) lived in Corona with his wife Lucille from 1943 until his death. The house is furnished with original furniture and many souvenirs and is open to the public.

Louis Armstrong House

❶ 34-56 107 St., between 34th and 37th Ave.; subway: 103rd St./Corona Plaza; Tue–Fri 10am–5pm, Sat, Sun noon–5pm; admission $10; tel. 718-478-8274, www.satchmo.net

The Quaker John Bowne's house dating from 1661 is one of the oldest buildings in the city, today a museum. The furnishings (both furniture and utensils) for the most part go back to the 17th and 18th centuries.

Bowne House

❶ 37-01 Bowne St., Flushing; subway: Main St., currently closed for renovations; www.bownehouse.org

The nature reserve Jamaica Bay Wildlife Refuge lies south of John F. Kennedy Airport and can be reached by subway directly from Manhattan. It is also known as Birdland, a place for bird-lovers all year round. More than 300 varieties of birds live in the bay, which is protected from the Atlantic by the Rockaway Beach peninsula. An almost 3km/1.8mi-long nature trail winds through marshes and high ground. There are beautiful views from here, including views of Manhattan. The only village, Broad Channel, lies along Cross Bay Boulevard.

*Jamaica Bay Wildlife Refuge Center

❶ Subway: Broad Channel, from here about a 20-min walk to the visitor centre; daily 8.30am–5pm; guided drives and hikes are also offered, tel. 1 718-318-4340, www.nyharborparks.org

** **Rockefeller Center**

E 11

Location: Fifth Ave., between 47th and 52nd St.	**Tel.** 1 212-698-2000
Subway: Rockefeller Center	**Admission:** $15
Tours: daily from 10am	**www.rockefellercenter.com**

The Rockefeller Center is a complex of 19 skyscrapers between Fifth Ave. and the Avenue of the Americas. It was built by the richest citizen of America, John D. Rockefeller Jr., whom New York also has to thank for Rockefeller University, Fort Tryon Park with ▶The Cloisters, and the UN headquarters (▶United Nations), for which he donated the land.

City in the
city

The 4ha/9.8ac plot originally belonged to Columbia University, from which John D. Rockefeller bought it in 1928. Between 1931 and 1940, during the worst depression years, 228 houses had to be torn down first so that, with its 12 buildings, the largest private business and entertainment complex in the world could be built. In 1932 the RCA Building (today GE Building) was opened. A team of seven architects was responsible for the plans, including Wallace K. Harrison, who designed the United Nations Headquarters and the Lincoln Center. From 1957 a second building phase and a further five buildings followed. Alongside countless offices, which see 250,000 people enter and leave daily, the Rockefeller Center has 30 restaurants, dozens of shops on ground level and, in the underground passages, television studios, exhibition rooms and in the winter an **ice rink**. The gener-

Rockefeller Center, a city in the city

ously sized plazas are virtually a museum featuring frescos, sculptures and reliefs. More than two dozen artists are represented with over 100 works. At the end of 1989 the Japanese Mitsubishi Estate Company bought 51% of the Rockefeller Center from the 88 Rockefeller heirs. Since 2001 the entire complex has belonged to the real estate company Tishman Speyer, which had to raise $1.85 billion to pay for it. In the meantime the value has probably risen in the face of increasing real estate prices in Manhattan.

The following description of the Rockefeller Center begins at the entrance to the pedestrian walkway Channel Gardens (Fifth Ave., opposite ►St Patrick's Cathedral). To the right and left are two seven-storey buildings, on the right the British Empire Building (1932), on the left the Maison Française (1933). Between these the 70m/75yd-long promenade **Channel Gardens** (named after the English Channel) leads to the Lower Plaza, which is used as a skating rink in the winter and as a terrace for cafés and restaurants in the summer. During the Christmas season the most impressive Christmas tree in the USA stands here. A marble tablet quotes John D. Rockefeller's credo. The gilded statue of **Prometheus** (1934, Paul Maship), who according to legend brought fire to humankind, stands in front of the west wall of the sunken garden. The flags of the countries accredited by the UN wave around the plaza.

> **? MARCO ● POLO INSIGHT**
>
> *Did you know*
>
> Construction workers set up the giant Christmas tree at the Rockefeller Center for the first time in 1931. They wanted to make a positive statement in economically difficult times – a tradition that continues to this day.

GE Building

Immediately behind the sunken garden is the main building of the Rockefeller Center, the 250m/820ft-high GE Building (General Electric Building; until 1990 the RCA Building standing for Radio Corporation of America). It houses the studios of the radio and television company NBC, which are open to the public (tel. 1 212-664-3700). Above the main entrance (30 Rockefeller Plaza) is the relief *Allegory of Wisdom and Knowledge* by the American sculptor Lee Lawrie. The main hall is decorated with murals by José M. Sert. Originally a fresco by the Mexican Diego Rivera was here, which Rockefeller however found to be too political. On the 65th floor the restaurant **Rainbow Room** has re-openend. On the 70th floor, 260m/852ft high, the **visitor's platform** known as ****Top of the Rock** gives a breathtaking view of the city's skyline. Above all, it is impressive to see the Empire State Building amongst the skyscrapers.

❶ Entrance 50th St., between Fifth and Sixth Ave.; daily 8am–midnight; reservation for a viewing time: www.topoftherocknyc.com, tel. 1 212-698-2000; admission $25

*Radio City Music Hall	To the north-west, behind the GE Building, is Radio City Music Hall. It was built in 1930 by Edward Durrell Stone in Art Deco style and houses a theatre auditorium with 6,200 seats in which, since film showings ceased, sporadic shows and appearances by popular stars and rock groups take place. The elaborately interior of the music hall can be viewed outside show times.

❶ 1260 Ave. of the Americas; tours: daily 11am–3pm,; admission $25; tel. 1 212-247-4777, www.radiocity.com

Detour to Sixth Avenue

For those interested in architecture, a short detour from Radio City Music Hall to Sixth Ave., also called Ave. of the Americas, is worthwhile. At the corner of 47th Street stands the Celanese Building, which was built in 1973 by Harrison, Abramovitz & Harris. This office also designed the next two skyscrapers, the McGraw Hill Building and the 1251 Avenue of the Americas Building, which is named after its address today (originally Exxon Building).

In front of the McGraw Hill Building (no. 1221) is a sundial, *Sun Triangle* (Athelstan Spilhaus, 1973). The point of the steel triangle shows the sun's position at the solstices and the equinoxes.

The curves of the blue-painted steel *Cubed Curve* (William Crovello, 1971) provide an effective counterpoint to the straight lines of the Time & Life Building behind it, built in 1959 (1271 Sixth Ave.).

Equitable Center

Between 51st and 52nd St. stretches the Equitable Center (1285 Sixth Ave. to 787 Seventh Ave.). The focus is the 54-storey Equitable Tower (Edward Larrabee Barnes, 1985). In its lobby (entrance from Seventh Ave.) Thomas Hart Benton's fresco cycle *America Today* (1930) can be seen, depicting everyday life in America during the boom of the 1920s. The atrium is dominated by Roy Lichtenstein's *Mural with Blue Brushstroke* (1984–85). The Equitable Gallery is also in the atrium, in which there are temporary exhibitions of modern art.

CBS Building

The CBS Building, built in 1965, is home to one of America's three media giants (Columbia Broadcasting System). The architect was the Finnish Eero Saarinen (1910–61), whose only high-rise is also called »Black Rock«. The E. F. Hutton Building rises up behind the CBS Building (31 W 52nd St.; Roche, Dinkeloo and Assocs., 1987). The small plaza between the two buildings is dominated by the sculpture *Lapstrake* by Jesús Bautista Moroles (1987).

At the end of 1989 on Sixth Ave., between 52nd and 53rd Street, a work by the pop artist Jim Dine, *Looking on the Avenue*, has been erected – three bronze sculptures, about 4, 6 and 7.5m high (13, 19 and 25ft), portraying variations on the famous Venus de Milo, not only without an arm, but also without a head.

✶✶ St Patrick's Cathedral

✦ E 11/12

Location: Fifth Ave., between 50th and 51st St.
Subway: 47–50th St./Rockefeller

Center, Fifth Ave./53rd St.
❶ Daily 6.30am–8.45pm

The Roman Catholic cathedral, seat of the archbishop, is New York's finest Gothic Revival building and the largest cathedral in the United States.

It was built of light-coloured marble between 1858 and 1888 to plans by James Rentwick in High Gothic style, and in 1910 dedicated to the Irish patron saint. At that time the Roman Catholic population of the city numbered 200,000, most of them Irish.

19th-century High Gothic style: St Patrick's Cathedral

The Lady Chapel on the east side was added in 1905. The cathedral, with two slender towers each 101m/331ft high and a rose above the main portal which has a diameter of 8m/26ft, is especially beautiful in the evening when illuminated. The dignified interior is 93m/102yd long and 38m/42yd at its widest and has around 2,500 seats. Massive marble columns support the dome. Among the rich furnishings, the stained glass windows, the main altar crowned with a canopy (dedicated in 1942) and the numerous side altars are especially striking; also look out for the figure of Elizabeth Ann Seton (1774–1821), who in 1975 became the first woman from the USA raised to sainthood, and is the founder of the order of the Sisters of Charity. The main organ has over 9,000 pipes.

Olympic Tower   The Olympic Tower (▶Fifth Avenue) built in 1976 stands next to the cathedral. East of the cathedral on both sides of the choir are the neo-Gothic rectory and the residence of the archbishop of New York (both also built by J. Rentwick in 1880).

*Villard Houses   Immediately opposite the rectory are the three-storey Villard Houses (457 Madison Ave.), which were built in 1884 according to plans by McKim, Mead & White for Henry Villard, a Bavarian who emigrated to the USA in 1860 under the name of Heinrich Hilgard and quickly attained wealth and respect as the publisher of the *New York Post* newspaper. The houses imitate the Palazzo della Cancelleria in Rome and are among the most effective neo-Renaissance buildings in New York. In the 1970s they were scheduled for demolition because the value of the land had grown enormously. The solution was to sell the air rights to the Helmsley Group, which built the 50-storey Palace Hotel instead. Today the south wing of the Villard Houses is the elegant hotel entrance.

* St Paul's Chapel

✦ **B 18**

Location: 209 Broadway, between Fulton and Vesey St.
Subway: Fulton St. and Broadway/Nassau St.

❶ Mon–Sat 10am–6pm
Sun 9am–4pm
www.saintpaulschapel.org

Fulton Street leads from the East River to the oldest church in Manhattan.

Built in 1764–66, it is not the oldest building in New York, but of those that have survived from the 17th and 18th centuries it is the only public building that has not been changed substantially. The architectural model was probably St Martin-in-the-Fields in London, whose architect James Gibb was also the teacher of Thomas McBean, who built the New York church. The tower and veranda were completed in 1796. The chair marked with a »G« on the left of the elaborate interior was used by George Washington. The exhibition Unwavering Spirit is a reminder of the days after the attack on the nearby World Trade Center in 2001, when workers from the Ground Zero site used the church.

The small cemetery is an oasis of quiet especially in the spring and autumn; a monument is dedicated to the actor George F. Cooke. ►City Hall and the Woolworth Building (►City Hall & Civic Center) are nearby.

Cemetery

✴ **SoHo**

——————————————————— ✴ **B/C 16/17**

Location: Between Ave. of the Americas, Broadway, Houston and Canal St.

Subway: Spring St., Bleecker St.

SoHo, an acronym for South of Houston, has of course nothing to do with the neighbourhood in London. It is bordered by Houston St. in the north, West Broadway (SoHo's main street) in the west, Canal St. in the south and Broadway in the east,

Only 40 years ago, this neighbourhood was a sleepy collection of warehouses and small factories. Then artists discovered it and set up their studios and living quarters in the large open industrial spaces, many of which were then turned into sleek and expensive lofts. Over time, galleries, interesting shops, restaurants, jazz and rock joints sprang up all around. Rising rents and property prices were the result, driving most artists to more affordable neighbourhoods, such as West Chelsea. SoHo is the best example of life after gentrification. Once a colourful hub for artists, writers and intellectuals, it is now largely an upscale shopping district with trendy designer boutiques. Admittedly, the streets and beautiful buildings are very inviting, especially on weekends when the streets buzz with activity.

Nowhere else in America is there such a continuous ensemble of so-called cast-iron houses as in SoHo (next to West Broadway particularly in Greene St., and also in Broome St.). These buildings are more than 100 years old. The use of cast iron made it possible to reproduce columns, arches, gates and other building parts, even whole façades, very cheaply: for the first time in the history of building, pre-fabri-

»Cast Iron«

Little Singer Building is a good example for cast iron

cated, standardized building parts could be used. This led to an unforeseen variety of details which can still be admired today, including bizarre fire escape ladders. The elaborate decorations on the buildings belie the fact that SoHo was an area given over mainly to industrial production. The façades have unusually large windows for the time, through which light can reach the workplaces deep inside the building, and the elevated ramps on the streets make deliveries easier. A unique feature of these buildings are the cast-iron floor plates with hundreds of glass lenses through which daylight could reach the lower floors as well. These can still be seen in many places in SoHo. In the 1960s the houses were almost demolished to make way for a street. The plan was stopped at the last moment. Today all of SoHo is protected heritage.

A stroll through SoHo, which neighbours ►Greenwich Village to the south, reveals galleries, boutiques and other interesting or way-out shops, as well as restaurants and bars. The most striking buildings include the **Singer Building** (561–563 Broadway), built in 1904 by Ernest Flagg as the offices and warehouse of the sewing machine company of the same name, the neighbouring house with its Italian Renaissance style (565 Broadway) and the **Haughwout Building** (488 Broadway), built in 1857. At the corner of Prince and Greene St. a mural by Richard Haas in trompe l'oeil technique from 1970 imilates the cast-iron façade. Those interested in the history of firefighting will enjoy dropping in at the **NYC Fire Museum**, a fire station built in 1904 in the Beaux Arts style (▶p.135).

Sony Building

━━━━━━━━━━━━ ✦ E 11

Location: 550 Madison Ave./56th St.
Subway: 53rd St.

Built in 1984 as the headquarters of the telephone company A T & T, what is now the Sony Building attracted attention like no other in the post-war era.

It was constructed at a time when dollars were short, when the old rule that the higher the building the more important was the owner was no longer completely true. Instead originality was called for, and the postmodern era dawned. But it was the cause of some amazement that Philip Johnson, the grand master of New York architects who had studied under Walter Gropius and Marcel Breuer, who had brought Mies van der Rohe and Le Corbusier to the USA and who had propagated the International Style in the 1930s based on the German Bauhaus, was the one to introduce a new era of architectural history in the 1980s. His A T & T Building, which he designed with his partner John Burgee, is considered to be the first postmodern skyscraper in the world. From 1984 to 1991 the 38-storey building of pink and grey granite, which was »only« 195m/639ft high, served as the headquarters for the telephone company A T & T, after which Sony took it over. Its trademark is the individually styled broken gable – critics say that it looks like a Chippendale dresser – and the massive, six-storey-high arched portal. Since the change in ownership the atrium, which once left a rather cool impression, has been transformed into a friendly public plaza. In the **Wonder Technology Lab** Sony exhibits its most modern communications technology.
Wonder Technology Lab: Tue–Sat 10am–5pm, Sun noon–5pm; by appointment only, tel. 1-212-833-8100, admission free, www.sonywodnertechlab.com

590 Madison

A little north of here is the former IBM Building which since the change in ownership has been named after its address, 590 Madison. The 183m/600ft-high, 43-storey skyscraper made of dark green granite and green toned glass represents an important enrichment of the New York skyscraper scene. It was built in 1984 to plans by Edward Larrabee Barnes. An especially popular spot is the four-storey-high, glazed bamboo garden at the foot of the building, a good place to flee

The Sony Building (centre) is an important work of Postmodern architecture

the noise of the city. Outside the entrance stands a sculpture by Alexander Calder and in the glass house there is a sculpture by J. Chamberlain. Through the lobby of the 590 Madison Building, visitors can enter the **Trump Tower**, which stands in the same block facing ▶Fifth Avenue.

✷ South Street Seaport

✷ B/C 19

Location: On the East River
Subway: Broadway-Nassau St., Fulton St.
❶ May–Sept daily 10am–8pm, rest

of the year until 5pm; adm. $10
www.southstreet seaport.org

South Street Seaport, once the core of New York Harbor and the gateway to the city, lies south of ▶Brooklyn Bridge.

The goods for overseas trade that made New York so large and important were sent on their way from harbour buildings and piers which are still standing today or have been restored. In the 1860s, when shipping changed from sail to steam, the harbour moved from the eastern shore to the western shore of Manhattan on the Hudson River, where ships with greater draught could anchor and there was more room to expand the pier. The area on the East Side declined and only the fish market remained. In 1967 the neighbourhood was carefully restored and transformed into a Living History Museum, with historic houses and cobbled streets from the 19th century. Today South Street Seaport is one of the most popular sites within the city, attracting more than 13 million visitors annually. Not only tourists but also New Yorkers visit the outdoor museum with its old ships, although the restaurants and shops in the small mall are not of a high standard. The museum buildings, galleries and the historical ships charge admission; ask at the ticket booth about guided tours.

Southstreet Seaport Museum

Between Pier 15 and 17 several historic ships are anchored. The showpiece is the four-mast bark **Peking**, built in 1911 by Blohm & Voss, with Hamburg as home port. It belonged, like its sister ships the Passat and the Pamir, which sank in 1957, to the legendary Flying P Liners, a total of 17 large sailing ships owned by the Hamburg shipping company Laeisz, which voyaged between Europe and South America. The Peking, which could load 4,700 tons, was sold to England in 1932 and served as a stationary school ship under the name of Arethusa. In 1975 she found her final

Historic vessels
A   Ambrose (light ship; 1908)
B   Lettie G. Howard (schooner; 1893)
C   Pioneer (schooner; 1885)
D   Peking (four-mast bark; 1911)
E   Wavertree (three-mast sailing vessel; 1885)
F   W.O. Decker (tug; 1930)

mooring here in New York. The lightship Ambrose, built in 1908, is also moored at this pier. From May to September the schooner Pioneer, built in 1885, casts off for two or three-hour **harbour tours**.
❶ Reservations: tel. 1 212-748-8600

In the so-called **Museum Block**, between Fulton, Water, Beekman and Front St., there are 14 renovated buildings from the 18th and 19th centuries, which today primarily house museums. The **visitor centre** and the museum shop are in the house at 12 Fulton Street. An exhibition here shows the history of the harbour; there is also information here on current events. In the Cannon's Walk block, Water St. no. 207, 211 and 215, is the 19th-century printing house **Bowne & Co.** The series of buildings constructed in 1811 and commissioned by the ship owner Peter Schermerhorn, the so-called **Schermerhorn Row**, is the showplace of the South Street Seaport. Once they were warehouses, later in great demand as real estate. The Fulton Market Building (Benjamin Thompson & Assocs., 1983) is already the fourth market house on its location. Opposite was once the Fulton Fish Market. From about 1821 until the end of 2005 fish was sold here. Now the fish market is in the Bronx, in the north of the city. In 1985 the old Pier 17 was roofed over; the new **Pier Pavilion 17** (Benjamin Thompson & Assocs.) with many shops and restaurants enjoys great popularity. The view from the terrace is beautiful. At no. 41 **Peck Slip** Richard Haas has painted a trompe l'oeil mural on the house, which shows a row of houses with shops as well as the Brooklyn Bridge.
Museum Block, visitor centre: 12 Fulton St.; daily May–Sept. 10am–6pm, Oct–April until 5pm; admission $10; tel. 1 212-748-8600

Staten Island

✣ **B/C 19**

Location: to the south of Manhattan

With just about 400,000 residents, 22km/13.5mi-long and 12km/7.5mi-wide Staten Island is the smallest and also least important part of New York. For this reason it is referred to jokingly as »the forgotten borough«.

The first settlers came in 1661, and for more than two centuries the island was mainly agricultural. It was incorporated into New York in 1898. Since 1964 the 1,298m/1,420yd-long Verrazano Narrows Bridge has connected Staten Island with Brooklyn.

Nostalgia at South Street Seaport

Staten Island

Staten Island Lighthouse
Bayonne Bridge
Kill Van Kull
Snug Harbour Cultural Center
S. I. Botanical Garden
Richmond Terrace
Staten Island Ferry
Staten Island Borough Hall
Goethals Bridge
Castleton Avenue
Forest Avenue
Bay Street
Forest Avenue
Clove Road
Silver Lake Park
Manor Road
Staten Island Zoo
NEW JERSEY
South Avenue
Staten Island Expressway
Clove Lakes Park
Alice Austen House
Vanderbilt Avenue
Bay Street
West Shore Expressway
Willowbrook Park
Travis Avenue
Victory
Boulevard
Staten Island Expressway
278
Verrazano Narrows Bridge
Sand Lane
New Jersey Turnpike
95
Fresh Kills Park
Richmond Avenue
Forest Hill Road
Richmond Hill Road
The Greenbelt
★ J. Marchais Center of Tibetan Art
Seaview Avenue
Lincoln Avenue
Midland Avenue
Ft. Capodanno Boulevard
La Tourette Park
★ Historic Richmond Town
Richmond
Miller Field
Arthur Kill Road
Amboy Road
Guyon Avenue
Hylan Boulevard
Arthur Kill
West Shore Expressway
Huguenot Avenue
Arden Avenue
Richmond Parkway
Great Kills Park
Woodrow
Bloomingdale Road
Amboy Road
Clay Pit Ponds Park
Blue Heron Pond Park
Great Kills Harbour
Outerbridge Crossing
Richmond
Parkway
Seguine Avenue
Amboy Road
Atlantic Ocean
Page Ave.
Amboy Road
Wolfe's Pond Park
Hylan Avenue
Conference House
1 mi
2 km
©BAEDEKER

★Staten Island Ferry

Insider Tip

The 20-minute ride on the Staten Island Ferry is a special experience which has the added bonus of being free of charge. The ferries run all year around the clock between the southern point of Manhattan (Battery) and the northern point of Staten Island (St George Station). En route, passengers enjoy the views of Manhattan's skyscrapers, the Statue of Liberty and Ellis Island, Governor's Island opposite, the quarters of the Coast Guard with a red-brick fort and the elegant Verrazano Narrows Bridge. Among the famous visitors to Staten Island are Giuseppe Garibaldi (1807–82), who lived here in exile before returning to Italy, and Francis Ford Coppola, who filmed *The Godfather* here in 1971. Less glorious Staten Island characters include »Big« Paul Castellano, head of the Gambino gang and the most powerful mafia boss in New York, who had his headquarters here until he was shot in 1985; the island also boasts the world's largest rubbish dump.

SIGHTSEEING ON STATEN ISLAND

In addition to a large number of well-kept homes from New York's period of expansion, Staten Island offers several tourist sights scattered some distance apart. Most can be reached by bus from the ferry landing St George Station, and the bus ride is also very interesting since it offers a view of this rural area.

❶ www.statenislandusa.com

The largest private collection of Tibetan art in the Western world can be found on a hill on Staten Island. The building's architecture imitates a Tibetan monastery with a terraced garden; the museum's treasures were collected and donated by the New York art dealer Mrs Harry Klauber, who also sold Asian art under the name of Jacques Marchais. Next to Tibetan art, which constitutes the main part of the collection, there are also examples of art from China, Korea, Japan, Southeast Asia, India and Persia.

*Jacques Marchais Center

❶ 338 Lighthouse Ave.; from the ferry landing take bus 74; Apr–Nov Wed–Sun 1pm–5pm; rest of the year only Fri–Sun, admission $6, www.tibetanmuseum.com

In Richmond, almost the centre of Staten Island, are 27 former seafarers' homes which give an excellent impression of life in colonial times. The oldest of the buildings, Voorlezer House, dates from 1696 and is the oldest schoolhouse in America. In the Moravian Cemetery is the mausoleum of the Vanderbilt family (▶Famous People). Demonstrations of old crafts are given regularly, and information and a schedule is available here which also identifies which houses are open to the public.

*Historic Richmond Town

❶ 441 Clarke Ave.; atrom the ferry landing take bus 74; Wed–Fri 1am–5pm, tours Wed–Fri 2.30pm, Sat and Sun 2pm and 3.30pm; admission $8; tel. 1-718-351-1611,www.historicrichmondtown.org

The American photographer Alice Austen, born in 1866, lived in this small cottage until her death in 1952. Today a selection of her pictures are displayed, giving an impression of what life was like on the island.

Alice Austen House

❶ 2 Hylan Boulevard; from the ferry landing take bus 51; open: Thu–Sun noon–5pm; admission $3; tel. 718-816-4506

Snug Harbor Cultural Center

Snug Harbor was founded in 1831 in a park above a waterway into Upper New York Bay. Once a hospital with several residences for former seamen, today it is a cultural and event centre. The complex also includes the Newhouse Center for Contemporary Art, the Staten Island Children's Museum and a botanical garden.

❶ 1000 Richmond Terrace, Building C; from the ferry landing take bus 40; daily from sunrise to sunset; admission $8

** Statue of Liberty

 Outside the city centre

Location: Liberty Island
Subway: South Ferry; ferry from/to Battery Park, daily 9.30am–5pm
Admission: $17 (reservation required)

Tel. 1-201-604-2800
www.nps.gov/stli
www.statuecruises.com

In the Upper Bay, about 4km/2.5mi south-west of the Battery, on the approx. 5ha/12.3ac Liberty Island (Native American Minissais, later Bedloe's Island, since 1956 Liberty Island), the »Statue of Liberty Enlightening the World« stands on the foundations of a fort built in 1811. The statue, 93m/305ft high including the foundation and base, is a world-famous symbol for the USA.

The monumental statue, presented to the USA on its 100th anniversary by France, was designed by Frédéric Auguste Bartholdi (1834–1904, from Colmar) and was originally intended for the northern entrance to the Suez Canal. It was inaugurated on 28 October 1886 in the presence of US President Grover Cleveland, F. A. Bartholdi and F. de Lesseps, the builder of the Suez Canal. The statue consists of steel scaffolding covered with 300 copper plates (Gustave Eiffel), is 46m/150ft high to the point of the torch in the raised right arm, which is illuminated after dark, and weighs 225 tons. The goddess of liberty, crowned with a radiant diadem, stands on the broken chains of slavery and holds the Declaration of In-

> **!**   *Plan ahead*   **Insider Tip**
>
> **MARCO ⊕ POLO TIP**
>
> To avoid queues, order your ferry tickets online well in advance. Tickets, reservations and schedules: www.nps.gov/stli and click on »Plan your visit«
> Crown tickets are available only by advance reservation.
>
> Expect queues to enter the pedestal of the statue, which offers panoramic views

dependence in her left hand with the historic date »July 4, 1776« inscribed upon it. The massive star-shaped base was designed by Richard M. Hunt. The construction materials could only be financed after private fund-raising. From the planning of the statue to its unveiling in New York, 20 years passed. Carved into the base is an excerpt from a sonnet composed by **Emma Lazarus** entitled *The New Colossus*: *»Give me your tired, your poor,*
Your huddled masses yearning to breathe free,
The wretched refuse of your teeming shore.
Send these, the homeless, tempest-tost to me,
I lift my lamp beside the golden door!«

For millions of immigrants who came to the United States by ship, the Statue of Liberty was the first thing they saw of the New World and the manifestation of their hopes. But before they could disembark they had to endure the procedures on ▶Ellis Island. The **Statue of Liberty Museum** in the base of the statue, the **observation deck** at a height of 50m/165ft (lift) and the crown are open to the public

Visiting

A symbol of freedom worldwide: the Statue of Liberty

Big and Bigger

The Statue of Liberty, the emblem of New York, is one of the world's largest statues and has often been copied. It is the principal work of Frédéric-Auguste Bartholdi (1834–1904), a sculptor from Alsace.

101m/333ft

92,9m/305ft

75,2m/247ft

©BAEDEKER

Name	The Motherland Calls!	Statue of Liberty	Siegessäule
Artist	Y. V. Vuchetich	Frédéric-A. Bartholdi	Heinrich Strack
Construction	1959 – 1967	1866 – 1886	1864 – 1873
Height of figure	85m/280ft	46m/151ft	8,3m/27ft
Height of base	16m/53ft	46,9m/154ft	66,9m220ft
Location	Volgograd / RUS	New York / USA	Berlin / GER

The Statue of Liberty around the world
Many copies of the Statue of Liberty
exist across the globe.

▶ Other works by Bartholdi
Bartholdi was a sought-after
artist in his day who created his
first work at the age of 17.

Name	Lion of Belfort
Location	Belfort (F)
Height	10,7m/35ft
Unveiled	1880

▶ Monuments compared
Until 1959 the Statue of Liberty was
the world's tallest monument.

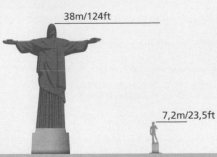

38m/124ft

7,2m/23,5ft

Cristo Redentor	David
Heitor da Silva Costa	**Michelangelo**
1922 – 1931	1501 – 1504
30m/98ft	5,2m/17ft
8m/26ft	2m/6,5ft
Rio de Janeiro / BRA	Florence/ ITA

Name	Bartholdi Fountain
Location	Washington D.C.
Height	9,1m/30ft
Unveiled	1876

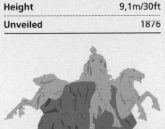

Name	Fontaine Bartholdi
Location	Lyon (F)
Height	4,85m/16ft
Unveiled	1889

Immigration – a Growing Trend

»Give me your tired, your poor, your huddled masses yearning to breathe free,« is the inscription on the base of the Statue of Liberty, which France gave to the USA in 1886 as a 100th anniversary gift. And between 1892 and 1954 more than 15 million people did emigrate to the land of opportunity.

No other US city saw as many immigrants pass through its gates as New York. Indeed, the expression used for the United States, the **melting pot**, originally referred to New York. The history of the city is the history of this melting pot, which has not been without its conflicts. In part, as Anthony Burgess once said, it is »the story of immigrants fighting against immigrants«.

From Every Corner of the World

The first European settlers in Manhattan were Walloons, who founded the settlement **Nieuw Amsterdam** in 1624 on the orders of the Dutch West Indies Company. In the following years Huguenots, Dutch, English and Germans joined them. Soon New Amsterdam developed into the North American colony with the most European cultures represented: in 1643 the roughly 500 residents spoke 18 different languages. They were not spared ethnic animosities and class conflicts, such as the Leisler Rebellion (1689 until 1691), in which Dutch artisans and small shop owners clashed with English and Dutch traders. In the 18th century, when New York became the leading port of the New World, the flow of immigrants continued to grow and the population became more and more **ethnically and culturally diverse**. The number of Black Africans grew as well; in 1712 and 1741 there were even slave rebellions. In 1790 New York was the second largest city in the new nation after Philadelphia. Among the 33,000 residents most were of English or Dutch descent. Between 1815 and 1915 more than about 33 million people from all over the world emigrated into the United States, three quarters of them through New York. They fled hunger, epidemics, political and religious persecution. A large number of **Irish and German Roman Catholics** also appeared in the city on the Hudson River, which disturbed the predominantly Protestant and Anglo-Saxon population. Street fights between native gangs and Irish immigrants were part of everyday life in the middle of the 19th century.

Second Wave of Immigration

In the mid-19th century New York was **the largest city situated entirely in the western hemisphere**, with over 600,000 residents. The approximately 175,000 Irish were the largest ethnic group, followed by about 96,000 Germans, who set-

Originally designed for the entrance to the Suez Canal, this monumental statue has greeted generations of immigrants to the USA.

tled on the Lower East Side in »Little Germany«. In the late 1880s a second immigration phase began when Russian and Polish Jews, southern Italians, Greeks, Poles, Hungarians, Romanians as well as other southern and eastern Europeans fled changes similar to the ones that northern and western Europeans had fled in the first half of the century. In 1907 twice as many people came into the country as in 1882, but the share of immigrants from northern and western Europe sank from 87% to 19% at that time. The immigrants around the middle of the century usually settled in ethnic neighbourhoods – the founding of **Little Italy** and **Chinatown** in southern Manhattan goes back to this time. The First World War had serious consequences for people of German descent. German language instruction was prohibited, the German theatre had to close, hamburgers were renamed »Salisbury steaks« and sauerkraut was called »liberty cabbage«. While Germans were still proud of their heritage before the war, afterwards they tried to hide it.

Fear of Aalienation

In 1920 about 20% of the residents of New York had been born abroad. The largest percentage consisted of Jews and Italians. Out of a fear of alienation a **quota** was introduced in 1924; every nation was permitted a certain annual quota of immigrants. This law was aimed above all at Jews, Italians and southern and eastern Europe-

Immigrants having English lessons (about 1919)

an immigrants; Asians were not allowed to enter at all anymore. The law was not even repealed during the reign of **National Socialism in Germany**, when the persecuted tried to find refuge in the USA. After the Second World War the flow of Spanish-speaking immigrants began and has continued to this day, at first predominantly from the American territory Puerto Rico, then also from the Caribbean and Central and South America. In 1965 the quota system was repealed, Congress instead fixing maximum numbers. Currently 675,000 immigrants are allowed to enter every year (excluding family members and political refugees).

Immigration Continues

Currently more than 100 nationalities live in New York City, and speak about 120 different languages. About 90,000 immigrants settle here every year. Those who cannot make it legally try to enter illegally. The »tired, poor and huddled« still see a Mecca of freedom in New York – this is an unbroken trend. The terrorist attacks of 11 September 2001 on the Twin Towers of the World Trade Center have done nothing to alter this image. Immigration has not decreased since then, though the process has slowed down, primarily because the immigration regulations have been made stricter.

following a costly restoration that was needed for safety reasons. There is an extraordinarily beautiful view of New York from the observation deck. Until 1916 it was possible to climb into the torch of the Statue of Liberty. Access to the **crown**, a dubious pleasure, as the 354 steps have to be climbed in a narrow, claustrophobic stairwell, is severely limited. A tour by ferry from Battery Park includes ▶Ellis Island. To do all of this, allow at least five hours, starting by noon at the latest. A one-hour wait before reaching the security check is normal. A good alternative is the (free) view from the Staten Island Ferry.

** Times Square

⬥ D 12

Location: Intersection of Broadway and Seventh Ave. between W 42nd St. and W 47th St.
Subway: Times Square

Times Square, a symbol of the Big Apple, is the long intersection of Broadway and Seventh Avenue, between West 42nd and 47th St. Some 40 playhouses in its side streets make it the centre of the theatre world.

Here, where city regulations require that all advertising be illuminated, the neon heart of the metropolis beats. An estimated one and a half million pedestrians cross the »world's intersection« daily, and more than 20 million tourists come here every year. Every New Year's Eve hundreds of thousands of revellers stand here and take part in the traditional countdown to the new year.

In the 19th century it was called »Longacre Square« and was the site of coachmen, saddleries and horse stables. The area was notorious, and the intersection of Broadway and Seventh Ave. was nicknamed »Thieves' Lair«. In 1904 the **New York Times** moved into its new publishing house Times Tower at the southern end of the square, which from then on carried its name (the editorial offices later moved into a new building by Renzo Piano on Eighth Ave., between 40th and 41st St.). The narrow high-

Times Square today

rise with the address »1 Times Square« has since then changed owners several times.

The square's rise to become the centre of New York's entertainment district began with the opening of the first house of the Metropolitan Opera in the year 1883 and the opening of the Olympia Theater two years later by Oscar Hammerstein. In 1903 the oldest of the remaining houses, the Lyceum Theater (149 W 45th St.) followed, as did others. In the 1920s there were 80 houses in the Theater District, in which Charlie Chaplin, the Marx Brothers, Sarah Bernhardt, Houdini and others performed. The stars stayed in elegant hotels like the Astor. The illuminated advertisements were an attraction in themselves. For a few years Broadway was Times Square, and Times Square was New York – the »apotheosis of electricity«, as the Odette Keun wrote in 1930. A slow **decline** began with prohibition in the 1920s. The change became dramatic in 1929 with the stock market crash, whose consequences restricted life in the theatres, varieties, restaurants and hotels. Striptease clubs opened in 42nd St., between Seventh and Eighth Ave. Prostitution, drugs and violence became a symbol of urban decline, which all visitors came to see but which invited no one to stay.

Change in the early 1990s At the beginning of the 1990s the situation turned around when businesspeople united with the authorities in a »clean-up« campaign. Then Disney invested, and many others followed. The first sign of success was the opening of the Marriott Marquis Hotel (1985). The opening of a branch of the exclusive Gap department store in 1992 at Broadway and Seventh Ave. served as a signal. In 1996 Disney opened a giant store on 42nd Street and Seventh Ave., in December 1996 the curtain rose again in the Victory Theater, the oldest theatre on Broadway, which first opened in 1900, and in May 1997 in the New Amsterdam Theater opened. Where once the Ziegfeld Follies appeared, Disney shows are now performed. Along with cinemas and stylish restaurants, more and more tourist attractions are being opened, including **Madame Tussaud's** wax museum (▶p.138) and the **NASDAQ Market Site**, the visitor centre of the technology stock exchange for those interested in stocks.

NASDAQ Market Site: 4 Times Square; open daily

TriBeCa

✦ **A/B 17**

Location: South of SoHo (Downtown)
Subway: Canal S.

TriBeCa, an acronym for Triangle Below Canal, is the neighbourhood between West Broadway, Canal, West and Chambers Street.

The area was actually called Lower West Side until a clever real estate agent invented the acronym, which has meanwhile been generally accepted. Old warehouses and former factory buildings dominate, many of them brick built. In the 1980s, primarily artists who could no longer afford to live in ▶SoHo moved to the TriBeCa neighbourhood (bordering Soho to the north). Film producers such as Harvey and Bob Weinstein and Robert de Niro set up film studios here. Robert de Niro is also the co-founder of the TriBeCa Filmfestival, and he is also at the culinary forefront as the co-owner of the TriBeCa Grill restaurant. Many clubs and businesses followed the artists to Tribeca. Today, the industrial spaces creatively transformed into affordable living and work quarters by the artists were converted into sleek and expensive lofts, condos and studios. Excellent restaurants, nightclubs, bars and live jazz and rock music venues are abound, and there are a number of art galleries here. TriBeCa has become one of the most desirable and most expensive neighbourhoods in NYC.

Attractions

The most striking buildings in TriBeCa include the eight built between 1804 and 1828 in the Federal Style on **Harrison Street**, though six of them were »imported« from other streets. The **New York Telephone Company Building** (32 Ave. of the Americas) was built in 1918 to designs by Ralph Walker in the Art Deco style and has an opulent lobby. Another Art Deco building is the **Western Union Building** from 1928 (60 Hudson St.). In the south, between Chambers and Greenwich St., is the small **Washington Market Park**, which gives an impressive view of the high-rises in ▶Battery Park City.

✷✷ **United Nations Headquarters**

✦ **F 13**

Location: First Ave. between E 42nd and E 46th St.;
Subway: Grand Central Terminal
Tours: $18, only in session period and only with tickets purchased in advance, no tours on Sat and Sun; children under 5 years are not

admitted; entrance 47thst./1st Ave.
❶ Visitor center: 43rd St./1st Ave., Mon–Fri 9.45am–4.45pm, Sat and Sun 10am–4.30pm tel. 1 212-963-8687
www.un.org/tours

The United Nations (UN or UNO, both expressions are acceptable) was founded in 1945 in San Francisco as the successor organization of the League of Nations in order to secure world peace and to promote international cooperation. The UN headquarters are in New York, and in addition there are other »UN cities« such as Geneva and Vienna.

The main organizations are the General Assembly (UNGA; it meets once a year from mid-September, but cannot pass any laws); the Security Council (UNSC) with the five permanent members USA, Russia, People's Republic of China, Great Britain and France, and ten other members from the General Assembly who are elected for two years; the Economic and Social Council (ECOSOC); the International Court of Justice (IJC) with its seat in The Hague (Netherlands); and the Secretariat (UNSG) headed by the Secretary General. The original 51 states have now become 191 member states. On 24 October, the official founding day, the »Day of the United Nations« is celebrated.

Buildings   The UN headquarters stands in an area which was once the domain of slaughterhouses and small industry. It was bought with money donated by John D. Rockefeller Jr., while the construction costs of $67 million were paid by means of an interest-free loan from the United States. The land is exterritorial – neither the USA nor the City of New York have any say there – and has its own police and post office. The building complex was built in 1949–53 to plans by an international team of architects, including Le Corbusier from France, who later distanced himself from the project, the Brazilian Oscar Niemeyer and the Swede Sven Markelius. The American Wallace K. Harrison was in charge of the project. Four individual buildings were constructed, decorated with the flags of all member states displayed in alphabetical order according to the English alphabet. The glass front of the relatively narrow 39-storey **Secretariat Building**

(154m/505ft) dominates and is the seat of the UN administration and the Secretary General, whose office is on the 38th floor. In the conference room there is a remarkable Swiss world clock. In the pool in front of the building is the abstract sculpture *Single Form* by Barbara Hepworth (1963). The flat **Conference Building** connects to the curved **General Assembly Building** with the domed, elliptical auditorium in the middle. The entrance to the UN complex between E 45th and E 46th St. leads into the lobby, where several works of art can be admired, including an ancient statue of Neptune, a Russian sputnik and to the rear on the right a stained glass window by Marc Chagall. Jean Bernard Foucault's 65m/213ft-high pendulum, a gift from the Netherlands, demonstrates the revolving of Earth on its axis. On the lower floor there is the UN gift shop, where arts and crafts and souvenirs from all member states are sold, and a bookshop. Stamp collectors will enjoy a visit to the UN post office, also on the lower floor, where letters are specially stamped and franked. How-

UN headquarters with Chrysler Building in the background

The United Nations

The world holds its talks on the East River. Founded in the realization that the disaster of the Second World War must never be repeated, this community of nations has since then made efforts to keep peace around the globe – with mixed success...

1945 FOUNDATION
ARTICLES IN THE CHARTA **111**
9,000 STAFF IN THE SECRETARIAT

51 **2,200** TONS OF PAPER CONSUMED PER YEAR
COUNTRIES FOUNDED THE UN
2 WORKING LANGUAGES
OFFICIAL LANGUAGE
193 MEMBER STATE

▶ Finance

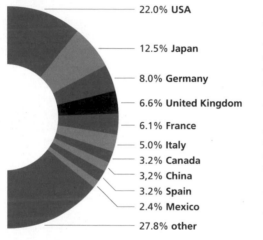

- 22.0% **USA**
- 12.5% **Japan**
- 8.0% **Germany**
- 6.6% **United Kingdom**
- 6.1% **France**
- 5.0% **Italy**
- 3.2% **Canada**
- 3,2% **China**
- 3.2% **Spain**
- 2.4% **Mexico**
- 27.8% **other**

5,152,000,000 US
was the budget in 2012/13

The United Nations is financed by fixed contributions from its member states. Each state contribut between 22% and 0.01% o the budget, depending on its ability to pay. Personnel and infrastructure costs are covered by this. These fixed contributions represent about one third of the UN' resources. Specialized agencies, peace-keeping missions etc. are financed b voluntary contributions.

▶ Peace-keeping missions
United Nations peace-keeping troops are the armed forces of member states, made available for establishing and maintaining peace.

Uniformed personnel: about 97,000

Missions (17 in 2012):

2,000 **soldiers**
14,000 **police**

81,000 **military observers**

Kosovo
Cyprus, Lebanon, Syria
West Sahara
Haiti
Liberia, Ivory Coast, Sudan, DR Congo
India, Pakistan, Afghanistan
East Ti

Principal organs
The UN has six principal organs.

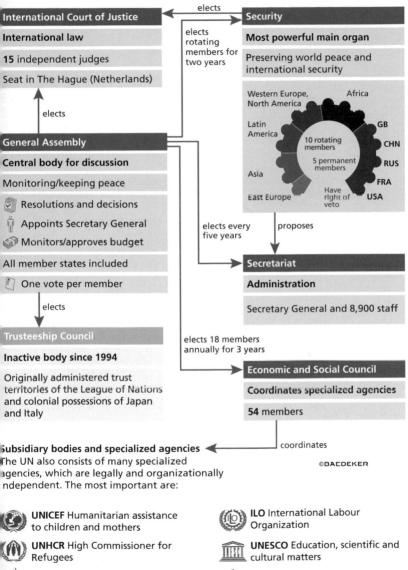

International Court of Justice

International law

15 independent judges

Seat in The Hague (Netherlands)

elects

General Assembly

Central body for discussion

Monitoring/keeping peace

Resolutions and decisions

Appoints Secretary General

Monitors/approves budget

All member states included

One vote per member

elects

Trusteeship Council

Inactive body since 1994

Originally administered trust territories of the League of Nations and colonial possessions of Japan and Italy

elects

Security

Most powerful main organ

Preserving world peace and international security

Western Europe, North America

Africa

Latin America

Asia

East Europe

10 rotating members

5 permanent members

GB
CHN
RUS
FRA
USA

Have right of veto

elects rotating members for two years

elects every five years

proposes

Secretariat

Administration

Secretary General and 8,900 staff

elects 18 members annually for 3 years

Economic and Social Council

Coordinates specialized agencies

54 members

coordinates

Subsidiary bodies and specialized agencies
The UN also consists of many specialized agencies, which are legally and organizationally independent. The most important are:

©BAEDEKER

UNICEF Humanitarian assistance to children and mothers

UNHCR High Commissioner for Refugees

UNHRC Commission on Human Rights

ILO International Labour Organization

UNESCO Education, scientific and cultural matters

WHO World Health Organization

ever letters and cards have to be deposited in mailboxes within the building in order to be mailed. The murals in the General Assembly are by Fernand Léger.

Dag Hammar-skjöld Library   South-west of the General Assembly Building is the Dag Hammarskjöld Library, named after the second UN General Secretary, who was killed in an aeroplane crash in the Congo in 1961. The building was constructed in 1962 according to plans by Harrison, Abramovitz & Harris and is a gift of the Ford Foundation.

Sculptures   To the north of the UN building complex along the East River lies a beautiful park with numerous sculptures from different countries, including the bronze statue Reclining Figure, a gift from the Henry Moore Foundation (1982), the sculpture Swords to Ploughshares, a gift from the former Soviet Union (1958), the bronze sculpture Climber by the East German Fritz Cremer, the White Horse by the German artist Elisabeth von Janota-Bzowski, the *Statue of Peace* from Yugoslavia as well as the peace sculpture *Non-Violence* by the Swedish artist Karl Frederik Reutersward, a gift from Luxemburg in the year 1988.

Surroundings   Anyone visiting UN headquarters should also take a look at some of the surrounding buildings and plazas, such as 1 UN Plaza (First Ave. / 44th St.), built in 1976 by Roche, Dinkeloo and Assocs. as a hotel and office high-rise, Tudor City and the building of the Ford Foundation on 42nd St. (►Grand Central Terminal). At United Nations Plaza and 46th St. is the **African-American Institute**, where exhibitions of African art are held on the ground floor. Sculptures are displayed in rotation on Dag Hammarskjöld Plaza.

** **Whitney Museum of American Art**

✦ F 9

Location: 9Washington & Gansevoort St..
Subway: 77th St.

❶ Wed, Thu, Sat, Sun 11am–6pm, Fri 1pm–9pm
Admission: $20
www.whitney.org

The Whitney Museum of American Art is the only museum in New York that is exclusively devoted to twentieth-century and contemporary American art. The museum grew out of sculptor Gertrude Vanderbilt Whitney's art collections. She is considered a leading patron of American art.

In 1907, Gertrude Vanderbilt started to purchase and show the works of living American painters who had been ignored by the traditional art establishment. Seven years later, in 1914, when she had a sizeable collection, she established Whitney Studio in Greenwich Village. This was at a time when museums, art galleries and art collectors in the United States still preferred European art. Gertrude Vanderbilt's aim was to introduce the works of American artists to a wider audience and draw attention to the artistic talent that was not overseas but right there in the country. Finally in 1931, the Whitney Museum of American Art was opened. As the collections grew, the museum had to change locations, and in 1966, the museum was moved to its current location on Madison Avenue.

History of the museum

The present building that houses the museum's collections was designed by Bauhaus-trained Marcel Breuer und Hamilton Smith in a distinctively modern style that give the museum a striking presence. The most unique features of the architectural design are the staircase exterior made of panels of granite and the external upside-down windows. The Whitney, as lovingly referred to by New Yorkers, will soon be moving for the fourth time. The future Whitney located in the Meatpacking District in lower Manhattan is currently under construction and is expected to open to the public in the spring of 2015. The eight-storey building between Hudson River and High Line Park with its steel grey façade was designed by Italian architect Renzo Piano, the world-famous architect who made a huge splash in the architecture world with his design of the Centre Georges Pompidou in Paris. The Whitney will have three times the exhibition and programming space that it has in the current building. There will be several terraces and a museum shop as well as a restaurant on the ground floor and a café on the roof-top terrace   .

The Whitney Biennale, an exhibition of contemporary American art, is held every two years in May. This event began in 1932 and is one of the leading art shows in the world. The exhibits showcase the work of mostly young and lesser known artists and have in the past helped to bring artists like Georgia O'Keeffe and Jackson Pollock to fame.

Whitney Biennale,

The Whitney has a collection of some of the most significant work created by artists in the United States and consists of more than 21,000 paintings, sculptures, prints, drawings, photographs, films, videos and new media (Art in New York, p.49). A number of works from the museum's permanent collection are always on view at the Whitney Museum, among them such works as Alexander Calder's »Cirque Calder« (in foyer) as well as works of Edward Hopper, Georgia O'Keeffe and Alexander Calder (5th floor). Most other treasures in the museum's collection are rotated. Regular exhibitions and touring exhibitions are there to enjoy as well.

Collection

✦✦ 9/11 Memorial & One WTC
✦ A 18

Location: between Church, Vesey, West and Liberty St.

Subway: Cortland St., World Trade Center, Chambers St.

At the site where 9/11 left a gaping wound in the heart of lower Manhattan is now a super-tall tower once again, the »One World Trade Center«. It was constructed in place of the original Twin Towers of the World Trade Center that were destroyed in the 11 September terrorist attacks

Old World Trade Center

The Twin Towers of the World Trade Center were built between 1966 and 1971, the North Tower at a height of 417m/1,368ft and the South Tower at 415m/1,362ft, both with 110 floors. At the time the towers were built, they were the tallest buildings in the world. The Twin Towers, along with the five smaller buildings of the World Trade Center complex, stood as a symbol of American economic power (architectural design: lead architect Minoru Yamasaki and associate architects Emery Roth & Sons). Some 50,000 people worked in the towers, while another 140,000-200,000 visited or passed through each day. After the two planes crashed into the Twin Towers on 9/11, they collapsed after burning for quite a while. At 9.59 am, the South Tower collapsed after 56 minutes and at 10.28 am, the North Tower after 102 minutes. The structural steel frames of the towers did not withstand the airliner crash, a fact around which there was much speculation. The collapse of the towers destroyed 3 WTC (Marriott Hotel). The 7 WTC building collapsed eight hours later. 4 WTC, 5 WTC and 6 WTC were badly damaged and later demolished. About 3,000 people lost their lives as a result of the attacks.

Reconstruction

Reconstruction of the WTC complex has progressed very slowly. There were several reasons for the delay. Six weeks before the terrorist attacks on 9/11, Larry Silverstein of Silverstein Properties acquired the World Trade Center for $3.2 billion. Silverstein had plans to rebuild, but a dispute with his insurers went on for some time before a settlement was reached. Financing was one of the major issues, however. Disputes between Silverstein and the Port Authority of New York and New Jersey delayed reconstruction as well. Previously, the World Trade Center site was under the control of the Port Authority. In 2006, the Port Authority reached a deal with Silverstein, which ceded control of One World Trade Center to the Port Authority and Tower Five, while Silverstein retained rights to build Towers 2, 3 and 4.

A phoenix from the ashes: the new World Trade Center

Tall, Taller, Tallest

Although Chicago and not, as you might think, New York is the birthplace of the skyscraper, the Big Apple undoubtedly has the most impressive skyline of all US cities. Following the destruction of the Twin Towers, new giants are reaching for the sky. They may be getting taller and taller, but they cannot match the elegance of the old-time skyscrapers.

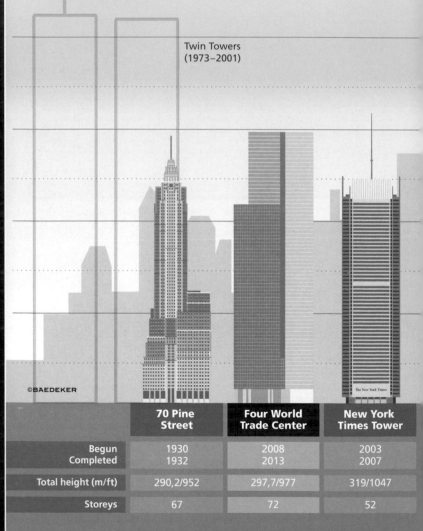

Twin Towers
(1973–2001)

©BAEDEKER

	70 Pine Street	Four World Trade Center	New York Times Tower
Begun Completed	1930 1932	2008 2013	2003 2007
Total height (m/ft)	290,2/952	297,7/977	319/1047
Storeys	67	72	52

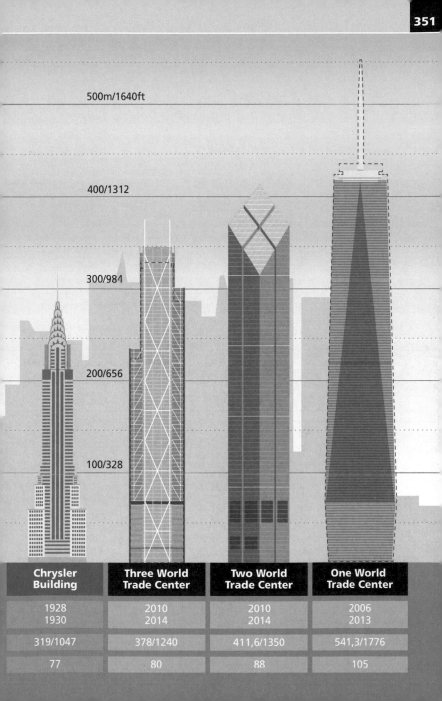

500m/1640ft

400/1312

300/984

200/656

100/328

Chrysler Building	Three World Trade Center	Two World Trade Center	One World Trade Center
1928 1930	2010 2014	2010 2014	2006 2013
319/1047	378/1240	411,6/1350	541,3/1776
77	80	88	105

Then, in 2008, a full-blown financial and economic crisis hit the United States, which delayed the reconstruction process even further. Some of the towers have been completed, while others have been put on hold.

New WTC   Daniel Libeskind of Studio Daniel Libeskind is the master plan architect for rebuilding the World Trade Center site. His initial plan proposed five towers standing in a semicircle facing west, each tower, from south to north, higher than the next. However, his plan was rejected. Of the new buildings on the World Trade Center site, the northernmost and highest building is **One Word Trade Center** (1 WTC). 1 WTC, formerly called the »Freedom Tower« is a compromise between the designs of the master plan architect of the World Trade Center Daniel Libeskind and project architect of the tower David Childs. Libeskind's original plan for the 1 WTC tower »Memory Foundations«, proposed a building with aerial gardens and windmills and an off-centre spire and was a dramatic piece of architectural art, whereas Childs and Silverstein's concept was much more pragmatic and traditional. Nevertheless, the tower's final design is striking; the glass-clad structure tapers octagonally as it rises. In May 2013, the final piece of the spire was placed on the top of the One World Trade Center (1 WTC) building, making it, at the time it was built, the tallest

building in the Western Hemisphere and third tallest in the world. The building reaches its symbolic height of 1776 feet (541.3 metres). The 4th of July 1776 marks the day when the Thirteen British Colonies in North America joined together to declare independence from Great Britain.

The other buildings of the WTC were designed by various other architects. **7 WTC** (250 Greenwich St, 228m/743ft) was also designed by Childs and has been completed. The construction of **3 WTC** (175 Greenwich St, 352m/1,155ft), designed by Richard Rogers of Rogers Stirk Harbour + Partners, is on hold for financial reasons. **4 WTC** (150 Green St, 298m/978ft) designed by Fumihiko Maki has been completed. **2 WTC** (200 Greenwich St, expected height of 390m/1,270ft), designed by Norman Foster with sloping roof consisting of four diamonds, is also on hold for financial reasons and disagreements over design and height, and the future of **5 WTC** (architects: Kohn Pedersen Fox) is uncertain. The visionary new World

Trade Center Transportation Hub was designed by architect Santiago Calatrava and set to be completed in 2015.

The core of the WTC complex is the National September 11 Memorial & Museum, which commemorates and honours the nearly 3,000 people killed in the terrorist attacks of 11 September 2001 at the World Trade Center site. The memorial was designed by architect Michael Arad of Handel Architects and landscape architect Peter Walker of Peter Walker and Partners.

*9/11 Memorial & Museum

The **underground museum** on the site at bedrock level with its aboveground entry pavilion was designed by architectural firms Davis Brody Bond (museum) and Snøhetta (pavilion). The memorial consists of a plaza with a field of trees around two large square pools that mark the footprints of the Twin Towers. The names of the victims are inscribed on bronze plates around the edges of the memorial pools. The museum space is 21m/70ft below street level and is assessed through a glassy pavilion. The gradual descent »from daylight into darkness« passes alongside the Vesey Street stair remnant, the »Survivors' Stairs«, which provided an escape for hundreds of people on 11 September. Some of the monumental artefacts on display include a mangled 58-ton steel column, part of one of the hijacked planes and a crushed fire truck. The more intimate exhibits show personal objects that were salvaged from the wreckage in an attempt to show that the victims were real people with unique lives not unlike our own. The visit ends in a cavernous space with a 36-foot steel beam known as the Last Column and the huge slurry wall, a retaining wall of the Twin Towers constructed to keep the Hudson River back — and that withstood the devastation of 9/11.

The **9/11 Tribute Center** (Tribute WTC Visitor Center) provides photos, artefacts and personal stories. Here, the 9/11 community can gather and share their personal 9/11 experiences with each other and the public.

9/11 Memorial & Museum: Entrance: Liberty/Greenwich St; Subway: Fulton St; Memorial: daily 8.30am – 8.30pm; Museum: daily, 21 May – 21 Sept. 9.00am – 8.00pm, otherwise until 7.00pm; Admission: $24, free admission on Tue after 5pm; www.911memorial.org

9/11 Tribute Center: 120 Liberty St; Mon – Sat 10.00am – 6.00pm, Sun 10.00am – 5.00pm; Admission: $15; Guided tours: »Tribute Center Walking Tours« Sun – Thu 11.00am, 12.00pm (noon) and 1.00, 2.00 and 3.00pm; Fri 10.30 and 11.00am and 12.00pm (noon) and 1.00, 2.00, 3.00pm, Sat. at 12.30pm (noon) and 1.30pm; $20, www.tributewtc.org

PRACTICAL INFORMATION

How do you get from the airport into town? Which sbway goes to brooklyn? Do you give a tip in restaurants? What about background reading? Look it up here – preferably before the trip!

Arrival · Before the Journey

HOW TO GET TO NEW YORK

By air Most visitors arrive in New York by air. There are scheduled and charter flights from all major airports in the UK, Ireland, Australia, New Zealand, and of course from other airports in the USA. The **flying time** from London is around 7 hours. Keen competition results in lucrative special offers, but the pricing system can appear impenetrable. Information is available in travel agents, from the internet or in travel magazines. The website www.cheapflights.co.uk allows you to compare prices.

Note
Service numbers that charge for calls are marked with an asterisk: *0180 …

All three of New York's **airports** are outside the city centre. The traveller can get information on how to get into town or to another airport at the Ground Transportation Centers.

By ship Apart from cruises New York can only be reached with one passenger ship line: the Cunard Line (Cunard Seabourn Ltd, Mountbatten House, Grosvenor Square, Southampton, SO15 2BF; tel.: +44 (0)23 8071 6500, www.cunard.co.uk) operates the luxury liner Queen Mary 2 from April to November once to three times a month in five days from Southampton to New York.

! *Carry cash!* **Insider Tip**

MARCO ⊕ POLO TIP

It is advisable to carry a small amount of cash (both notes and coins) at all times. Taxis and museums, for example, only accept cash, and bus drivers do not give change. Moreover, taxi drivers are not required to accept notes over $20 and owners of small shops and stores can rarely be persuaded to provide change.

It is not advisable to drive to New York in a hire car. **Parking spaces are extremely rare**, and hotels charge up to $25 for 2 hours in parking spaces, while towing costs at least $185 plus the fine. It is also not unlikely that the car will be stolen.

There are **two railway stations** in Manhattan, Grand Central Terminal and Pennsylvania Station. There are subway stations directly under the railway stations, and bus stations directly outside. Amtrak, the state-owned railway, can be contacted in the USA on tel. 1-800-872-7245; in the UK, contact Leisurail (tel.: (0800) 698 7545 or (0870) 750 0222 / 443 4483, www.leisurail.co.uk).

AIRPORTS
J. F. Kennedy International Airport – JFK

Location: 26km/16mi outside town, on Jamaica Bay (Queens)
Information: tel. 1 718-244-4444
www.panynj.gov
Airtrain: Connection between various airport terminals (free of charge) and the subway stations ($12, 5 min) Howard Beach (continue on line A to Brooklyn and Manhattan, 65 min) and Jamaica Station Beach (continue on lines E, J, Z or LIRR (Long Island Rail Road) to Manhattan, $12, 35 min). Returning: only line A towards Far Rockaway/Mott Ave. or Rockaway Park Beach as far as Howard Beach/JFK Airport, or take the LIRR
Shuttle: Supershuttle runs mini-buses from JFK to Manhattan ($20–30).
Taxi: From J. F. Kennedy Airport to Manhattan: $52 flat rate plus tunnel toll as well as tip, total approx. $60. Travel time 60–75 min.
New York Airport Service: bus service from 6:15am until 11pm every 20 to 30min between the airport terminals and Manhattan (Grand Central Terminal, Penn Station, Port Authority Bus Terminal – Eighth Ave. / 42nd St. – and many hotels); tel. 1 718-706-9658; fare $15; travel time 60–75 min.
Helicopter Flight Services: tel. 1 212-355-0801, www.heliny.com

LaGuardia Airport – LGA
Location: 13km/8mi outside the city centre, in the north of Queens
Information: tel. 1 718-533-3400
www.laguardiaairport.com
New York Airport Service: buses between the terminals of La Guardia and Manhattan, ►JFK; fare $12; travel time 40–70 min.

Taxi: fare approx. $16–30, plus bridge and tunnel toll and tip; travel time approx. 30min
Bus: M60 (New York City Transit Authority, 5am–1am) via 125th to 106th St. / Broadway with connection to subway lines.
Helicopter: ►JFK

Newark Liberty International Airport – EWR
Location: 24km/15mi south-west in New Jersey
Information: tel. 1 973-961-6000
www.newarkairport.com,
www.airtrainnewark.com
Airtrain: Transfer (included in NJ Transit or Amtrak ticket) between terminals and Newark Penn Station; from here continue with the trains NJ Transit or Amtrak to Penn Station in Manhattan; $15–§30, travel time approx. 30 min.
Taxi: about $80 plus bridge or tunnel toll and tip
Airport Express: Buses (6am–1am every 15 or 30 min.) to stations in Manhattan (Port Authority Bus Terminal, Fifth Ave. /Bryant Park, Grand Central Terminal); travel time 40–50 min., $15.
Express bus: SuperShuttle from door to door; fare $15–20; travel time 40–50 min. to Manhattan, tel. 1 800-258-3826
Helicopter.►JFK

AIRLINES
Virgin Atlantic
Tel. 1 800 862 8621 (USA);
0844 209-7777 (UK)
www.virgin-atlantic.com

British Airways
Tel. 1-800-AIRWAYS (USA);
0844 493-0787 (UK)
www.ba.com

American Airlines
Tel. 1-800-433-7300 (USA);
0844 3699 899 (UK)
www.aa.com

Delta Airlines
Tel. 1 800-241-4141 (USA);
tel. 0871 2211-222 (UK)
www.delta.com

United Airlines
Tel. 1 800-864-8331 (USA)
www.united.com

RAILWAY STATIONS
Grand Central Terminal
42nd St. / Park Ave.
Information: tel. 1 212-532-4900
www.grandcentralterminal.com
Open: daily 5.30am–1.30am

Main station for the commuter trains
going north and east of New York, to
Connecticut and Westchester County.
There is a subway station in the lower
floor, and bus stops outside.

Penn (Pennsylvania) Station
Seventh Ave. / 33rd St.
Information: tel. 1 63 12 31 LIRR (LIRR)
and 1 800 8 72 72 45 (Amtrak)
Tickets: daily 5.10am–9.50pm
Station under Madison Square Garden,
commuter trains go from here, and
trains to New Jersey and Amtrak trains.
There are subway stations in the lower
floor, and bus stops outside.

Port Authority Bus Terminal
42nd St. / Eighth Ave.
Information: tel. 1 212-564-8484

By bus or coach If a visit to New York City is part of a USA holiday, the **Greyhound** bus line (tel. 1-800-229-9424, www.greyhound.com) can be used to connect to the largest cities. The Ameripass is an all-inclusive ticket which can be purchased for 4, 7, 10, 15, 21, 30, 45 or 60 consecutive days. The passes cost significantly less for foreign visitors than for Americans, but they need to be bought before arrival in the USA. Seat reservations are not accepted but if the bus is full an additional bus is provided.

ARRIVAL AND DEPARTURE REGULATIONS

Travel documents Citizens of member states of the European Union are eligible for the Visa Waiver Program (VWP), and can enter the USA as tourists or for business purposes without a visa for a period of up to 90 days if they arrive with a recognized airline or shipping company and have a return ticket. On arrival digital fingerprints are taken of all fingers and a digital portrait photo is taken. On leaving, too, visitors are fingerprinted. The permitted duration of stay is individually specified according to the reason for travel. Extension is possible only for holders of a visa. The latest day on which the visitor must leave the USA is stamped in the passport. Only a machine-readable passport is accepted. Children must have their own passport. Visitors from countries participating in the Visa Waiver Program must produce an electronic (ESTA), which costs $14 currently and can be applied for on the internet at https://esta.cbp.dhs.gov, and is valid for all further journeys to the USA for a period of two years. Further information is available at the Department of Homeland Security under www.dhs.gov.

At present a full national **driving licence** from most countries is accepted in the USA for up to one year. An international driving licence is not required, but helpful when travelling in remote areas. It is a good idea to check on the requirements of car hire companies before renting a car in New York.

Driving licence

Customs regulations on entry: Adults over 21 may bring one litre of wine or spirits and 200 cigarettes or 50 cigars (but not from Cuba) or 1300g/46oz of tobacco duty free. Children and adults may bring along gifts worth up to $100/£50 duty free. Meat, plants, fruit and obscene articles and publications may not be brought in. Up to $10,000/£5,000 may be carried upon arrival. Visitors who need medication containing drugs should bring a sufficient supply along with a doctor's attestation of the need (in English) in order to prevent the possible suspicion of drug smuggling. The same applies to injection needles for diabetics. Information is available at consulates or U.S. Customs, 1301 Constitution Ave. NW, Washington D.C. 20229.

Customs

Departure: In general the customs regulations of the country of destination apply. The following may be brought into the UK (from the age of 17 upwards) and other EU states. tobacco (200 cigarettes, 100 cigarillos, 50 cigars, 250g of loose tobacco), alcohol (1 litre of spirits over 22%, 2 litres below 22%, or two litres of sparkling wine and two litres of still wine), coffee (500g/17.6oz coffee and 200g/7oz instant coffee), scent (50g/1.8oz perfume and 0.25l/9fl oz. eau de toilette), medicines for personal use and all other goods up to a value of €430/£390 (for under-15s €175/£160), excluding articles for personal use.

Travel insurance is strongly recommended for a visit to New York, since all medical costs must be paid in cash or with a credit card. The costs will be reimbursed when the receipts are presented to the insurance company. It is advisable to ensure that diagnoses, prescriptions and costs are listed in detail.

Travel insurance

Electricity

The mains supply is 110 volts AC. Those bringing European norm (set switch to 110!) electrical appliances need an adaptor which can be purchased at the airport or department stores, but also at large local department stores.

110 Volts AC

Emergency

Ambulance, police, fire department: **Tel. 911**

Etiquette and Customs

Thanks to its many immigrants, almost no other city in the world is as cosmopolitan as New York. Visitors coming into contact with New Yorkers (which can happen quickly) soon notice that life in this city, at least for the middle and upper class, is marked strongly by **status symbols**. Conversations in New York – or more precisely Manhattan – naturally revolve around the most expensive shops like Takashimaya, the breathtakingly expensive food in one of Alain Ducasse's restaurants, and the name and address of employers: the higher the floor where the desk is, the lighter and larger the office, the better the job – and the better the pay, which the New Yorker who has arrived talks about openly. At the very top, naturally, are the bosses in suite-like luxury offices, and even the executive secretary or security personnel enjoy the view through the glass walls. At the bottom the rank and file work in mostly musty, tiny and often windowless cubicles.

Noise Be it an outdoor lunch in a Central Park restaurant, the intermission in a musical theatre or the best restaurant: Europeans notice the **extreme noise level** – caused not by music, but by people talking so loud that it seems as if they haven't seen each other in years and need to make up for lost time in a cascade of conversation. But that's life here: New Yorkers love nothing more than to be the star of their own show – to talk about where they eat, where they shop or how their love life is shaping up.

Rush hour The **haste** of Manhattanites is the stuff of modern legend. There is a good reason why the expression »rush hour« comes from New York, where the first subways went into service at the beginning of the 20th century. Particularly after 5pm, a hectic mass of people is set into motion all over the city – driven by the wish to get home as quickly as possible. Enjoy the hustle and bustle instead of cursing it: it's part of a dynamic city.

Small talk In New York, as in the rest of the USA and for that matter many places in the world, there are **clichéd expressions** and behaviours that shouldn't be taken too seriously: for example an invitation to »do lunch someday« is polite, but often not meant literally. Even if you get an address or telephone number, it will normally be the office number where there is no time for personal calls. An evening date is different however. The person who invites you out to dinner, an evening in the opera and a bar, or even to a party is serious, and accepting the invitation for a date equally so – in every respect, since 3.1 million singles live in New York.

New Yorkers call it **hyping**: magazines, tour brochures, radio and TV adverts, self-appointed columnists or posters promise wonders – the best food, the cheapest tickets, biggest sale ever and so on. Even if it could all be true, it doesn't have to be. In the USA, above all in New York, advertising using comparatives (and superlatives) that are not taken very seriously – so the best advice is to stay sceptical.

Hype

Drinking alcohol on the street is prohibited in New York. Smoking is banned in all public buildings, public transport including taxis and inside ferries, in pubs and clubs, and since 2011 in parks and on beaches – this includes Central Park, Herald Square and Times Square. In hire cars and many hotel rooms smoking is also forbidden. Airports and some restaurants have small smoking zones – the *Zagat New York City* guide lists restaurants where smoking is possible.

Alcohol, smoking

Last but not least there is the call of nature to take care of. In the USA, don't ask for the toilet: that's considered rude. Ask for the restroom, bathroom or the ladies' or men's room. Public restrooms are rare in New York City. Use the ones in one of the many fast-food restaurants.

Toilets

Usually restaurant prices do not include a service charge, and the waiters usually earn very low wages. A tip of 15 to 20% is therefore usual. A good rule of thumb is simply to double the amount of sales tax (8.375 %) shown on the bill. Either add the tip to the credit-card payment or leave cash on the table. Some waiters put the tip on the bill on their own initiative, so be sure to check it and ask whether a tip is included if you are unsure.

Tipping

Cloakroom attendants get $1, hotel porters $1 or $2 per bag, hotel chambermaids $1 or $2 per day after a few days' stay. Also give $1 or $2 to the concierge for getting a taxi, and 15% of the amount on the meter to the taxi driver – or maybe 20% on a short trip.

Health

In American **drug stores** prescription medication is only a small part of the stock, and many look like small department stores. Drug stores are listed in the Yellow Pages. They are open daily from 9am to 6pm, some until 9pm or midnight.

Pharmacies

PHARMACY
Open 24 hours
Rite Aid, 50th St. / Eighth Ave. Tel. 1
212-247-8384
Duane Reade 244 57th St. / Broadway
Tel. 1 212-358-9206

AMBULANCE · POLICE
Tel. 911

HOSPITALS
Dial 411 to locate the closest private or
public hospital with a hospital emergen-
cy room.

New York Downtown Hospital
170 William St.
Tel. 1 212-312-5106

Bellevue Hospital Center
462 First Ave./27th St.
Tel. 1 212-562-4141

St Luke's Roosevelt
111 Amsterdam Ave.
Tel. 1 212-523-4000

Mount Sinai Medical Center
1 Gustave L. Levy Place
Tel. 1 212-241-6500

New York Hospital
525 E 68th St.
Tel. 1 212-746-5454

Hospitals The city clinics are mostly overcrowded, the private hospitals expensive. There is a list of private hospitals in the blue pages of the telephone book. Information is also available from **Travelers' Aid**, a US
organization for tourists headquartered in Washington DC (tel. 1
202-546-1127, www.travelersaid.org).

Information

IN USA
*New York City's Official Tourism
Organization*
NYC and Company
810 Seventh Avenue
New York, NY 10019
Tel. 1 212-484-1200

IN UK
NYC and Company
(London Marketing Office)
Hills Balfour, Notcutt House
36 Southwark Bridge Road

London, SE1 9EU
Tel. +44 (0) 207 202 6367
www.nycvisit.com
Information on accommodation, restaurants, events, shopping, business concerns

IN NEW YORK
*New York's Visitor Information
Center*
810 Seventh Ave.
(between 52nd and 53rd St.)
Tel. 1 212-484-1200

Mon–Fri 8.30–6pm, Sat, Sun 9am–6pm
www.nycvisit.com
Information on hotels, sightseeing, City
Pass etc.

Times Square Visitor Center
1560 Broadway
(between 46th and 47th St.)
daily 8am–8pm
www.timessquarenyc.org
All suseful information, Metro-Cards,
Broadway tickets, postage stamps.

Additional tourist offices
The Brooklyn Tourism Council
647 Fulton St.
Tel. 1 718-855-7882
www.brooklynx.org
Bronx Tourism Council
198 E 161st St.
Tel. 1 718-590-2766
www.ilovethebronx.com
Welcome to Harlem
2360 Frederick Douglas Blvd. Suite D
Tel. 1 212-662-7779
Mon–Fri 11am–3pm
www.welcometoharlem.com
Queens Tourism Council
Queens Borough Hall
Kew Gardens
Tel. 1 718-263-0546
www.discoverqueens.info
Staten Island Tourism Council
www.visitstatenisland.com

NY State Division of Tourism
www.nylovesu.com
www.iloveny.com

Further Information
Weather report
tel. 1212 274 1212
Lost and found
taxi: tel. 1 212-869-4513,
subway and bus tel. 1 718-625-6200

US EMBASSIES ABROAD
In UK
24 Grosvenor Square,
London, W1A 1AE, Tel. (0)20 7499-9000
http://london.usembassy.gov
US Consulates General in Cardiff, Edin-
burgh and Belfast

In Republic of Ireland
42 Elgin Road, Ballsbridge
Dublin 4
Tel. +353 1 668-8777
http://dublin.usembassy.gov

In Australia
Moonah Place, Yarralumla, ACT 2600
Tel. (02) 6214-5600
http://canberra.usembassy.gov

In Canada
490 Sussex Drive
Ottawa, Ontario K1N 1G8
Tel. 613-688-5335
http://can-am.gc.ca/new-york/

CONSULATES IN NEW YORK
British Consulate General
845 Third Avenue
Tel. 212-745-0200
www.gov.uk/government/world/organisa-
tions/british-consulate-general-new-york

Consulate General of Ireland
Ireland House
345 Park Avenue, 17th Floor
Tel. 212 319-2555
http://consulate-new-york.com/ireland.html

Australian Consulate General
150 East 42nd Street, 34th Floor
Tel. 212-351-6500
www.newyork.usa.embassy.gov.au

Consulate General of Canada
1251 Avenue of the Americas

Tel. 212-596-1628
http://geo.international.gc.ca/ can-am/
new_york

INTERNET
www.newyork.citysearch.com
Information of all kinds, including
events, theatre, museums, shopping etc.

www.nyc.gov
The city's official website
www.nycgo.com
Includes hotel reservation service
www.visitnewyorkguide.com

Digital travel guide, updated monthly
nymag.com

www.allmy.com
Events listings, nightlife, restaurants, etc.

www.timeout.com/newyork
Website of the weekly city magazine
with information on events, restaurants,
nightlife etc.

www.villagevoice.com
Website of the well-known city newspaper

Literature

Non-fiction **Kenneth T. Jackson (ed.)**, The Encyclopedia of New York City, Yale University Press and The New York Historical Society, New Haven & London / New York 1995. Here is everything you ever wanted to know about New York, from A to Z.

Italo Rota, Not Only Buildings, Te Neues Publishing Company 2000. A kind of field guide on the buildings in Manhattan, in which all are depicted in the form of hand-coloured postcards from the first half of the 20th century.

Bill Harris, Jörg Brockmann, 1000 New York Buildings, Black Dog & Leventhal Publishers 2005. Brockmann photographed New York's architecture, and Harris wrote the sober explanations.

Georges Perec, Robert Bober, Ellis Island, New Press 1995. A poetic volume about the history of emigration and an account of the millions of immigrants who passed through Ellis Island between 1862 and 1942.

Gil C. Alicea, Carmine DeSena, The Air Down Here, Chronicle Books 1995. A Hispanic American teenager reflects on life in the South Bronx.

Time Out New York, Penguin Books. Annually updated New York guide with many important tips.

Beyond the above there are numerous novels that take place in New York. **Paul Auster** captured the character of the city especially well in The New York Trilogy, Moon Palace, The Brooklyn Follies, Henry Holt and Co. 2005.

Novels

Kevin Baker, Paradise Alley, Harper Perennial 2003. This exciting novel brings historical New York to life. It takes place on three days in July 1863, considered to be the three most awful days in the history of New York until 11 September 2001. The novel is part of a trilogy.

The following novels are also recommended: **Rita Mae Brown,** Rubyfruit Jungle, 1973 **Truman Capote,** Breakfast at Tiffany's, 1958 **Herbig Jerome Charyn,** Metropolis New York, 1973 **Max Frisch,** Montauk, 1975 **F. Scott Fitzgerald,** The Great Gatsby, 1925 – a morality tale from old Long Island **Tama Janowitz,** Cannibal in Manhattan, 1987 **Toni Morrison,** Jazz, 1992 **John Dos Passos,** Manhattan Transfer, 1925 **Joseph Roth,** Job: The Story of a Simple Man, 1930 **Hubert Selby,** Last Exit to Brooklyn, 1951 **Lynne Tillman,** No Lease on Life, 1998 **Tom Wolfe,** Bonfire of the Vanities, 1987 **Paul Auster, Joachim A. Frank,** City of Glass, 2004 **Candace Bushnell,** Sex and the City, 2001

Films in and about New York i►MARCO POLO Insight p.44

Media

In spite of its size New York has only three daily newspapers: The *New York Times* is the most respected newspaper in America. The weekday editions are 72 to 124 pages long, the Sunday edition 300 to 500. The boulevard papers *Daily News* and *New York Post* are quite sensationalist. The quickest source of information is the nationwide publication *USA Today*.

Newspapers

News-stands sell papers from the UK and Republic of Ireland, but they are normally a day old. Some publications, such as the UK newspaper *The Times*, are available in a US edition the same day.

UK and Irish newspapers

Money

The US monetary unit is the **dollar** (US$), colloquially called the »buck«. Apart from notes, or bills, worth $1, 2, 5, 10, 20, 50 and 100 (there are also larger notes for bank business), there are coins in cir-

EXCHANGE RATE
1 US$ = 0.61 £   1 £= 1.62 US$
1 US$ = 0.79 €   1 € = 1.26 US$
Current exchange rates:
www.oanda.com

LOST CREDIT CARD
American Express 1-866-549-6426
Mastercard 1-800-627-8372
Visa 1-800-847-2911

culation worth 1 cent (penny), 5 (nickel), 10 (dime), 25 (quarter) cents, and more rarely 50 cents (half-dollar) and 1 dollar. It is better to exchange money in your home country – part of it into traveller's cheques, which are accepted almost everywhere.

Opening times of banks are Mon–Thu 10am–3.30pm, Fri until 4.30pm. At weekends and on public holidays, only the banks at international airports are open.

Currency import
Up to $10,000 may be brought in to or taken out of the country freely. Larger amounts must be declared in the customs declaration form which non-residents are required to complete during the flight.

Traveller's cheques and foreign currency
Traveller's cheques are accepted like cash in hotels, restaurants and shops, though often a passport or driving licence has to be shown. If they are lost or stolen, they are replaced immediately by the issuing company if the document of issue is presented.

Credit cards
The most common method of payment is the **credit card**; Euro/MasterCard, Visa and American express are the most common. When renting a car a credit card is required for the deposit; most hotels require them as well. ATMs (automatic teller machines) are available at many locations around the clock. Most UK bank cards enable you to withdraw money from ATMs in New York, though there will probably be a charge incurred and the exchange rate is likely to be less advantageous than that offered by banks and bureaux de change at home. Of course, the PIN number is necessary for withdrawals.

Post and Telecommunications

Post
Post offices are open on weekdays 8am–6pm, and on Saturdays until 3pm; the **main post office** (General Post Office, 421 Eighth Ave. / 33rd St.) is open around the clock.

Postal rates
Postage for letters within the United States is currently 49 cents for up to 3.5 ounces (98g, ▶Weights, Measures, Temperatures); postcards cost 34 cents. Postage for letters and postcards to Europe is $1,15.

COUNTRY CODES
Calls from New York
to UK: 0 11 44
to Republic of Ireland: 0 11 353
to Australia: 0 11 61
to Canada: 1

Calls to New York
from UK and Republic of Ireland: 00 1
from Australia: 0011 1
from Canada: 1

DIRECTORY INQUIRIES
Tel. 411 and www.411.com

The zip code is placed after the two-letter abbreviation for the state (for example New York, NY 10017; variable four-number additions for different parts of the city). **Zip code**

The operator, who can be reached free of charge by dialling 0 will answer any questions. Calls using a **telephone card** (a prepaid card for $5, 10, 20 or 50), which can be bought at news stands, are reasonably priced and easy. Dial the number of the provider first (providers are listed on the card), enter the PIN and telephone worldwide. **Mobile phones** (cell phones) work only if they have a multi-band facility (tri, or ideally quad), and the charges can be very high with an international roaming agreement. It is best to buy a pre-paid SIM card from Cellular One or Verizom. Telephone numbers often have **letter combinations**, for example »USA-WIND«. These correspond to the letters on the telephone keys. There are also toll-free telephone numbers for hotels, airlines etc., which mostly begin with 800, 888, 866 or 877, and operate only within the USA. Don't confuse them with the 900 numbers, which are used for commercial services that can be very expensive. **Telephone**

In New York the **area code** (Manhattan 212, 917 or 646, Bronx, Brooklyn, Queens and Staten Island 718 and 347) is part of the telephone and fax numbers. When calling within New York always dial 1 + area code + 7-digit telephone number. **Area code**

Prices and Discounts

Students and senior citizens (often starting at the age of 58) get numerous discounts, for example for museum admissions. Children (almost) always pay less. **Admission**

The **City Pass** ($109 for 9 days) allows reduced admission of about 40% to the six biggest attractions, the **New York Pass** ($85–$230, for 1– 7 days) gives free entry for about 80 attractions (almost all of the

?

MARCO ⊕ POLO INSIGHT

What does it cost?

Subway ticket: $2.50
Double room: from $180
Simple meal: from $10

Restaurant prices: ►p.109
Hotel prices: ►p.66

city's main attractions); both include a tour on the Circle Line. The passes are available online (www.citypass.com, www.newyorkpass.com; recommended) as well as at participating attractions and the Visitor Information Center (►Information).

Note when shopping that price tags usually show the **pre-tax** amounts.

Time

From the last Sunday in October until the first Saturday in April **Eastern Standard Time** is in effect; in the remaining months **Eastern Daylight Saving Time**. New York's time zone is five hours behind Greenwich Mean Time/British Summer Time. Depending on when the clocks are changed, the time difference in April can be seven hours, in October five hours. Time check: tel. 212-976-1616

Transport

PUBLIC TRANSPORT

Finding the way

Thanks to the street grid introduced in 1811, finding the way in New York is no problem. **Avenues** run north–south, **streets** run east–west. Fifth Ave. divides Manhattan into the East Side and West Side. The street numbers east of Fifth Ave. have an E for East, those west with a W for West. Broadway is the only important exception. The streets north of Washington Square are numbered continuously. Most avenues have numbers from 1 in the east to 12 in the west, but in between and east of First Ave. there are some with names and even letters of the alphabet (in the lower part of the city).

By ship, harbours

Thanks to its location New York has always been an important port. Manhattan was surrounded by a border of piers up to about 100th Street. The restored historic core of the old harbour, **South Street Seaport**, is reminiscent of bygone days. Only a few piers are used today for passenger transport, such as the Passenger Ship Terminal between 48th and 52nd Street. Most of this traffic consists of cruise ships that stop here on the way to the Caribbean; only one shipping line (▶p.356) still travels between Europe and New York. The large container ships dock mostly on the side of New York Bay that belongs to New Jersey.

Staten Island Ferry, from Manhattan to Staten Island Departure: Battery Park, subway: South Ferry, Bowling Green daily every 30 min, during rush hour every 15 to 20 minutes, from 9.30pm to 5.30am every hour Information: www.siferry.com
This is the cheapest entertainment in New York (free) with the nicest view of the Manhattan skyline. The ferry goes to Staten Island and back, past the Statue of Liberty and Ellis Island.
Circle Line, to the Statue of Liberty and Ellis Island Departure: Battery Park, subway: South Ferry, Bowling Green Information: tel. 1 866-977-6998, www.circlelinedowntown.com
Hoboken Ferry, from Manhattan to Hoboken (New Jersey) Departure: from the pier below the World Financial Center across the Hudson River to Hoboken. Get off here – then back on again to return to Manhattan. Information: tel. 1 800-53-FERRY
The boats of **New York Water Taxi** run from May until October. They stop at various landings and are an alternative in getting around town. Tel. 1 212-742-1969, www.nywatertaxi.com.

By ferry

Long-distance and local buses from the **bus terminal**, the Port Authority Bus Terminal at the intersection of 42nd Street and Eighth Avenue. **Local transport** is covered by countless bus routes, almost 40 of which are found in Manhattan alone. Buses run on all avenues and along the most important streets. All bus stops are request stops; people who want to get off have to ring the bell. Passengers must have the fare ready when they get on. The MetroCard (▶ below) can also be used on the bus. Regular buses stop on every street corner, limited stop buses only at every third or fourth corner, and express buses (increased fare) go directly to the suburbs. Bus stops can be recognized by the yellow curb stones and blue signs.

By bus or coach

Metropolitan Transportation Authority (tel. 1 212-330-1234; www.mta.info)

Information

The underground railway system, known as the **subway**, connects all parts of the city except for Staten Island. It runs around the clock, during rush hour usually every 2 to 5 minutes, during the day every 10 to 12 minutes, between midnight and 5am about every 20 minutes. Those wishing to know more about the subway will find out in the New York Transit Museum (▶Brooklyn). Most of the lines run between Uptown (North) and Downtown (South). **Express** trains only stop at the most important stations; **locals** at all stations. Gener-

Subway

Limousines Those who would like to be driven around Manhattan for longer periods, or would like to get to know other parts of the city or the neighbouring New Jersey, can order a limo with chauffeur from the doorman. Limousines have no meters, and the price must be agreed in advance. A limo with room for up to four passengers can be rented starting at $30. Even a so-called stretch limousine, in which any Joe Shmoe will feel like a VIP and which has room for up to nine people, is available starting at $50 an hour. Cars with drivers are available at: Arrow Transportation, tel. 1 212-431-1900, BLS Limousine Service, tel. 1 718-267-4760 Carmel Car & Limousine Service, tel. 1 866-666-6666 www.carmellimo.com. Golden Touch Transportation, tel. 1 718-886-5204 www.goldentouchtransportation.com LimoRes, tel. 1 212-527-7461, www.limores.net

> **MARCO ⊕ POLO** TIP
>
> ❗ *Enjoying a cab ride* **Insider Tip**
>
> A taxi ride can be an entertaining, amusing and eventful experience, or vexing and frustrating – depending on the traffic and the driver. A good tip is to give the closest cross street with the address: this can save you and the often uninformed driver costly detours.

An unusual means of transportation is the **cable car**, which goes from Second Ave., corner of 58th Street, every quarter of an hour to Roosevelt Island. It was built in 1976 and was supposed to disappear after Roosevelt Island was connected to the subway system in 1989, but was kept in service because of its popularity (►Bridges in New York).

Citi Bike Citi Bike programme provides rental bikes at some hundred stations (listed on www.citybikenyc.com). To rent a bike you need a credit card.

CAR RENTAL

In New York it doesn't make sense to drive your own or a rented car because of the heavy traffic and the lack of (or costly) parking spaces, especially since public transport and taxis work so smoothly. But for travellers for whom New York is the starting point of a longer trip, or those who want to explore the area around the city), a car is indispensable. Generally it is much cheaper to book a hire car from home before the trip. Those wishing to rent a car must be at least 21 years old (and in some cases 25). A driving licence and – don't forget! – a credit card are required.

Avis
Reservations in UK:
Tel. 0808 284 5566
Reservations in New York:
Tel. 1 800-331-1212
www.avis.com

Alamo
Reservations in UK:
Tel. 0800 028 2390
Reservations in New York:
Tel. 1 877-222-9075
www.alamo.com

Budget
Reservations in UK:
Tel. 0808 284 4444
Reservations in New York:
Tel. 1 800-527-0700
www.budget.com

Sixt/Holiday Car
Reservations in UK:
Tel. 0844 248 66 20
www.sixt.co.uk

Dollar
Reservations in New York:
Tel. 1-800-800-3665
www.dollar.com

Hertz
Reservations in UK:
Tel. 0843 309 3099
Reservations in New York:
Tel. 1-800-654-3131
www.hertz.com

National Car
Reservations in New York:
Tel. 1 877-222-9058
www.nationalcar.com

Thrifty
Reservations in New York:
Tel. 1-800-847-4389
www.thrifty.com

BOAT EXCURSIONS

Departure: Pier 83, 42nd Street/West Side Highway, on the Hudson, and Pier 16, South Street Seaport, between Burling Slip and Fulton St. on the East River; information: tel. 1 212-563-3200, www.circle-line42.com A three-hour tour goes down the Hudson and into New York Bay to the ▶Statue of Liberty, up the East River and around Manhattan, and back to the departure point. A guide describes the sights – this is a classic among the guided tours and especially recommended for short visits. There is also a two-hour trip down the Hudson, up the East River to the UN Building and back. Circle Line Statue of Liberty and Ellis Island Ferry ▶ p.369. **Circle Line Cruises**

Departure: Pier 78, W 38th Street/West Side Highway, on the Hudson, and Pier A, W 38th St., Battery Place; information: tel. 1 800-533-3779, www.nywaterway.com Various tours, among them an all-day tour up the Hudson to the »Rockefeller Castle«, the home of the famous family. **NY Waterway Sightseeing Cruises**

Shearwater Sailing	Departure: Hudson River, between Liberty and Vesey St.; information: tel. 1 212-619-0907, www.manhattanbysail.com. From April to October various tours are available on a yacht built in 1929.
Further information	Staten Island and Hoboken Ferry ▶By ferry, p.369

Travellers with Disabilities

Many public buildings, museums, theatres and hotels in New York are accessible to the disabled. Sidewalks have ramps at the corners so that wheelchair users can cross streets easily. Buses have special lifts for wheelchairs, and the hard of hearing can rent headphones and the like in theatres. In Avery Fisher Hall, concert programmes are available in large print. The brochure **A Guide to Accessible Travel in NYC** is available free of charge from New York Mayor's Office (100 Gold St., between Frankfort and Spruce St., tel. 1 212-788-2830; Subway: Chambers Stand Brooklyn Bridge-City Hall). The website www.access-able.com is also very informative. The brochure published by Hospital Audiences Inc. (tel. 1 212-575-7676) provides information on the accessibility of theatres, museums and other cultural institutions. Information for the **deaf and hard of hearing**: New York Society for the Deaf (161 William St.,11th floor, between Ann and Beekman St., tel. 1 212-777-3900, www.perceptions4people.org). Information and literature in Braille for the **blind**: Lighthouse International (111 E 59th St., between Park and Lexington Ave., tel. 1 800-829-0500, www.lighthouse.org).

Weights, Measures, Temperatures

LINEAR

1 inch (in;) = 2.54 cm	1 mm = 0.03937 in
1 foot (ft;)= 12 in = 30.48 cm	1 cm = 0.033 ft
1 yard (yd;) = 3 ft = 91.44 cm	1 m = 1.09 yd
1 mile (mi;) = 1.61 km	1 km = 0.62 mi

AREA

1 square inch (in²) = 6.45 cm²	1 cm² = 0.155 in²
1 square foot (ft²) = 9.288 dm²	1 dm² = 0.108 ft²

1 square yard (yd²) = 0.836 m²   1 m² = 1.196 yd²
1 square mile (mi²) = 2.589 km²   1 km² = 0.386 mi²
1 acre = 0.405 ha   1 ha = 2.471 acres

VOLUME
1 cubic inch (in³) = 16.386 cm³   1 cm³ = 0.061 in³
1 cubic foot (ft³) = 28.32 dm³   1 dm³ = 0.035 ft³
1 cubic yard (yd³) = 0.765 m³   1 m³ = 1.308 yd³

LIQUID
1 gill = 0.118 l   1 l = 8.747 gills
1 pint (pt)= 4 gills = 0.473 l   1 l = 2.114 pt
1 quart (qt)= 2 pt = 0.946 l   1 l = 1.057 qt
1 gallon (gal) = 4 qt = 3.787 l   1 l = 0.264 gal

WEIGHTS
1 ounce (oz.) = 28.365 g   100 g = 2.527 oz
1 pound (lb) = 453.59 g   1 kg = 2.206 lb
1 cental (cwt.) = 45.359 kg   100 kg = 2.205 cwt

°F	°C
110°	43°
100°	38°
90°	32°
80°	26,5°
70°	21°
60°	15,5°
50°	10°
40°	4,5°
32°	0°
30°	-1°
20°	-6,5°
10°	-12°
0°	-18°
-10°	-23°
-20°	-29°
-30°	-34,5°
-40°	-40°

TEMPERATURE
Fahrenheit: 0 10 20 32 50 68 89 95   **Celsius:** -18 -12 -6.5 0 10 20 30 35
Conversion: Fahrenheit = 1.8 x Celsius + 32

$$Celsius = \frac{5\,(Fahrenheit - 32)}{9}$$

CLOTHING SIZES
Men's clothing For men's suits, coats and shirts measurements are identical in the UK and the USA.

Men's shoes:	**UK** 7 8 9 10 11
	US 8 9 10 11 12
Women's clothing:	**UK** 3 4 5 6 7 8
	US 5.5 6.5 7.5 8.5 9.5 10.5
Women's shoes:	**UK** 8 10 12 14 16 18
	US 6 8 10 12 14 16
Children's sizes:	**UK** 3-4 yrs 4-5 yrs 5-6 yrs 6-7 yrs 7-8 yrs
	US 3 4 5 6 6X

When to Go

New York City lies at the same latitude as Naples. In general the weather is good in New York (250 to 300 sunny days per year), since low pressure zones generally pass quickly and high pressure zones are stable. The best time to visit is May and from mid-September until the beginning of December. The summer months should be avoided: even though most buildings are air conditioned, the high humidity out of doors can be oppressive.

Temperatures The **average temperatures** vary between 28°C/83°F in June (average 10 hours of sun, 7 days with precipitation) and 4°C/39°F in January (average 4 hours of sun, 3 days with precipitation). There is rarely snow before January. The highest summer temperature ever measured in New York was 41°C/106°F, the lowest winter temperature minus 24°C/minus 11°F. The general rule: if it turns cold, then it gets really cold. Blizzards that swoop in from Canada often bring the traffic to a halt; in these circumstances snowfall of over 50cm/20in in one night is not unusual.

Weather forecasts Weather reports are made regularly in almost all news programmes on TV and radio. Weather reports are also available by telephone, tel. 1 212-976-1212, as well as on the internet at www.weather.com.

Index

List of Maps and Illustrations

Photo Credits

Publisher's Information

1st Edition 2015
Worldwide Distribution: Marco Polo
Travel Publishing Ltd
Pinewood, Chineham Business Park
Crockford Lane, Chineham
Basingstoke, Hampshire RG24 8AL,
United Kingdom.

Photos, illlustrations, maps::
171 photos, 28 maps and and illustra-
tions, one large city map
Text:
Achim Bourmer, Monika Hausner-Schön-
felder, Ole Helmhausen, Thomas Jeier,
Wolfgang Liebermann, Carin Drechsler-
Marx, Silwen Randebrock, Anja Schlieb-
itz, Jörn Trümper, Wolfgang Veit, Jens
Wassermann
Revision:
Sebastian Moll
Editing:
Anja Schliebitz, Robert taylor, John
Sykes
Translation: Barbara Schmidt-Runkel,
John Sykes
Cartography:
Christoph Gallus, Hohberg;
MAIRDUMONT Ostfildern (city map)
3D illustrations:
jangled nerves, Stuttgart
Infographics:
Golden Section Graphics GmbH, Berlin
Design:
independent Medien-Design, Munich

Editor-in-chief:
Rainer Eisenschmid, Mairdumont
Ostfildern

Printed in China

Despite all of our authors' thorough
research, errors can creep in. The publishers do not accept any liability for thi
Whether you want to praise, alert us to
errors or give us a personal tip Please
contact us by email or post:

MARCO POLO Travel Publishing Ltd
Pinewood, Chineham Business Park
Crockford Lane, Chineham
Basingstoke, Hampshire RG24 8AL
United Kingdom
Email: sales@marcopolouk.com

FSC
www.fsc.org
MIX
Paper from
responsible sources
FSC® C011918

MARCO ⊕ POLO

HANDBOOKS

New York Curiosities

A competence test for street buskers, tickertape parades, why the taxis are yellow – and many more strange and unusual facts about New York

►Tickertape parades

More than 200 such parades have been held to celebrate great achievements with a blizzard of paper in the »Canyon of Heroes« on Lower Broadway. The first tickertape parade took place in 1886 for the inauguration of the Statue of Liberty.

►Subway musicians

The buskers in subway stations have to pass a rigorous selection procedure before they are allowed to make music underground. Some famous artists have been among them.

►Foreign languages

More than half of all New Yorkers above the age of five speak a different language than English at home.

►Central Park

Central Park covers an area larger than the Principality of Monaco.

►Yellow cabs

New York taxis are yellow because this is the colour that the human eye can recognize best, as company founder John Hertz found out.

►Manhattanhenge

Two days in summer (around 28 May and 12 July) are reminiscent of Stonehenge: sunset is then aligned with the street grid in Manhattan, and the sun goes down at the end of every street at right angles to the main avenues.

►City of a million

Until 1989 Brooklyn was an independent city, and would be the fourth-largest in the USA today after New York, Los Angeles and Chicago.

►A grim place

Washington Square Park was originally a cemetery for victims of yellow fever and the site of public executions.

►Capital city

New York enjoyed the status of capital city of the United States for only a few months between 1789 and 1790.